Miss Vera's Finishing School

for **BOYS**

who want

to be

Girls

DOUBLEDAY
CELEBRATES
100 YEARS OF
EXCELLENCE

Miss Vera's Finishing School

for BOYS who want to be Girls

Veronica Vera

MAIN STREET BOOKS

New York
London
Toronto
Sydney
Auckland

A MAIN STREET BOOK
PUBLISHED BY DOUBLEDAY
a division of Bantam Doubleday Dell Publishing Group, Inc.
1540 Broadway, New York, New York 10036

MAIN STREET BOOKS, DOUBLEDAY, and the portrayal of a building
with a tree are trademarks of Doubleday, a division of Bantam
Doubleday Dell Publishing Group, Inc.

Book Design by Amanda Kavanagh, ARK Design

Library of Congress Cataloging-in-Publication Data
Vera, Veronica.
Miss Vera's finishing school for boys who want to be girls: tips,
tales, and teachings from the dean of the world's first cross-
dressing academy / Veronica Vera.
p.   cm.
1. Transvestism.   2. Transvestites.   3. Sex role.   I. Title.
HQ77.V46   1997
305.3—dc21   97-18736
CIP
ISBN 0-385-48456-9
Copyright © 1997 by Veronica Vera
All Rights Reserved
Printed in the United States of America
November 1997
First Edition
10 9 8 7 6 5 4 3 2 1

This book is based on the true-life exploits and experiences of Veronica Vera and Miss Vera's Finishing
School for Boys Who Want to Be Girls. To protect the
privacy of those whose paths have crossed the author's, some events have been altered, and many
names have been changed.

To my sisters, Georgia and Connie, for their love and compassion;
to my nieces, Meredith and Maureen, for their hope;
and to the sissies of the world for their courage.

Contents

Introduction   1

Preface   How the Academy Came to Be   9

Chapter 1   Think Pink   23

Chapter 2   Venus Envy   29

Chapter 3   The Student Body   37

Chapter 4   Herstory   55

Chapter 5   Hair Dressing   59

Chapter 6   Bodybuilding   71

Chapter 7   Makeup Test   85

Chapter 8   Fashion Assignment   97

Chapter 9   Best High Heel Forward   109

Chapter 10   Home Ec   119

Chapter 11   Girl Talk   129

Chapter 12   Field Trips   137

Chapter 13   Etiquette for Macho Girls   157

Chapter 14   Sex Education   165

Chapter 15   Coming Out   181

How to Become an Academy Debutante   191

Recommended Reading and Sources   192

List of Courses   195

Acknowledgments   197

Author Biography   200

Introduction

From the time I established Miss Vera's Finishing School for Boys Who Want to Be
Girls, the world's first male-to-female
cross-dressing academy, my pink Princess phone
began to ring incessantly. At the other end of the
line were the often nervous, usually husky, sometimes breathy, mostly polite and always excited
voices of the men—the Stephanies and Jennifers, Denises and JoAnns the prospective
students, all of whom wanted to explore
what they felt as their feminine side.
They felt her like children feel an
imaginary friend. Often, she had
been with them since childhood. Some could look in the
mirror and see her in their
eyes. In reading about the
academy they felt they had
found someone who be-
lieved in her too. Most
callers asked me if the
school was for real.
Could I actually help
them to "pass" as fe-

male? When I answered, "Yes," it was as if someone had confirmed the existence of Santa Claus or, as I prefer to think of myself, Cinderfella's fairy godmother.

Eric Kroll

Cinderfella's fairy godmother.

I quickly felt myself riding the crest of a wave of success, uplifted on the broad shoulders of a sea of grateful men in skirts. Not only had I put my well-manicured finger on the pulse of every cross-dresser's dream but I had tapped into the rich mother lode of the male psyche. Having gone through my own process of woman's liberation, I understood my students as the flip side of the feminist movement. When women felt the need for balance in their lives, to share more in the male experience—to move from the home to the workplace, from the bedroom to the boardroom, to be financially independent, and sexually autonomous—we created the women's movement. Men, too, have this need for balance, to share more in what they view as the most desirable aspects of the female experience: to be pampered and protected, to be glamorous and sexually desirable, and, yes, even to do housework—many of the "privileges" that we women saw as confining. Cross-dressers are more fortunate than most men because their affinity for the clothing gives them access to these feelings of Venus Envy. The academy offers a mode of action. For every woman who burned her bra, there is a man ready to wear one.

The academy is my own private laboratory. With the matriculation of more than 500 on-campus students, I have been able to witness the positive aspects of this unique form of behavior modification. Contrary to what many assume, the student is not "finished" when he puts on a dress and learns to carry himself like a debutante, but rather when he can take the lessons and insights of his femmeself and integrate them into his male persona.

Robert is a student who came to the academy every six weeks. One of our early classes consisted of a field trip during which Robert and I visited a tiny lingerie shop in Chelsea. With the help of the shop's proprietress, we chose some frilly bra and pantie sets and lacy nighties for Robert to try on in the shop's private dressing room. Our plan was to leave the store with our purchases, to have dinner together, and then return to the academy where with the aid of cosmetics and prosthetics Robert would become Roberta and model her new finery.

During dinner I was aghast as I watched Robert eat. He hunched over his

My
NAME IS RALPH.

BUT

MY FRIENDS

CALL ME RACHEL.

People are full of surprises. Just like the cross-dressing phone classes at Miss Vera's Academy.
Call 1-900-884-VERA ($2.99/min. Adults only.)

MISS VERA'S
FINISHING SCHOOL
For Boys Who Want To Be Girls

WATCH FOR MISS VERA'S BOOK FROM DOUBLEDAY PUBLISHING COMING IN 1997.

MVA

Our breakthrough ad campaign created by Jeff Griffith and Joe Lovering.

plate and shoveled the food into his mouth. "Roberta will need lessons in table manners," I told him. Robert explained that his professional life as a doctor left him no time for table manners. Eating for him was just something he needed to accomplish in order to go on cutting people up. He proceeded to tell me that his schedule was overbooked, that he did not know how to say "no" to people, and that he feared for his health as he learned of colleagues who had heart attacks at an early age. Here was a man who wanted to dress in soft delicate clothes but was still imprisoned in a tough male hide.

But clothes alone do not make the woman. As I tell every student: Understand that when you dress there may be things that you also need to *address.* I saw very clearly that Roberta, the femmeself, could, through lessons in etiquette and table manners at the academy, learn to eat more slowly and with more appreciation for the nourishing pleasure of food. Robert would thus be led to a longer and happier life. As the butterfly Roberta emerged from her cocoon, she lessened Robert's chances of dropping like a fly. I am sure that *her* lessons with the knife and fork improved *his* skill with a scalpel.

Such success stories are the goal of Miss Vera's Finishing School. Are we encouraging a band of defectors? Undermining the male power structure? I prefer to think that we are responding to a need. The tremendous popularity of the academy attests to the fact that people want to believe that there is a place where men can learn to be more like women. This is an idea whose time has come.

In those other academic circles, gender is a discipline; in publishing, it's a genre; in cyberspace, an option; in show business, it's a gimmick. The topic has captured the international zeitgeist. Now more than ever there is great awareness that gender roles are in a state of flux. Witness the popularity of megastars like David Bowie and Michael Jackson, whose phenomenal success is deeply rooted in their fascinating androgeny, and drag artists such as Barry Humphries aka Dame Edna Everage; John Epperson, who is Lypsinka, John Kelly's Joni Mitchell, writer/actress Charles Busch. Mr. Television, Milton Berle, spent lots of time in skirts. Theater, from Shakespeare to Broadway and the movies, has provided steady employment for the male crossdresser. The stories of transformation are as timeless as Cinderella and as up-to-the-minute as RuPaul. On a visit to the academy, you will find our pretty pink walls lined with photos of Jack Lemmon and Tony Curtis as Daphne and Josephine in *Some Like It Hot;* Flip Wilson's feisty Geraldine; Dustin Hoffman's Tootsie; Robin Williams' Mrs. Doubtfire, and Tim Curry's Dr. Frank-N-Furter from *The Rocky Horror Picture Show,* as well as portraits of our students. In 1993, Tony—make that Antoinette Perry—Award winners for best musical, *Kiss of the Spider Woman,* and best play, *Angels in America: Millennium Approaches,* relied heavily on cross-dressed males. Most recently, we have Julie Andrews swinging the other way in *Victor/Victoria* and before that there was *La Cage aux Folles* and then *The Birdcage.* Male actors seem to almost fly into those heels and hose: witness Terence Stamp and the traveling girls in *The Adventures of Priscilla, Queen of the Desert;* that pretty trio of beefcake cum cheesecake—Patrick Swayze,

Wesley Snipes, and John Leguizamo in *To Wong Foo, Thanks for Everything! Julie Newmar;* and the movie that has come closest to portraying an academy girl, *Just Like a Woman,* starring Adrian Pasdar and Julie Walters. Perversely, even the psychoseamstress of *Silence of the Lambs* is further proof that transvestites have come of age. If a minority is strong enough to withstand such a vicious and malicious characterization, it is a sign that reality is well understood. But it was the phenomenal success of Neil Jordan's film *The Crying Game* that really struck at the heart of the matter. In *The Crying Game* the macho warrior is debunked as he is despunked by a cross-dressed lover, proving that the sword melts at the touch of the lipstick wand.

All of this reflects the public's fascination and awareness of the current SNAFU (or Situation Normal, All Frocked Up). It is the male role, in particular, that is held up to the mirror as Pentagon generals grudgingly acknowledge the contributions of gay men in the military; Robert Bly scores a huge best-seller with *Iron John,* in which men are encouraged to beat the bush and find their origins in Mother Nature; and authors such as Warren Farrell, Ph.D., question *The Myth of Male Power.*

When headlines shrieked the scandal of "nannygate" because the woman whom President Clinton had nominated for the position of Attorney General had illegally employed a housekeeper, I viewed the situation from my own academic perspective. More than a hundred years after suffragettes fought for women's rights and planted the seeds of the feminist movement, women were still plagued with babysitter problems, yet I was housemother to a unique sir-ority, many of whom envied the fifties' housewife and yearned to be in her place. At Miss Vera's Finishing School for Boys Who Want to Be Girls, we do our best to iron out the nation's domestic problems.

Students of the academy, most of whom identify as heterosexual, are not Broadway babies or drag queens, though that is the level of expertise to which many aspire. The great drag performer Divine is one of the academy's patron saints. Drag queens, who are usually gay, work it every day. They constantly perfect their performance personae. Students of the academy do not. They are often married and well established in their occupations.

Abe Fraindlich

Miss Vera and student in typical drab.

But as cross-dressers, they have been touched with a heavy dose of the same magic that inspires the drag queen and made the shamans dance, the power of the combined masculine and feminine energies alive within each of us.

Cross-dressers were recognized in society long before theater evolved. From earliest times, the North American Plains Indians identified men who dressed as women as *berdaches.* Among the Aztecs and Incas, they were called *bardage;* in Tahiti, *mahoos* and Brazil *cudinas.* Cross-dressing and the androgynous spirit it celebrates have long been part of harvest and fertility rituals. In his book *Dressing Up,* Peter Ackroyd, citing early Roman sources, reports that on the island of Cyprus, male priests dressed as women and honored a bearded Aphrodite. From ancient through modern times, god or the forces of creation and chaos have been represented by a man in a dress.

The ubiquitous presence of cross-dressers on talk shows during the ratings months attests to the fact that this practice can still draw faithful audiences to the altar. In fact, when the media learned of the existence of the academy, we practically had to fend off the talk show hosts with a stick. Television seemed to offer little real information to people, though it deserves credit for increasing public awareness to some degree and, in some cases, even saving people's lives, as evinced by a cross-dresser in the recent documentary from Cajun Films, *All Dressed Up and No Where to Go.* Still, I was reluctant to submit myself or my students to the process, unless I could refer them to my book for the real story.

This book is my attempt to bring Miss Vera's Finishing School for Boys Who Want to Be Girls directly to you with the same care and style we devote to each lucky neophyte who finds his way to our door, and I want to share this exciting tale. In essence, this is our academy textbook. Perhaps you are a man who identifies as our students do. Like thousands of men, you may have been dressed in girls' clothes when you were a child and those early experiences have inspired the creation of your female persona—or as we call that amalgam of feelings and needs—your femmeself. You want to know more about her. Take a look at her. Help her to be the best she that a he can be. This book will show you how to do that. Maybe you are the wife or partner of a male cross-dresser and would like to be more informed for the purpose of enhancing your emotional and sexual life. This book will help you to do that, too.

I want to enable more women—g.g.'s, or genetic girls, as we call ourselves at the academy—to understand and appreciate male cross-dressers. I and the other deans find ourselves the objects of schoolgirl crushes from a whole group of very eligible bachelorettes and we want to share the wealth.

Perhaps you are a man who is simply curious to see how the other half lives. Even a man who has never had the desire to see himself in a skirt can benefit from the lessons of our academy. In the process he will come to understand not only the ways in which men differ from women but the ways in which we are similar.

A former boyfriend who did not cross-dress once said to me, "I wish I could be a woman for a while. If I were, I'd be able to wrap men around my little finger." I have heard other men make similar claims.

Usually they are convinced that, given the right equipment, they could be femmes fatales. Here, we welcome all who want the chance to prove it.

Cross-dressing is an act that offers new options. Why not discuss business over tea rather than beers or martinis? (It could definitely help in those deals with the Orient, and, while strengthening the bottom line, preserve the waistline.) Academy students learn to accommodate their shoes and take a rest from the rat race. They discover how lipstick can color their lives. Do not forget that while it is the clothing of the female that is being adopted, in many ways the clothing is merely a prop. This book dares the student to allow his male ego to be miss-taken and miss-guided.

It has been suggested that men like to cross-dress because it helps to relieve stress. This far too simplistic explanation supports the myth of the dominant male and grossly underestimates female potency. Think about which values the female or mother has supported compared to that of the male or father. Traditionally, Father represents strict adherence to rules of performance; Mother represents unconditional love. On the other hand, men know how to work; women know how to play. And Miss Vera knows how to play very well. Having grown up in the era of "Father Knows Best," I sing out that "Girls Just Want to Have Fun." One way to define the academy is to say that our business is education and re-creation. We teach people to have fun.

What you will find here is a step-by-step guide to a male-to-female transformation. Ours is the holistic approach. We emphasize the physical changes, but do not dismiss the underlying feelings—pay atten-tion to nylons and crinolines, but do not overlook the Freudian slips. Students spend several hours at a time with us, or several days. Courses include makeup application, herstory, girl talk, flirting fundamentals, ballet one and tutu, etiquette, home economics, field trips (Our girls go everywhere!) . . . Most of these are excellent subjects for any man to know, no matter what his fashion statement.

I am very proud of our students. They offer us the uplifting support of a tightly laced corset. They are our mainstays. You will meet some of them in these pages and follow them in their miss-adventures, as well as be introduced to the academy's deans . . . For Miss Vera's Finishing School for Boys Who Want to Be Girls is not all brick and concrete, not even all lipstick and lace, but a living, breathing reality that rests in the hearts and high-heeled souls of its students and teachers.

The revelation that the late FBI Director J. Edgar Hoover spent considerable leisure time in ball gowns is one example of many that men in high positions like to dress up. But cross-dressers cross societal borders. Students of the academy, when not dressed in female clothes, lead very traditional lives. Many are family men with mainstream jobs. They come from all walks of life: professionals and proletarians, young and old, married and single. They come in all body types, and bring to the academy different-sized endowments.

The femmeself, as a creature of the imagination, is born to be uninhibited emotionally and sexually. How far the invisible woman goes when she becomes a material girl depends on the man. Some of our students entertain the idea that they might live full time as a female, but for the great majority this is only a fantasy. A defining characteristic of transsexuals is that they are people who feel they have been born into the wrong body and want to change it. Recent scientific advances have made it possible for the transsexual to choose better living through chemistry, i.e., hormones and surgery. Christine Jorgensen, whose sex change operation made headlines in the fifties, and tennis pro Dr. Richard Raskind, who became Renee Richards, are two of the best-known transsexuals. Cross-dressers or transvestites, who comprise the majority of our students, want only to change their clothes. We help them with their outfits and their attitudes.

Our goal at the academy is to bring out the female persona for the purpose of learning from her. Listen to her voice. What does she have to say? What does she like to do? How does she feel? What does she need—and where will she shop for it? We put the clothes in the closet and let the girl out.

For a long time, I have lived my life as a student, taking in information. Now that I am the teacher, I find that I still learn from my students. One of the things they have taught me is an appreciation of the power and passion of the female. Miss Vera's Finishing School for Boys Who Want to Be Girls has also helped to balance my energies. Assuming my role of Dean of Students has given me more creative outlets, more assurance, more financial security than I have ever known. Putting men in dresses has enabled me to wear the pants in my own life.

What has it done for the men? Often, even after the orientation interview, a student arrives for his first class and makeover with his face very tight in a grimace of nerves. How gratifying it is to see that same student emerge with a grin that spreads from earring to earring. He has taken a brave step. Most of our students have never shared this side of themselves with anyone. It is a privilege for us to be with a student at that moment when he is literally facing his greatest desire and his greatest fear in the mirror and to help him see that she is beautiful.

An academy transformation is not merely about putting on a dress or learning to walk in a different way. It is about diving headfirst into the experience. It is about learning to trust yourself in a scary situation, "feeling the fear and doing it anyway." Ours is an empiric study that offers new options and choices and can lead to personal evolution, growth, and empowerment.

For years the man who enjoyed "feminine pursuits" has been labeled a "sissy." At the academy, we believe in *sissy power*. Our students' determination to liberate themselves and their feelings helps to liberate us all. In his quest to expand the idea of what it is to be masculine by embracing, celebrating, and surrendering to the feminine influence, each student helps to expand the idea of who we are as humans. As we step boldly toward the new millennium, I am glad to know that many more of us will be doing it in high heels.

Preface

How the Academy Came to Be

*H*ow does a person become Dean of Students at a cross-dressing academy? It is not a career choice listed by high school guidance counselors. But then, the single most important lesson that life has taught me is to forget about the woman that I am supposed to be and be the woman I am. That is why I am the perfect person to guide others in the process of female liberation.

Every one of us goes through her or his own personal evolution. For me, as for many of our students, the adventure

Most students cross-dressed in early childhood (Jennifer James).

began early on, and with a pair of panties. I literally got in touch with my self the day I put my fingers in my underpants and felt those first moments of heavenly bliss. I ran to my mother, for I was eager to announce my thrilling discovery. Clearly not sharing my enthusiasm, she stopped me in my tracks with the words "God does not like that." With the wisdom of a child, I knew that something did not ring true. My mother tried to speak with authority, but I saw fear in her eyes. I had not gone looking for trouble. If I was not supposed to touch that spot why did it feel so inviting? Motivated by my natural curiosity, a healthy libido, and the innate knowledge that I was essentially good, I determined that I would find my own answers. Outwardly, I accepted my mother's decree and hung my head in shame; subconsciously, I stamped my Mary Janes in protest, flung my baloney curls to the wind, and set out on a quest to discover my sexual identity and validate my independence. This journey of the body and the soul would occupy my life; take me, literally and figuratively, all around the world; and be the research that prepared me for teaching.

There were some signposts along the way, but it is only now that I can look back and recognize them as such. At ten, I squeezed into my mother's lap, and proudly confided my plans for the future. First, I would be chosen queen of the May procession, the highlight of our church's calendar. Each spring, during an evening high mass, all of the boys and girls in St. Elizabeth's Roman Catholic grammar school marched down the church aisle in their best suits and frocks. There were other processions throughout the year, but this was the only one in which the girls had boy partners, and it was the only one that took place at night, which contributed an exciting air of romance. Sometimes our outfits would be color coordinated: fourth-grade girls, all in pink; fifth-grade girls in blue . . . but only one girl wore white. She floated down the aisle at the very end of the procession, wearing a dress that looked like a wedding gown. We all wore flowered wreaths, but this girl wore the coveted rhinestone tiara and—though she was on her way to crown the statue of the Blessed Virgin Queen of May—we all knew the real queen was the girl in the wedding gown. What could be a more worthy goal than to crown the queen: I could be glamorous and good at the very same time.

As my lofty speech was designed to persuade my parents to continue financing my dancing school lessons, which were in jeopardy due to my supposed lack of enthusiasm, I continued to prophesy that following lifelong lessons in tap, toe, and ballet, in which I would excel, and upon being graduated from college, I would become a famous ballerina, and when I was too old to dance, I would be the seamstress who embroidered vestments for the priests. I waited, expecting that, at any moment, my mother would clutch me to her bosom, thrilled with my impressive choices. Instead, she looked me square in the eyes and said that at my age, I could not be sure what my future would be. If there had been a musical accompaniment to that moment, Doris Day would have warbled it over the radio: "Que sera, sera . . . Whatever will be will be . . ." My mother was more right than she could have ever imagined—and so was I. Ballet,

Mary Veronica and little sister Connie.

ers "the intelligentsia," but a mediocre typist, so I wound up in Wall Street where I learned to trade over-the-counter stocks.

My mentor was Crazy Norman, a cross between his idol comedian Don Rickles and Emperor Napoleon. Crazy Norman's schtick—a loud, rapid-fire, hopping-up-and-down, song and dance delivered via telephone in which he pleaded for additional eighths and quarters in one moment ("C'mon . . . It's my birthday") and punctured his target with withering insults the next ("Sold to you, you old douche bag!")—was my first encounter with performance art. On Wall Street, I met a cast of characters worthy of another book, learned lessons of supply and demand that I had never learned in school, and became acquainted with some of the inner workings of the male power establishment.

brides, and ball gowns all figured in my future. I never did learn to sew, but I have put a lot of men in dresses and crowned more than my share of queens.

The ambition about which I grew most serious was to be a writer—to smoke a pipe and live in a house in Connecticut—but what the world seemed to want was for me to be a typist. In the early seventies, as the National Organization for Women was being formed, the first question still asked of female college graduates was, "How fast can you type?" I was a Dean's List student who had edited my high school and college newspapers, a member of what was termed by our teach-

My next foray into the world of finance was in the Fifth Avenue office of petroleum engineer Bob Albrecht, a real straight-arrow guy who taught me the meaning of those words. Billie Bob (as he was called very briefly in those days) and I traveled to Utah where I helped him set up an office and learned how to fish. Our prime quarry was not the trout at the end of the lines, but the ranchers who fished beside us holding poles in one hand and in the other dangling leases for land which we hoped to acquire for Billie Bob and his partners' independent oil company. We hooked lots of fish. As a result of his brains, charm, and professional expertise, Billie Bob's company made money for everyone and true to his word, he gave me a share. I had financial security, but something was missing.

Many times a student's first visit to our academy coincides with a particular trauma: divorce, a life-threatening illness, the death of a loved one. The student gets a taste of mortality and decides to explore this part of himself that seems to have been with him forever and does not look as if it is going away. My own wake-up call came in the middle of the sky, in a tiny twin-engine plane over Utah, when the radio squawked my name and announced that I must call home. My beloved mom had died just one day prior to my scheduled return home. Her heart gave out during an act of love: She had been joyfully cleaning the house for my homecoming. Dad discovered her slumped over the Electrolux and the Dustbuster. (Like cowboys who die with their boots on, it is not uncommon for a woman to die while vacuuming.)

Faced with the fact that I would not live forever, I decided to write or forget my fantasy to be a writer. My mother had always encouraged my writing; ironically, the subject I chose to write about was the only one that she feared. The sole person I knew who was making her living as a writer was editing a sex magazine. Her name is V.K. McCarty and she still edits *Penthouse Variations*. V.K. and I met during the late seventies, the swinging years of Plato's Retreat, the infamous orgy club, and the miracle of birth control pills. As a New York bachelorette, freed from the constraints of living with my family, I was quite actively exploring my sexuality. V.K. and I had partied together

and she knew that I was pretty uninhibited. She invited me to try writing for *Variations*. I knew that sex was important in my life, so I thought, "Why not learn to write about it?" What I did not know was that with this very first assignment a whole world would open for me. Sex became my field of research, my language, my favorite method of communication, my yellow brick road, and the path on which I would meet little Mary, the girl I left behind.

My childhood Mary Janes grew to "come-hither" pumps. For over a dozen years I explored the elysian fields of sexual research. Unlike other academicians, I pursued my studies not in theories, but in practice. As a sex journalist, I wrote about my own sex life and interviewed other people about theirs: commercial sex workers, booth babies in peep shows, expensive call girls, strippers, love acts who did it on stage— five times a day—fetishists, s/m aficionados, swingers, and transgenderists, as well as clergymen, college students, construction workers . . . the fields of my research spanned from orgy to temple. Many of the articles were done in collaboration with Annie Sprinkle, who was well on her way to being a blue movie legend when we became bosom buddies. Annie womanned the camera in what we dubbed our high-heeled journalist team. Presaging Nike by about a dozen years, sex goddess Annie advised, "Never let anyone talk you into doing something that you do not want to do, but if there is something you really want to do, just do it!"

My previous ventures in the business world had left me with some capital. I could pick and choose what I wanted to do. So I did it with the best, people who

SPRINKLE & VERA

FROM THE SCHOOL OF
HIGH-HEEL JOURNALISM

Annie Sprinkle & Veronica Vera, bosom buddies.

explored sex with a passion and an artistic point of view. In collaboration with Robert Mapplethorpe, I created images of my body that grace the walls of international museums and galleries. Gerard "Deep Throat" Damiano directed my first X-rated performance in a quasi-documentary entitled *Consenting Adults.* I was not supposed to perform sex in the movie, but one day I just jumped into a scene. It was a very liberating experience. Given my religious upbringing, life as a nun might have seemed more appropriate. Instead, repression inspired my exhibitionism. Eventually I understood that the person I most wanted to expose myself to was me.

My personal quest was political, and my goal was to support information over ignorance. I became a sex rights activist, testifying in Washington for freedom of expression before a Senate Judiciary Committee chaired by Arlen Specter. I campaigned for the decriminalization of prostitution, helped to reorganize PONY (Prostitutes of New York), and lectured at other institutions of higher learning like Yale and Dartmouth.

I traveled. First to France—where I lived for six months and returned often, because every writer has to live in Paris—but then all over the globe. With my friend Robert Maxwell, I traveled around the world in eighty days: to Rio, Johannesburg, Nairobi, Katmandu, Bangkok, Perth, Singapore, Manila, Hong Kong, Tokyo, and India. "Max" collected *objets,* I acquired fabrics and costumes so that I could better identify with the women of those lands. In India we visited the erotic temples of Khajuraho and learned of the Tantric yogis and their reverence for sexual energy.

Human sexuality is a fun and fascinating subject, but it was all the more interesting because of the women who became my teachers, my friends, and my colleagues. In the early eighties, at a show of rubber fashions at Annie's home, the Sprinkle Salon, I met the designer Jeanette Luther aka Mistress Antoinette. During a summer internship at her lovely home in Southern California, Antoinette taught me the importance of clothing as a prop to the psyche and introduced me to the complexities of dominant/submissive behavior. The world of dominance and submission, with its emphasis on ritual, power, and permission, was the perfect complement to my religious background. Antoinette and her husband Dick, a well-known physician also known as the photographer "Zorro," had created *Reflections: The Magazine for the Exotic Life.* Through the magazine and the video company that followed they discovered an enthusiastic market for the fetish fashion designs that were Antoinette's forte. The company Versatile Fashions was aptly named because while Jeanette had begun designing clothing for herself and other women, she was soon deluged with orders from cross-dressers. Her clientele expanded along with her size chart. They welcomed an enthusiastic assistant in what I termed their kinky conglomerate, but what Zorro liked to call "a mom and pop operation." In exchange for my summer apprenticeship, Antoinette, Zorro, and their transvestite office manager, Reb Stout aka Rebecca H. Heels, gave me a crash course in exotica that helped to make me the glamour girl that I am.

Antoinette was also the person who encouraged me to "come out" to my dad and let him know that I had chosen human sexuality as my field of research. "I love you," he said, his voice quivering, "just be careful." Up until that time I had told my dad that I was writing and being published but I had never shown him a thing I had written. He was not thrilled with my choice of subjects—to say he was "terrified" would not be exaggerating—but he was relieved that we were finally communicating on an honest level. Dad feared I would be exploited by men, but it was always the women, bold pioneers, who most powerfully influenced me.

Artist and sex educator Betty Dodson taught me the personal and political ramifications of self-love. We were already friends by the time I took her famous "Bodysex" workshop in which a group of women lie naked in Betty's loft, "the temple of the goddess," share personal stories, examine their own and one another's genitals or femalia, learn to give themselves pleasure and in these ways reclaim not only their sexual selves but their lives. Nearly a dozen years before, in 1973, at the first sexuality conference sponsored by the National Organization for Women, which was then in its infancy, Betty had presented a slide show from one of her first Bodysex workshops. One thousand women saw photos of the femalia of fifteen workshop participants, up close and personal, and one thousand women stood and cheered Betty and this varied bouquet. She has continued to educate women in this

Club 90 (left to right: Annie Sprinkle, Gloria Leonard, Veronica Vera, Candida Royalle, Veronica Hart).

Michele Capozzi

simple, fun, honest, and powerful style ever since. Betty understands the words "political body" in every sense. Guilt, shame, or ignorance around the body can silence the voice and cause political impotence. I admired Betty's directness and was inspired to not beat around the bush.

Religion, sexuality, and art all came together for me the summer Annie Sprinkle and I spent in residence with performance artist Linda Montano at her Art/Life Institute in Kingston, New York. Linda, who had almost been a nun, called the internship "summer saint camp." There were many highpoints of our stay, even the quiet moments. Linda's credo is "Life Is Art" and it is that feeling, that belief, that this Mother Superior looks to inculcate in each of her novices. Each day was devoted to meditation, fasting, and performances. One of the most significant performances was when Linda baptized me and Annie as artists. Accepting myself as an artist put everything in perspective.

Since 1983, I have been part of the support group Club 90, which consists of five former adult movie stars. Besides myself, they are Jane Hamilton aka Veronica Hart, who successfully balances a career as a producer/director in adult entertainment with a beautiful family—a devoted husband and two fine sons; Gloria Leonard, a savvy businesswoman and "stand-up constitutionalist," who traveled the lecture circuit on First Amendment issues and now lives comfortably in Hawaii enjoying her new granddaughter and helping to raise another generation of women; Candida Royalle, who took the world by storm when she created Femme, Inc., the groundbreaking, intelligent, and passionate line of erotic videos from the women's

point of view; and Annie Sprinkle, internationally acclaimed performance artist and educator. Like these bold women, I understood that my reputation as an uninhibited sexual explorer left me to choose whether I was pariah or paragon. Like them, I opted for the higher path and, ten years later, when I created the academy I was determined my students in their journey of femmeself discovery would learn to do the same.

Founding
Our
School

Necessity is the mother of invention. I began to feel the need to write a book to communicate what I had learned about human nature through my sexual periscope. The academy was a direct result of my need to support myself while I worked on that book.

As any freelance artist knows, in order to survive, you must learn to be versatile. So when my friend JoLynne approached me with a business proposition, I listened. JoLynne White—who wrote a column for *Transgender,* the journal published by the Massachusetts-based International Foundation for Gender Education—had established a reputation as a fashion consultant to cross-dressers. It might surprise you to learn that this has become a professional specialty, but it would not surprise any Mary Kay or Merle Norman rep, or the proprietress of your favorite lingerie shop, all of whom have for years been doing a healthy business with transvestites. (Now you know Victoria's secret!) An out-of-town client of JoLynne's wanted to come to New York and spend the weekend dressed as a female. At the time, JoLynne was preparing to move out of the state and did not feel she could commit to organizing this weekend, so, knowing that I had a lot of ideas and connections in the real world of make-believe, JoLynne asked me if I wanted to speak to her client and perhaps, guide him.

Jack was a thirty-eight-year-old attorney within whom dwelt a twenty-one-year-old "bimbo airhead" he identified as Sally Sissyribbons. Jack and I established a rapport via telephone. I knew there was an event coming up called the Dressing for Pleasure Ball, an annual convention of people who enjoy cross-dressing and wearing leather and rubber clothes, corsets, very, very high heels, and other fetish attire. DFP weekend consists of workshops, boutiques, a fashion show, and a dinner dance. "Why not come to town for this event?" I suggested to Jack. "I will organize a fabulous weekend for you with the ball as the focal point." I had one stipulation: In order to take on the responsibility of making his dream come true, I would need to hire a staff to help me—a makeup artist, photographer—and be paid a substantial fee myself. To his credit, Jack went for it.

He stayed dressed *en femme* for the entire weekend. I took him to be waxed for the removal of his body hair. We went to the ball, and all of the events associated with it, and on the last day of his stay I organized a photo shoot with the multitalented Annie Sprinkle, photographer, and my friend Leslie Lowe as makeup artist in which we turned Sally into a centerfold star.

Schedule of Miss Sally Sissyribbons:

Friday

8 A.M.	Leg and chest wax at Bonnie Brandt's salon. Arrive as Jack, leave as sissy boy Sally in short pants.
10 A.M.	Breakfast Chez Vera (pre-academy designation).
11 A.M.	Bubble bath for Sally. Dress in hose and short pants for shopping.
Noon	Lunch at Old Homestead restaurant.
1–4 P.M.	Shopping at Lee's Mardi Gras for Sally's wardrobe.
4:30 P.M.	Sally's diary writing. Relaxation.

From Sally's diary:

I am sitting here looking my prettiest. Right now I feel as though I have the right dress, the right makeup, the right hair, the right shoes, gloves, stockings, and accessories, and I am very happy and excited. From now on I'm not going to speak unless spoken to. I will do exactly what Miss Vera tells me to do because I want to be her little girl. I am a gay sissy transvestite, and I love it!
(punctuation and emphasis Sally's)

Sally Sissyribbons

6:30 P.M.	Dinner in. Miss Vera, Miss Viqui, and Sally.
8 P.M.	Theater, Charles Busch, The Lady in Question.
10:30 P.M.	Makeup removal.
Midnight	Beauty sleep for all.

Saturday

9 A.M.	Breakfast and bubble bath.
10 A.M.	Sally's makeover by Anthony McAulay.
12:30 P.M.	Miss Vera and Sally attend Dressing for Pleasure fashion show accompanied by Anthony.
4 P.M.	Lunch at La Taza d'Oro. Miss Vera, Sally, and Anthony.
6 P.M.	Makeup for Sally. New look.
7 P.M.	Miss Vera's friend Judy arrives to join our party.
8 P.M.	All depart for Dressing for Pleasure dinner dance.
1 A.M.	Club hopping.
3 A.M.	Sweet dreams, Sally.

Sunday

11 A.M.	Breakfast and bubble bath.
12:30 P.M.	Photo shoot at Sprinkle Salon. Makeup by Leslie.
6 P.M.	Dinner at Blue Hen.
7 P.M.	Miss Vera attends political meeting.
8 P.M.	Sally writes in journal and relaxes.

. . . As regards last night, I really enjoyed making my entrance as a little pink girl. I want to go further next time. Once I got over my initial nervousness I really began to enjoy being as girlish and fem as possible. I also enjoyed the looks and comments from other people upon greeting me, as if in confirmation that I am a little sissy entirely and everyone knowing it. Perhaps I can use this as a way of finding a new form of self-expression, complete surrender to lace and sissydom for Sally.

| Midnight | Bedtime. |

Monday

| 11 A.M. | Late breakfast. Chez Vera. Cleanup by Sally Sissyribbons. Packing. |
| 2 P.M. | Farewell, Sally! |

This was, quite frankly, Veronica, the most exciting experience I have had.

Thank you,
Sally Sissyribbons

Dear Sally,

It was a pleasure to help make your dreams come true. Remember to thank Jack for working so hard and for letting you have this very special weekend. Anthony, Annie, Leslie, Judy, Viqui, and all agree that you are a sweet, beautiful girl. You made me very proud of you.

Here are some things that I want you to remember:

1. *A warm, sweet-smelling bubble bath will always calm you down and help you to enjoy each moment.*

2. *A lady wiggles her hips, not her shoulders.*

3. *Always remember to say "please" and "thank you."*

4. *Seamed stockings must always be straight.*

5. *Good food is just as important as makeup.*

6. *Miss Vera knows best.*

Love and sweet sissy kisses,
Miss V.

By the end of the weekend, I knew I enjoyed working with cross-dressers and that I was good at it, and so did JoLynne. When she eventually moved away, I agreed to let JoLynne refer some of her clients to me. For two years I saw only referrals from JoLynne. Since she had already begun to cut back on her clientele, this consisted of about a half dozen persons. I continued to write articles for *Adam, Penthouse Forum,* and other adult magazines. I also continued to be welcomed in the art world. The urge to write a book stayed with me, so I left New York for the summer and joined pioneer feminist Kate Millett at her tree farm/art colony in Poughkeepsie, New York, where I learned that with patience and persistence I could create something from nothing. I underwent my own butch training, learning to lay a hardwood floor, transform a chicken coop into an artist's studio, and, with my last gasps, managed to put together a book outline and proposal. My sister artists were fascinated by the stories of my cross-dressing students and agreed that we could use a few transvestite maids to lighten the work load at the colony where we considered ourselves slaves to art. (It could have been worse. Had I been there at the beginning of the summer and not at the end, my duties would have been out in the fields pruning the dreaded Christmas trees, where instead of a hammered thumb, the chief occupational hazard was poison ivy.) The women, many of whom were lesbians, were intrigued both by my ingenuity and by the outfits. By the end of summer, I was carting wigs and fetish frocks to Millett farm so the younger dykes could dress up for the closing ceremonies.

Back in the city, I immersed myself in the luxury of writing an autobiography, and relished the time to slip deep into my feelings and reveries without the pressure of a deadline. I was also enjoying my work with cross-dressers, so, with an eye to expanding my business, I decided to place an ad in a magazine called *The Transvestian,* a racy, poorly printed tabloid with a national distribution of approximately ten thousand, and its sister publication, *Feminin,* which the publisher, Tania Volen, referred to as "the coffee table edition" because, unlike *The Transvestian, Feminin* contained sewing tips rather than sexy photos. With the appearance of the ads, my phone began to ring off the hook.

My next challenge was to do this work in a way that was fun and creative for me, as well as to be of service to the people who call. That is when I advanced the academy concept, for that is how I understood the need. These ladies-in-waiting wanted not only to be transformed, they wanted to look good. They did not want to parody women, but to emulate us. What these men wanted did not seem impossible. They wanted to learn how to do their own makeup, to walk and talk in a more feminine manner, and to get more in touch with this highly sensual feeling that they identified as female. I did not question whether these men had a right to do this. I had already dealt with that in my own life. These men, too, were in the midst of their personal evolutions. What they needed was a school—a finishing school. Every finishing school seems to be named after "Miss This" or "Miss That"—I already had the nickname Miss Vera, promulgated mainly by my late friend comedy genius

Michael O'Donoghue, who among other things, helped to create "Saturday Night Live." Michael was a man who appreciated the merits of getting all frocked up and was always ready to explore the offbeat and unusual, in his life as well as on paper. He had a collection of all sorts of different costumes and vintage clothes, as well as plastic kitsch, taxidermied bears, and his own watercolor masterpieces, which he painted by numbers and showed in galleries. One day, on a whim, I coaxed him into a children's clothing store on Fourteenth Street that I called Ropas par Niños because of the big sign that hung over the front. I tried on a size 14 girl's blue party dress, which we took back to Michael's and both wore. (His rock-and-roll lifestyle left him pretty slim.) After his death, Michael's wife Cheryl Hardwick offered his wardrobe to friends. There were smoking jackets, silk pajamas, a hand-painted leather jacket with the archangel St. Michael on the back. I did not spot the blue party dress that I had urged him to keep. He had probably given it away to some well-deserving little Miss Prim. But the academy's first graduation gown was a glowing white treasure that dangled from the racks of this collection. I have since dyed it pink. And Michael's playful, mischievous spirit is one of the ghosts that still watches over us . . . So the school would be Miss Vera's Finishing School but not for girls . . . for boys who want to be girls, even if just for a few hours. The name was funny and fun. It was right to the point and made the concept accessible. After that the rest was easy. This would be a process of education, a new you-niversity whose specialty was re-creation. Right from the start, I understood the academy would be a holistic experience, not just about putting on clothes but assimilating a consciousness.

With my friend, illustrator Viqui Maggio, who is now Miss Viqui, our Dean of Design and Assistant Headmistress, I designed the academy's crest with three symbols: the fleur-de-lis, my personal symbol (I have one by artist Spider Webb tattooed on my foot), the butterfly, which acknowledges the metamorphosis involved; and a high heel, which requires no explanation. Every academy needs a motto and I decided to forgo the Latin and opt for the French, *Cherchez la femme,* which means "Look for . . ." or "look to . . . the woman." What could be more appropriate? In looking *for* the women in themselves our students also looked *to* women for guidance.

I rose to the challenge.

Chapter 1

Think Pink

When Greenwich Village spilled over its northern border across Fourteenth Street into Chelsea, bohemia met the barrio. Later, through the process called gentrification, local bars and bodegas along Eighth Avenue gave way to trendy shops and restaurants, but the neighborhood has retained its relaxed "live and let live" spirit. This is the area that is home to our academy. In a long, low apartment house built like a stone fortress, the doorperson, Miss Betty, welcomes new arrivals. Though not employed by our school, she enjoys it when our students respond to her

The dedication ritual.

as the academy's receptionist and she thinks of herself as such as she announces each one and directs him to the elevator. He proceeds down a long corridor, his heart no doubt pounding loud enough to drown out the sound of the bell. The door opens and he enters, leaving behind the world as he knows it.

As the novice looks about the intimate studio that is our main campus, he discovers himself enveloped in pink: pink walls, pink sofa, rosy carpet and drapes. He is encouraged to think pink. *Pink* is the color of optimism: *Everything's coming up rosé.* Color analysts agree that a person dressed in pink stands the least chance of encountering aggression while walking down the street, a useful fact for a six-foot transvestite. Pink soothes and calms the soul. From the academy's inception, it was important to me to present the experience in a positive light and encourage personal responsibility. We are the teachers. We are definitely the ones in charge. But every student acknowledges that *he* is here because *she* wants to be.

So we begin each class with the dedication ritual in which the student lights a pink candle carved in the shape of a woman and repeats after me: *I dedicate myself to releasing all of the juicy female energy inside of me. I place my trust in Miss Vera and the deans of the academy and I thank myself for giving myself this gift.* What, you may ask, is the meaning behind the dedication ritual?

First of all, in requiring that the student purchase his own candle, we begin this adventure with a scavenger hunt. The candle ritual highlights the magical qualities of our academy. We send him to an oc-

cult shop located not far from our school. The atmosphere in this musty old shop encourages the student to expect the unexpected, for the academy is a place of experimentation and inquiry. By now the number of pink candle seekers who have entered the shop would nearly circle the block. When I was a girl, I was fascinated by a television program called "The Magic Cottage." At the beginning of each program, the female artist who hosted the show drew a picture of a character who would appear in that day's story. The viewer gazed at the drawing, the picture came to life, and the story unfolded. The academy is our magic cottage. The student's face is our drawing tablet and the mirror reflects fantasy made real. (I was also an avid viewer of "Ding Dong School," and I guess some of Miss Frances rubbed off on me, too.)

Buying the candle requires that the student go out of his way just that much more, and thus increases his awareness. At the academy, attitude and awareness are part of our AAA philosophy. The third element being action. That is why the neophyte must find the candle and bring it to class rather than have it supplied for him.

Before the academy came on the scene, when a cross-dresser went looking to become the girl of his dreams, the path often led to a house of domination. There he was encouraged to give up responsibility for his actions and place himself in the hands of a dominatrix who would order him to dress, usually with little makeup and in lingerie that had seen better days. The dominatrix would then humiliate and spank him, thus repeating a cycle from his childhood, the combination of sexual feelings accompanied by punishment, that had played so long in his brain it felt like love. Here we do not force the student to dress or to do anything; nor do we humiliate him once he is dressed. (No matter how much he begs.) I fully appreciate that many, many people enjoy such encounters and I am sure it is possible to find a whip-wielding mistress, compatible to these needs, but I can't even spank my cats. In my personal sexual evolution, I have found the fantasy realms of dominant/submissive behavior the perfect complement to the sexually repressive religious attitudes of my childhood. Exploring that behavior proved very liberating. But I do not choose to promote that aspect of a student's education or to perpetuate that discipline. In the male world of patriarchal religions and performance anxiety, any variation on the norm, even lusty desire, is treated as weakness. The irony is that there is no real norm. Therefore, everyone stays under control, dominated by guilt which has become so connected to sex and love that it is an aphrodisiac.

I dedicate myself implies focus, concentration, and commitment. Much care and energy go into the planning of our curriculum and the deans and I expect the same level of attention accorded a doctor, a lawyer, or any corporate chief. When I am dealing with a student, I find that even though he has applied for admission, even though he has taken the time to meet me for a half-hour preliminary consultation, and even though it is clear by his actions that he wants to come to class, a part of him may still resist. "I'm not sure when my schedule will permit a class," he might say, though at that moment no thought is more preeminent in his mind. It takes courage to enroll at the academy, but as brave as the student may be, he is also usually scared to the marrow, so he may try to hang on to what is familiar like a bitch to her bone. Our pledge of allegiance helps remind our lady-in-waiting why he is here.

To releasing all of the juicy female energy inside of me. Believe me, each student has plenty and it's ready to spurt. His femmeself is sexually less inhibited than his male persona. He is his own fertility goddess. The student cannot expect her to observe the same rules as he does, especially with regard to fantasy. In the world of sexually explicit media, from which I was graduated cum laude, "pink" refers to the female genitalia—or as we refer to the labia and environs, the *femalia*—when the lips are spread to reveal the entrance to the vaginal canal. At the end of the vaginal canal is the cervix and right in the middle of the cervix is a tiny hole through which the sperm enters to fertilize an egg. This tiny hole is also called "os." I have always been intrigued by the similarity of these names that each refer to a center of magic, mystery, and new life. Our rosy surroundings are a not-so-subtle invitation to the student's libido to awaken from her slumber and lead our Dorothy or Danielle or Jennifer or René on a pink highway to her personal Oz.

I place my trust in Miss Vera and the

deans of the academy. Not only is this line designed to help the student acknowledge his position but to let him know that we, his teachers, are aware that our position is one of privilege and trust. He has surrendered himself to our tutelage and it is about time. The world very much needs to surrender to the female influence, to approach a different balance, a harmony described by the ancient Greeks as homeostasis. The male world measures performance as power. Men have achieved positions of power but not without giving up much in the bargain. Men and women have much to teach each other. Besides fertility and sexiness, another essential quality associated with the female is that of the nurturer. The female is tolerant. The mother loves unconditionally. We tap into all of that energy when we begin to explore each student's femmeself. We strip him of his business suit, his army uniform, or other trappings of male drag that have become his emotional straitjackets. We immerse him in pink frillies, take him back to the security, safety, and sensuality of the womb, so that he has another chance to grow up. As the student enters, pregnant with feeling, our totally, positively, and permanently pink environment, he gives birth to his femmeself. The child is father to the man—and in this case, mother, too.

I thank myself for giving myself this gift. Shakespeare, who so often inspired men to wear dresses, gave Polonius the words, "This above all, to thine own self be true . . ." The student gives himself a gift of love and trust as he embarks on this exciting journey of femme self-discovery. He has, most likely, worked long and hard to pay for his tuition, so he thanks himself. He deserves it.

About that tuition, which at the time of the dedication ritual the student presents to me (in a pink envelope, of course) . . . A revolutionary aspect of the academy is that I have chosen to give financial value, and a hefty value at that, to female life experience. Gloria Steinem wrote in an issue of *Ms.* that women need to be prepared to open new vistas of employment. I doubt that Ms. Steinem, who has never appreciated the opinion of a woman in the adult industry unless she was crying for help, had our academy in mind when she wrote these words, but I totally agree. I did not grow up with the idea that I would become dean of the world's first male-to-female cross-dressing academy.

In early 1996, the *New York Times* reported that institutions of higher education across the country were forced to lower their tuitions due to lack of enrollment. I would suggest that one reason for this decline is these schools are not offering subjects that people want to learn. As enrollments swell at this institution of alternative education, we have been able to raise tuitions, thus bettering our services and offering our students increased opportunities. Clearly we are doing something right. In *Failure Is Impossible,* the story of Susan B. Anthony, biographer Lynn Sherr reports that in 1856, during a heated debate over a proposal by Susan B. Anthony and Elizabeth Cady Stanton that women be given property rights, the members of the New York state legislative committee ridiculed the idea, saying that any husband who followed his wife's lead and voted in favor of this proposal might more properly reflect their relationship by exchanging his breeches for her petticoats. True words are often spoken in jest. Our students, as cross-dressers, represent a threat to the political status quo. The patriarchy is dead, when we believe it to be so.

Vive la femme!

Chapter 2

Venus Envy

Our Founding Philosophy

reud got it half right. Penis envy does exist, but so does its counterpart. When women felt the need for balance, to expand our horizons and share more in the power of men, we created the women's movement. Men too have this need for balance, to share more in what they view as the most enviable aspects of the female experience: to be pampered and protected, to be desirable sex objects, to be of service (yes, even to do housework), many of the things that we as women have put down in recent years as too confining. Cross-dressers are more fortunate than most because their affinity for female cloth-

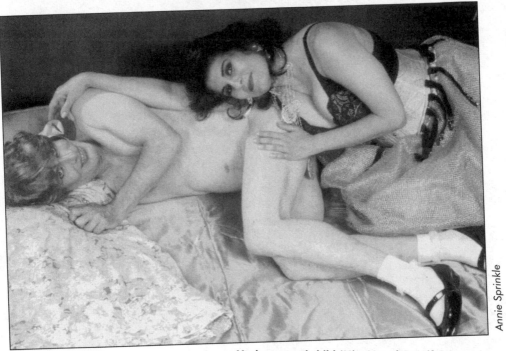

Madonna and child (Miss V and Jennifer James).

ing gives them access to these feelings of Venus Envy. Every stroke of his skirt puts him more in touch with his psyche.

Venus Envy is the founding principle of our academy. To deny this phenomenon is to deny the power of the female experience. (Let's not forget that it is the clothing of the female that is being chosen.) Most of us were raised primarily by our mothers. Dad brought home the bacon, Mom cooked it up and was responsible for the home, the area where we spent most of our time. Mom was home and home was security and comfort and safety. Even if home was hell, it was still home. Most students of the academy have been cross-dressing in some form since early childhood. A young boy may have crept into his parents' bedroom, that mysterious place where Mommy and Daddy did private things behind closed doors. He may have opened the closet and felt good, enveloping himself in the feel and the smell of Mommy that he found in her clothes. These sensations aroused in him what students have so often described as an alluring combination of relaxation and excitement. Out of the closet and into Pandora's box.

Mommy's Little Girl

Many of my students have told me that as little boys, they were dressed in girl's clothes by their mothers or sisters, an aunt, a female baby-sitter, or some other older or bigger woman in a position of power. Imagine this happening at the same time his little penis was getting hard those very first times. The clothing became linked with those early erotic stirrings. The connection stuck, usually to be reinforced, by accident or design, many times later, because it felt good.

A student named Cynthia told me that he was dressed by an aunt who preferred to see him in girls' clothes, and that as late as age fourteen, the rest of his family seemed to accept this, even got a chuckle out of it. (The family was very religious and included several generations of ministers, which may have prepared them for the idea of a man in a dress.) Cynthia enjoyed being the center of attention at those early dress-up sessions, which provided a break from an otherwise strict upbringing in which he was always expected to be a "good boy."

"My aunt had one sweetheart who died young," Cynthia told me, "then she never again took an interest in men. I think that she did not like them.

"Why do you think that some women like to dress male children in girl's clothes?" Cynthia asked.

The question gave me some pause. First, it presumed the existence of such women. I must admit, until Cynthia posed this question, I thought of this form of dress-up as more accidental than planned: big sister and her girlfriends wrestle pesky little brother to the floor at the pajama party and put him in lipstick and a slip or similar scenarios. But Cynthia's experience and those described by other students reveal that there are women who for various reasons enjoy dressing little boys as

little girls. Sometimes these women don't like or are frightened of men and boys; sometimes they like to treat children as dollies and little girl's clothes are much more fun and frilly than those of little boys; or maybe, they wanted daughters. Fathers are sometimes physically absent, or too busy to notice or to care. A father may also be a role model that the child feels unable or unwilling to emulate. Whatever the reasons, a lot of little boys are getting all frocked up and being left with lasting impressions.

At the nail salon I visit, a woman arrives for a biweekly appointment accompanied by her two-year-old son, who sits in her lap. As I watch the son snuggle close to his mother's bosom all during the manicure, I wonder if the boy will one day experience a strong desire to see himself in long nails, and then a dress, and then *voilà!* find himself on our doorstep. In Ireland, at one time, custom decreed that boys be dressed as girls until school age. The custom, based on legend, was supposed to protect the little boys from being stolen by the fairies who considered male children prize commodities. Ironically, saving them from the fairies could turn the boys into them. The academy has a parade of colleens.

Vested Interest

On the other hand, a boy can be inspired to cross-dress if he is deprived of his frock as well as forced into one. How many little boys begged to wear dresses but were turned down and told those were "girls' clothes." Then they saw girls fawned over, patted, and petted just because they looked so pretty in their dresses. To the young boy, the dress was invested with a magical

I've often referred to the academy experience as "therapy with props" because cross-dressing is not simply a matter of putting on clothing. The clothing represents feelings and emotions. The femmeself is the personification of feelings, emotions, needs, and desires. An actor who assumes a role puts on a costume to get closer to the part. And a good actor can use a role, and its costume, to help him learn more about himself. In Cynthia's and Loretta's cases, and in the case of every student who has found his way to our doors, there is a tremendous feeling of relief that accompanies being dressed in female clothing because it reconnects him to that time when putting on a dress did make everything okay. He felt saved or accepted or loved and he felt pleasure. But now his relief may be only temporary. When our student has the urge to dress, I tell him to dress, and to ask himself if there is something he needs to address. What else is going on in his life? Is his urge lust or loneliness? Is he anxious about his job or some other situation? Is putting on a dress going to benefit this other situation or just be like nail polish on a snag in his panty hose—sooner or later he's going to get a big messy run. For instance, if the student is dressing because he is lonely or horny, his femmeself can bring him intense sexual

Annie Sprinkle

Jennifer James with pussy.

power. Had he been allowed to try it on for size, he might have discovered early on that happiness is not a matter of fashion statement. (Or is it?)

Another student, Loretta, recounted to me that as a little boy he was beaten when he was disobedient, but his sisters were never hit. He found that when he wore his sisters' clothes, he was spared physical punishment, so he just kept on wearing them.

pleasure, but he may also need to get out more and meet people, join a social or service group, answer or place a personal ad. If there is stress at his job, he may need to communicate with his co-workers. Since our lady-in-waiting is no longer a boy, I encourage him to let his femmeself help him continue to grow into a man of action. Otherwise cross-dressing may become a frustrating experience.

Jung Ladies

Cross-dressing provides a break from the burdensome role of manhood into which he has been thrust, a role that comes with its own costume, an emotional strait-jacket. If it is so hard to be a man, why do men try so hard? What is the payoff? The payoff is power, control, and acceptance. A boy is educated with the idea that if he "acts like a man," he will attain wealth, power, and respect. He tries very hard to maintain his male persona, but his femme-self, or as Jung would call her, his *anima* knows better. According to Jung, every woman has a male inner life called her animus and every man an anima. The anima represents a man's experience with women, his subconscious knowledge of all women. By making the anima visible, we encourage him to have a chat with her, get to know her, and get to know himself better.

I have learned from hundreds of students that there are a lot of unhappy men. Many men do not like their jobs, no matter how financially rewarding. Some men resent their roles as providers because in order to be accepted and fulfill their commitments they have denied who they are. Many feel like Clark Kent forced into the role of Superman when they'd rather be Lois Lane. Others are bored or lonely. Men are unhappy because they are out of balance. The path of the man, the straight man, has become so narrow there is no room to progress without major change. I suggest he get up on his toes to be high-heeled and well healed. Femininity is a state of mind as well as a state of being.

Our ladies-in-waiting are taught lessons in ways of being that seem to be the opposite of how they are as men. This is not because men are the total opposites of women and vice versa, this is because as human beings, we are very similar. We are not taking something from outside the student, be it a dress, a mannerism, or a desire, and imposing it on him. We are drawing from an emotion or energy that is within the student and encouraging it to flower.

Of course, our girls usually do not understand all of this when they arrive. Although the students derive much pleasure from their femmeselves, many see her as trouble. She's got the allure of Kitty from "Gunsmoke" and the reputation of Calamity Jane. They also do not understand all of the complexities involved. If the students ran the school, they might spend most of their time putting on outfits and never see beyond the mirror. So we surround them with other educational opportunities. The deans provide their expertise in the arts as well as lessons from life experience. The academy library is filled with books and videos—most created by women—on all of the subjects in our curriculum, including biographies of female role models as diverse as Simone de Beauvoir, and Elizabeth Taylor. Many of my colleagues who emphasize human sexuality as a path to enlightenment are represented: author Susie Bright; anthropologist Helen

Fisher; the tantrika, Jwala; Candida Royalle; Annie Sprinkle; Betty Dodson; and more. It is through the student's sexuality that he has been led to our school. One of the key differences between a transvestite, which is how most of our students identify, and a transsexual is that the transvestite is sexually aroused by female clothing. The clothing just does not matter that much to a transsexual and she sure could do without her penis. Our girls have followed their erections to our door and now that we have got their attention we work on the total person. Ours is a holistic experience, a painless and pleasure-filled women's studies course for men.

Gender Euphoria

Since the academy's inception, I have been interviewed often. The most insightful of all of the interviewers so far has been Phyllis Burke, who visited our school while researching her book *Gender Shock*. Ms. Burke really understood what is going on here— the importance of learning from the experience of doing. The academy is a stark contrast to what Phyllis Burke describes as the "Orwellian" treatments imposed on young boys and girls who did not measure up to the expectations of their gender in behavior modification clinics that have existed since the 1960s. Young boys who played with dolls were subtly humiliated when they played with girls' toys and rewarded when they chose guns and war games. Young girls who were "tomboys" were reconditioned to conform to more traditional feminine behavior. Of course, not every boy or girl was sent to a behavior modification center, but the centers reflect the stringent gender boundaries that society has accepted as nor-

mal. A child who did not conform was said to be suffering from what was termed *gender dysphoria*. At the academy, we believe in *gender euphoria*.

The more we learn about the concept of gender, the less we seem to know. The first time I heard the word gender was in language class. In English, there were three genders: masculine for male, he and him; feminine for female, she and her; and neuter for it, things that were neither masculine nor feminine. Other languages offered only two genders: masculine and feminine. In French, the pencil is masculine, *le stylo;* the pen is feminine, *la plume*. The prevalent thinking was that a person's sex and her gender were the same.

In 1952 all of that changed. George Jorgensen underwent surgery and became Christine and all the world learned there were people in the world who felt out of sync with their bodies enough to change them and that such change was possible. In his brilliant chronicle *What Wild Ecstasy: The Rise and Fall of the Sexual Revolution*, author John Heidenry reports that it was around this time that Dr. John Money borrowed the term gender from its use in language and coined the terms "gender roles" and "gender identity" to use in his work with transsexuals at Johns Hopkins, which would become the first American hospital to perform sex change surgery.

Sex has come to refer more to physical acts or attributes, gender to social conditioning, and not everyone identifies those two within themselves as congruent. Now a third sex seems to have emerged, the transsex, those who want to be free to straddle the middle, sometimes physically as well as mentally. Advanced technology shows us that there is much variation in even the physical and chemical makeup of individuals. The more we know, the less we can be sure.

In November 1995 the theme of the annual conference of the Society for the Scientific Study of Sex (Quad S) was "Sex and Gender—What Is the Difference?" A fascinating presentation described what has been practice when a child is born with the ambiguous genitalia. If a child was born with a teeny, tiny penis or no penis, he was raised as a she with appropriate surgery, particularly because to reconstruct a functioning penis was, and continues to be, far more difficult than to construct a functioning vagina. What has happened is that years later some of these children decide that they would prefer to identify as the opposite gender. The prevalent thinking now is that early surgery can be a mistake and it is better to let a child develop independently without surgery, and make her or his own gender choice. Before Christine Jorgensen, transsexuality was a feeling. Technology has made it a physical state of being.

Students of the academy with only one or two exceptions, identify as men. Now that transsexual surgery has become so advanced it is easier to opt for an operation, but I hope that our students learn to

Annie Sprinkle

Jennifer grows from toddler to temptress.

transcend the confines of gender without surgery.

Sapphic Poetry

On a field trip with a student, some of the deans and I visited Crazy Nanny's, a lesbian bar in the West Village. Our student, Tammie Alberts, considered the bar a great testing ground to see if her maleness could really go undetected. Tammie claimed to be seriously considering sex reassignment surgery but she said if there was no hope for her to pass, why bother? I told her that if she really needed the surgery, how she felt on the inside might be more of a determining factor than how she looked on the outside. But if she wanted to visit a lesbian bar, we would take her.

Tammie was slim and young and very feminine. She could have fooled me, and I am an expert. Not even her voice gave her away. We made quite a few friends in the bar. Tammie seemed to be accepted quite easily. As a group of women left, headed for a pool tournament at another bar, one of them invited us to follow. Tammie could not resist confiding her story. She called the woman over and told her that she was a man. "That's cool," confided her new friend, "I'm gender neutral." As the woman spoke the words, I thought what a great term, gender neutral. What a great concept. I hope that our students will allow their own lives to approach closer and closer to gender neutral by first let-

ting in those aspects of themselves without prejudice that they otherwise might reject as too feminine.

Where is this all heading? What if we all were gender neutral—would we all end up the same, clones of each other? Not if we lived 5 million years. For example, we all have the physical capacity to experience bisexual pleasure, and we have always had that capacity, yet we all do not choose to do so. There are so many variables that go into the creation of an individual from within and without. The purpose of the academy is to increase the options.

We live in an amazing age. Technology humbles us all. It is only since 1920 that the sex hormones have been isolated, less than a century ago, just a sequin on the glittering ball gown of Father Time.

There are more things in heaven and earth, Horatio,
Than are dreamt of in your philosophy.

—*Hamlet,* I, v, 166

Chapter 3

The Student Body

*D*o you have many students?" When I hear this question from a prospective enrollee, I know it means "Are there many girls like me?" I assure him that he belongs to a very big sorority. According to the International Foundation for Gender Education, based in Wayland, Massachusetts, as much as 6 percent of the male population has the desire to cross-dress. Using figures supplied by the Department of Commerce and published in the 1996 World Almanac, which lists a United States population of 250 million people, approximately 74 percent of whom are over eighteen and 49 percent of whom are men, I calculated that to be about 6 million adult men, in the United States alone. From the number of phone calls we receive and the number of requests we get for brochures, I consider this to be a conservative estimate. We have the talent and connections to turn our girl into a centerfold star, but many of our students choose to be very private about their dressing and we honor that privacy.

Sometimes, during an interview, I am asked to name names. "Are there any people who come to your school whom we would recognize?" ask the gossipmongers. I tell them, "Look around at your lawyer, the cop on the beat, the man who delivers your mail, hauls the trash from your street, or runs the company where you are employed." Students of the academy come from any and all walks of life, all economic levels, all the colors of the human spectrum. All shapes and sizes. Many of our girls are football jocks, over six feet tall (in flats). Others fit into their wives' size-eight dresses. Dennis Rodman is not the only professional athlete who likes to get out of uniform and into a dress, but he is probably the least inhibited. One professional wrestler, a mountain of a man, telephoned to thank me for creating the academy. He told me that he longed to participate but was terrified of the consequences. His fear gripped him more strongly than any opponent's half nelson. Among the jocks we've put in frocks are baseball players, yachtsmen, football and tennis stars. All students bring with them different endowments: small, medium, and XXX. And every one is very proud of his legs. One of the first products I will create is Miss Vera's Panty Hose for Him. Joe Namath, the superstar quarterback and former L'Eggs pitchman, was way ahead of his time.

We average about one hundred new students a year and many returnees. Students arrive from across the country and around the world and many more study via our telephone extension classes at 1-900-884-VERA. There is one thing that all of these men have in common: an affinity for female clothing. For the typical student, these feelings began in early childhood. He loves the feel of it, the smell of it, the associations with love and security and sensuality. As a little child/animal he found comfort in this clothing and it made a lasting impression.

Initially, most of our students enrolled at about the age of forty, and why not? Forty is the age of self-acceptance. Life begins at forty. The student acknowledges that for most of his life he has fantasized about being a woman and this fantasy is not going to just go away, so he decides to get a bead on her. That is where we come in. Men in their twenties and thirties may still be trying to ignore these feelings, or hoping that they can make them disappear; older men who have been dressing in total privacy for many years may be too set in their ways to share this part of themselves with the outside world. However, now that the academy has been in business since 1992, we see more college-age co-eds and we sing happy birthday to more and more sixty-year-old debutantes who sigh wistfully and ask, "Where were you twenty years ago, [when I was still young and pretty]?" Actually, older men transform more easily.

The femmeself exists to liberate the man from the narrow confines of maledom. She represents qualities which may lie dormant within him and she offers new options. The more he knows about her—the more he can let her be his guide—the more he evolves as a person. Our goal at the academy is not merely to make the student a passable femme, but to encourage him to use what he learns when *en femme* and integrate this into his male persona so that the student can be a happier, healthier, sexier human being no matter what the fashion statement. Ours is the school from which no one wants to graduate. All classes are private involving one student and several teachers, depending on the curriculum he has chosen. A student will pursue his studies at his own pace. He might spend a couple of hours with us in a two and a half hour Sudden Beauty Seminar or opt for the four-hour Miracle Miss, and then we might not see him again for a year or six months. After sticking in his toe to test the waters, he may need to run back to shore. He might, especially if he comes in from out of town, spend a couple of days with us in a Femme Intensive, or he might visit us every six weeks on a continuing basis. The more time he spends with us, the more he learns. But no matter if he spends a couple of hours with us or a couple of years, the experience, as attested to by our students, is profound. People have asked me if I want to put every man in a dress. I do not. We already have our hands full with eager beavers. But I do think that any man who experiences an academy transformation will learn a lot. The students who have learned the most are the students who have spent the most time with us. It is a privilege and an honor to witness each one's evolution.

What sort of personality might a student ascribe to his femmeself? Sissy maid? Sexy vamp? Young wife? Sophisticated career woman? Streetwalker? Mommy's little girl? Conservative librarian? Fashion model? Mother-to-be? Or something else altogether? This question is included on the enrollment application that each student is required to complete before gaining admittance to our academy. He may pick more than one because a real woman can be both madonna and whore and all points in between. A preponderance of students identifies as sophisticated career women, though we do have a strong sissy maid contingent and plenty of aspiring fashion models. And there is a little whorish slut in every girl.

In a homework assignment entitled "Create a Herstory" (Chapter 4), the student is asked to answer some questions regarding the femmeself. The answers can be based in fact or in fantasy. If there is a trait the student has that he attributes to his femmeself—for example a love of reading—he might include that in the herstory. Or if there is something the femmeself might like to do, but does not yet know how to do, that may also be included in the herstory because we can make it happen. We have taught students to sew, clean, be good hostesses and dancers . . . the list goes on.

First in Her Class

One of my favorite herstories was submitted by Sally Sissyribbons. I find it so endearing because it is nostalgic—Sally was my very first student—but also because it is fun. Consider that this is coming from a hard-nosed litigator in his late thirties: "My name is Sally Sissyribbons and I am a twenty-one-year-old bimbo airhead . . . I am a virgin. Miss Vera is special in my life. I like movies involving romance, strong men, and pretty women. I very seldom read books, just magazines—my favorite is *Sassy*. My favorite season is autumn due to my innate melancholia. I do not participate in sports, though I've often dreamed of being a cute little cheerleader, the top of my head reaching the shoulder of some good-looking hunk. My car is borrowed from my mommy, I do not own one myself. I currently live alone. My favorite star is Madonna and supermodel Paulina, best hunks are Mel Gibson and Kevin Costner. I like to cook brownies, but I'm not very good at it."

In his male life Jack worked for a major corporation, wore pinstripe suits, read true-life crime stories, ran track, and could argue an opponent into the ground. Jack was not sure if he was straight or gay and did not understand that he did not need to choose. His greatest fear and his greatest desire was to have the world find out about Sally Sissyribbons. His position with his firm made him subject to intense security checks. Investigators might literally go into his underwear drawer. Yet, the "twenty-one-year-old bimbo airhead" inside of him loved the idea of being placed on display in all of her plumage at a crowded party, a rare bird amid a flutter of giggles and a flock of admiring glances.

Sally's herstory illustrates the childlike spirit inherent in cross-dressing. Before his first classes in high-heel training, even Sally's posture displayed his immaturity when opening up to his femmeself. He stood with his belly puffed out, like a baby in a diaper trying to be strong and stay erect. My best friend, Annie Sprinkle, the internationally known sex educator, performance artist, and former adult movie star, has said that in terms of our sexual

knowledge most people are still in kindergarten.

We begin our sexual evolution and might linger in place, sometimes forever, especially if that place feels good, and what feels good is usually what is most familiar. Cross-dressers are not alone in this. Another example is a man whose first sexual experiences were with a prostitute and who, despite his insistence that he is looking for a wife, still finds commercial sex most exciting. Or a woman who, though she is an avowed feminist who is responsible for her own orgasm, enjoys being the naughty girl who wants a good spanking. Exploring the femmeself, like exploring any aspect of sexuality, is a learning experience. It is part of growing up. Even those who have taken the bold step of contacting the academy display a childlike helplessness. Sometimes a prospective student will request information and then tell us he has no confidential mailing address at which to receive it. Because they are no longer children and need no longer be helpless, I say, "Rent a post office box."

Student Council President

Jennifer James is our student council president. Jennifer attained her position not by election, but by appointment. He appointed himself. From our very first meeting, James let me know that he was strongly in support of me and the academy concept. "You're on to something, girl, let me be the wind beneath your wings." (James likes to speak in pop phrases: "The squeaky wheel gets the grease"; "You win the clean plate award"; "High five to you"; "Keep your smile on . . .")

Student James is . . .

Annie Sprinkle

. . . Jennifer James.

When he enrolled at the academy, James was a nuclear engineer who worked in a power plant the size of a small city: three thousand employees, most of them men, entrusted with the weighty responsibility of the safety of whole communities, small fish in a big electrified pond. While James dressed in jeans and L. L. Bean sweaters, Jennifer's dress of choice was a pink satin maid's uniform with a short frilly skirt, layers of petticoats, ruffled rubber rhumba panties, and heels. A chatty exhibitionist, Jennifer could start up a conversation with ease and always knew the right thing to say. Unlike James, Jennifer never needed to fortify herself with brew in order to socialize, though she might have a Virginia Slim to relax. Never uptight when she was tightly laced, she took courage from the caress of her corset.

James is a small man with a big heart and piercing blue eyes. He is a jock in those sports that rely on speed rather than bulk, like baseball and track. He had been married for thirteen years but the marriage had ended in divorce, some of the turmoil having stemmed from the existence of James' female persona, Jennifer. Jennifer had "been 'round the block" as they say. James listed three Jennifers: 1, 2 and 3. Jennifer #1 had been born when James was a child. She was his deep dark secret and her meager wardrobe was stolen from his sister's drawers and neighbors' clotheslines. . . . Once James started earning money as an adult, Jennifer #2 came into existence. He found her in commercial sex magazines like *Penthouse Forum*. He learned that he was not alone, that men who liked to wear women's clothes were called transvestites. He bought her some clothes like those he saw in the magazines—a short frilly French maid's uniform that felt sensational—and eventually he told his wife. The Jennifer who matriculated in our academy is Jennifer #3: Jennifer James, a bachelorette, our most open and evolved girl to date.

Tall, Dark, and Handsome

On the opposite end of the physical spectrum was June G. Edwards, the G. for Georgette, after her mother. June arrived at the academy as Ed. Tall, dark, and handsome, he was six foot two, swarthy and square-jawed. Ed was a second-degree black belt who ran his own foundry. His second marriage had just ended and he felt devastated and suicidal. Rather than do himself in, he decided to give himself an academy weekend as a thirty-eighth birthday present. June, too, was a girl with a past, a kinky one.

She sported an "S" for slave branded into her bottom with a hot iron, but she longed to be mistress of her own fate.

Sargent Susan

I believe that every traditional male bastion of endeavor has cross-dressers high-stepping among the ranks. Susan Sargent took her name from her military classification. The other students who met her, such as Jennifer James and June, envied her ability to organize. She was the "goody two shoes" among the bunch. Susan's male persona, David, grew up in orphanages and foster homes. He had learned early on to have a place for everything and everything in its place. Susan arrived for class with a suitcase full of clothes neatly arranged in Ziploc bags: stockings, panties, bras, slips, gloves, wigs, and jewelry all sorted, folded, and inventoried with military precision. Susan told stories of having been a bodyguard to presidents and an adjutant to high brass in Vietnam. We suspected her stories might be exaggerated, but they were such good stories (and Susan told them with such sincerity) that we were captivated. She arrived quite suddenly, and as we were to discover, she would leave the same way, having made quite an impact. In her short tour of academic duty, she excelled as my aide de campus.

Star Pupil

Most students admit they are very nervous at the time of their initial consultations. Some try to mask their feelings with an air of bravado. Patti Harrington might have been nervous at our very first meeting, but what he projected was ingenuousness, an innocence and naïveté coupled with a determi-

Patti's androgynous look.

nation to explore. Pat at six four was one of our tallest girls. As a child, his size had been the source of many problems. Other boys enjoyed making a name for themselves by beating up this big kid who did not like to fight back. Like many of our students, Pat foraged through his sister's pantie drawer a few times as a child. He felt that his personal-ity was more suited to that of a girl. Pat's sexual experiences had been minimal, only one unconsummated encounter in a brothel he had visited with some pals from work. Any-time he felt sexual, he felt a discomfitting de-sire to be a girl, rather than to be with one and in repressing that wish, he repressed his sexuality. I had a virgin on my hands.

When he began to explore his femmeself, Patti's first stop had been an S&M house. He described being pushed in the direction of a pile of limp frillies and expected to take it from there. "I knew there must be a better way," he told me. And that is what led him to our door. Once a month, we transformed tall, bald, slouching Pat into beautiful, stately Patti. Our emerging femme fatale waged a fierce battle with the lonely pessimist who also lived inside of her. She had learned to walk with grace and do her own makeup though she still found it difficult to accept a compliment for any of her accomplishments. Patti also learned to sew her own dresses from complicated Vogue patterns. Pat's wardrobe pre-academy consisted mainly of Grateful Dead tee shirts.

Pat began to integrate more of Patti into his everyday dress: jeweled studs in his ears, a long ponytail trailing below his bald spot, manicured fingernails . . . One of his buddies, on noticing the gradual changes in Pat's appearance, remarked, "Harrington's looking more and more like Olive Oyl!" It felt right to Patti. She was the essence of Olive Oyl, pulled between valiant Popeye and villainous Bluto. Pat found an Olive Oyl tee shirt and added it to his wardrobe of Grateful Dead tees. Patti also began to think about dating. Our (big) little girl was growing up.

Our Admissions Policy

At the entrance to the kinky brothel owned by the infamous dominatrix Monique von Cleef in The Hague, there was a sign that read, "Are there any straight men left?" As I have said, about 95 percent of our student body identifies as heterosexual. Often, a student will say to me, "In my daily life I am heterosexual (about 60 percent of our student body is married), but when I am dressed anything goes." Some mean that only in fantasy—some are ready to be more adventuresome. Part of what the student learns when he comes to the academy is the line between who is straight, gay, or bisexual, especially when it comes to fantasy, is a very blurry line, more herringbone than black or white. Those of our students who identify as gay usually share the same sorts of mainstream jobs and the same embarrassments about dressing up as their sorority sisters. Out of one closet and into another.

After five years of the academy's existence, only one of our students has had a sex change operation. Many students have a fantasy to live full time as a woman, but it is usually a fantasy—a very strong fantasy, but still a fantasy. They derive enormous fulfillment and/or sexual pleasure from dressing up, but they are transvestites. They identify as hetero- (and occasionally homo-) sexual men and have no desire to lose their penises. Male-to-female transsexuals identify as hetero- (or homo-) sexual women and feel they have been born into the wrong body. Part of the reason the academy exists is to help students learn the difference between fantasy and reality, and also to learn how to make the two come together.

What we look for in a student is an upbeat attitude and the desire to explore. Not all applicants are accepted. Sometimes a student will make up an elaborate story to explain his desire to dress. When I asked one caller how he had learned of Miss Vera's Finishing School, he told me that he was not really a cross-dresser, but that his wife had seen our ad and recommended he enroll. Since, at the time, we were advertising only in an obscure tabloid, *The Transvestian,* which was available primarily in adult bookstores not known for high percentages of female clientele, I doubted that his wife would have dropped by for a copy. He elaborated. He and his wife were separated and she told him that if he agreed to come to the academy and live for one week as a female, she would take less in their alimony settlement. "It will save me thousands," he declared, in a vain attempt to keep his male ego intact. His dishonesty outweighed his imagination and so he was not accepted for enrollment. The pretense of having been forced to contact the academy is a popular defense mechanism that some prospective students employ to protect their fragile male egos and pride. One caller told me that his enrollment was his mother's idea. The idea of someone else, a wife or mother, having exerted her powers of persuasion allows the student to avoid facing the thought that he *wants* to dress up, and somehow legitimizes forbidden longings. We understand these rationalizations, but those who hide behind them are not ready for the academy. Every lady-in-waiting who actually crosses our pretty pink threshold acknowledges that she is here because he wants to be.

The Other Woman

Wives sometimes do give their approval and encouragement, and more and more have accompanied their husbands to the academy. One of the first couples to attend was Tom and his wife, Eileen. Tom was a tough guy: a trucker from the Bronx with the appropriate "dese" and "doze" speech patterns. He was pint-sized but powerful. A silk-stocking enthusiast, he spun from the mirror after checking that his seams were straight, and standing in his size-eight sequined dress announced to us during his first transformation, "When I was in high school, I was unhappy because of my size, but as Renée, I am just right." Tom was proud that his femmeself Renée Thomas could fit into Eileen's dresses, though Eileen was not expected to share them. The only item they fought over was the gold anklet that Tom had given Eileen for her birthday. Renée *wanted* that anklet.

By way of introduction, Tom had sent us a home video that he had made, which showed him as Renée at the sink doing the dishes. To accomplish this housework Renée wore white ankle-strap shoes with five-inch heels and a sophisticated pink suit with a slim skirt, which was protected by a frilly white apron. Occasionally the family dog walked past the camera and Eileen could be seen off to the side reading a book.

Renée Thomas, however, was tired of keeping her light under a bushel, and was ready to go out on the town. Eileen gave Tom a trip to the academy as a birthday present and we all went out together. For Tom and Eileen—for better, for worse, for richer, for poorer, in dresses or in pants—the evolution of Renée Thomas was an adventure they shared.

Hopeful Housewife

Student George was a union man. He wielded heavy equipment and hung with the crew. Like trucker Tom, in his work life George strove to maintain the image of he-man, not she-man. But George, too, had another side:

Growing up with two older sisters gave me an edge on dressing up and getting familiar with sexy clothes and perfumes. We spent a lot of time in the kitchen. Today, I am forty-four and still my favorite room is the kitchen where I am really happiest cleaning and cooking, watching cooking shows on TV, and serving appetizers and drinks to my girlfriend. I dream of being with a real career girl who wants to get into the boardroom with men as much as I want to get out of it and get my femmeself into the kitchen, the bathroom, and the bedroom!

My lady would arrive home after "a hard day at the office" and I greet her at the door in a dainty maid's outfit, bonnet, high heels, etc. "What would you like dear," I say as she settles in, "White or red? I bought a beautiful chardonnay today that I know you will love." I pour her a glass and prepare some fresh shrimp, cheese, and crackers, maybe some chicken wings. On the stove is a great pasta sauce and some linguine. There's fresh bread, and a salad in the fridge. We dine together and I serve her, hoping she comments on my outfit, my new perfume, and how clean the house is . . . It's my job to soothe her. I draw her bath, a hot bubble bath. I gently massage her feet. In the bedroom, I perform as her "boudoir girl." As Gina, I am very submissive to her wishes and very, very oral. I would rather please her. She soon forgets her hard day at the office. In the morning, I get up a half hour earlier than she and prepare fresh muffins and fruit and coffee. She goes off to work and I am left alone in my element, cleaning up after her and preparing to greet her again when she comes home. After all, I am her wife.

Gina's and Renée's dreams of domestic bliss are shared by many students of the academy. As a sophisticated career woman myself, it is easy to see the benefit to encouraging this obvious link to the house husband.

Old-Fashioned Girl

Stephanie nee Stephen was an attorney. (The academy could start its own distaff firm.) Unlike some students who have lived their lives trying to overcompensate for their femmeselves—forcing themselves to play football, signing up with the Marines, playing up their roles as sexual studs—Steve has always displayed a softer side to us. A supportive girlfriend helps Steve and Stephanie to evolve. The herstory of Steve's femmeself reads in parts like a romance novel:

Who is Stephanie? She is pink and sky blue and bright red. She is the spring rain and a gently falling winter snow. She is a sunset on a warm summer night, and the scent of a summer thunderstorm. She is my soul.

Stephanie is an old-fashioned girl. She lives alone in a sixty-year-old house which is decorated with period furniture from the twenties and thirties. She collects old books. She likes to stay at home, watch old movies, read, and enjoy the roses and lilies in her garden.

Stephanie makes her living as a lawyer, but she would adore being a cocktail waitress. She likes a sense of risk, but where there is some safety. She dreams of serving drinks to customers and being caressed by them— both men and women. She feels that if she were to make a scene, she would be fired, so she doesn't, and revels in the attention.

Stephanie loves to photograph people in their natural environment. She would love to be with men, yet be invisible to them, figuratively speaking, and photograph them doing the silly macho things men think they must do. She also likes to photograph women of different cultures to show their dignity and worth.

Stephanie plays tennis. Her heroines are Chris Evert and Martina Navratilova. Chris shows the grace and talent that make a true champion, *without the macho bragging and swagger common to many male athletes.*

Stephanie admires Eleanor Roosevelt, Susan B. Anthony, Jane Fonda, Miss Vera, Katharine Hepburn, Diane Arbus, and Mary Ellen Marks. Her favorite movie stars include Ingrid Bergman and Marilyn Monroe. She loves to cry for the tragic heroine, although she really does not wish to be one. Stephanie thinks Robert Mitchum is the sexiest hunk ever. She drools over him, and Clint Eastwood, as he was in the old spaghetti westerns. Paul Newman, Robert Redford, and Michael Douglas also make her itch. And she can't forget the male models in the International Male catalog. She spends simply hours gazing at the underwear ads. (Oh to have some of that in her mouth.)

Lonesome Cowgirl

While the majority of our students have come from the New York metropolitan area, there are many ladies-in-waiting inhabiting the hinterlands. For some men, the femmeself is often their best lover, a companion in what is sometimes a lonely existence. Charlene West was a cowgirl from Wyoming. Charlie described his earliest memories of Charlene in his herstory:

"Charlene began to know herself at about age twelve. Her sister, who was two years older, had a closet full of clothes that Charlene used to try on. Everything felt so nice then, and even better now. Then things changed as my sister went away to school and took most of her clothes with her. This left me without anything so I started buying various items. Not knowing any better, I had a terrible time with sizes. Then I found my sister's plastic raincoat and because it clung and felt like a skirt, everything was fine. Charlene still gets a lot of pleasure from wearing a raincoat, today."

Accompanying Charlie's enrollment application were two photos. The first showed Charlene standing in front of her fireplace, wearing a red skirt, a sweater set, and crimson ankle-strapped high heels. The second showed Charlie dressed in rubber waders, proudly holding a large trout. Charlie hunted deer and antelope and Charlene earned brownie points by marinating the steaks and serving them to the deans for dinner. For Charlene, the West was never so wild as our trip to the Lower East Side where we took her shopping to pick out a wardrobe (Chapter 8).

Graduation day.

Eric Kroll

Extracurricular Activities

Some of the students enjoy meeting each other. Some prefer to be private. An early pajama party attended by Jennifer James, June, and Stephanie resulted in the creation of our first class in how to walk in high heels (Chapter 9). On another occasion, with Susan Sargent in tow, Jennifer and Stephanie, as a photojournalist team, documented Wigstock, the Labor Day festival in which participants put on and let down their hair (Chapter 5). We have carried our pink banner, a gift from student Zondra, in the Gay/Lesbian/Transgender Pride parade (Chapter 12) and attended parties such as the Dressed to Thrill Ball in Los Angeles (Chapter 12). Night of 1000 Gowns (Chapter 15), the drag ball and coronation run by the Imperial Court of New York, has become an annual academy event. A group of students as French maids brought the academy its initial publicity in *New York* magazine (Chapter 12) and our girls have become our own supermodels, posing for the academy's award-winning advertising campaign.

While our girls certainly have a very big interest in common, they are also very different, and are not always compatible. There can be a stiff competition among them, not so much for gowns and gloves as for attention. Not all girls like to share the spotlight and though a student will be fascinated with the outward reflection of his femmeself in the mirror, if he is inwardly uncomfortable, he may be afraid to see his femmeself mirrored in the face of another student. It is a tricky thing putting students together, but well worth the effort because the students learn much from each other. The group events like pajama parties and galas are some of the highlights in the annals of academy herstory.

Miss Casting

Though the academy has received much publicity, there are those who do not realize we are a school for girls with something extra rather than the more traditional finishing school for girls. Because we are listed under schools in the Manhattan telephone directory as "Miss Vera's Academy" with no further explanation, we receive solicitations from all sorts of companies: colleges that offer a junior year abroad, amusement parks advertising their facilities for class trips, plumbing suppliers who offer to clean our pipes. Usually, I just read the flyers and chuckle, imagining our girls whitewater rafting in makeup and heels, or boarding the plane for a year at the Sorbonne. But one invitation inspired a response.

Dear Miss Vera,

We are a Hollywood casting agency looking for girls 14–20 to play opposite Leonardo DiCaprio in the major motion picture "Romeo & Juliet" to be directed by Baz Luhrmann (Strictly Ballroom). We will be in your area conducting auditions . . . If you have any students interested in trying out for the part, please let me know and I will be happy to fax you our audition procedures.

Sincerely,
Bill Kaufman,
David Rubin Casting

I immediately faxed back:

Dear Mr. Kaufman,

How brilliant of you to adhere to the traditions of the Bard and invite our girls to participate. I am sure when I put out the word, we will have a number of enthusiastic ingenues. My first thought is to recommend our student council president, Jennifer James. Jennifer is very versatile and can play any age from 4 to 40. As a sample of her work, I am faxing you a copy of one of our ads in which she is the model.

This note was followed by an ad that shows Jennifer James in a flowered gingham dress, above copy that explains our school in detail and a tag line that reads "Be the Sister You Never Had."

Unfazed, Mr. Kaufman fired back.

Thank you for your response. I see that your girls may not be who we are looking for, but I am sending you the casting procedures anyway. You never know . . . they may have daughters.

In the completed feature, Mercutio was played as a drag queen. Could this correspondence have provided an inspiration?

The Reluctant Debutante

Mr. Kaufman's invitation was not our first encounter with Hollywood. With the popularity of cross-dressing in movies and on television, it was not surprising that we have begun to have actors as students. In preparation for his role as the transvestite director Ed Wood, Johnny Depp received information on our academy and, though he did not have the time to study here, he generously publicized our school in interviews. Frank Beatty, a young actor on the CBS soap "Guiding Light" did learn feminine fundamentals at Miss Vera's Finishing School. The TV star spent several months as a TV villain who cross-dressed in order to facilitate a revenge plot. When the show's producers made initial arrangements with me, they asked that I keep Frank's lessons secret. "We plan to keep the viewing audience in the dark for the first few weeks," they told me, "and we don't want the soap opera press ruining the surprise." I thought it was kind of a stretch to ask Mr. Beatty to pull the deception off for so long, no matter how much latex makeup and padding of curves they planned to use, but I agreed to keep mum, not even telling the deans the whole story, just letting them know that he was an actor preparing for a part. Mr. Beatty had his own ideas. Upon meeting each dean he promptly announced that he was not one of our regular students, he was doing this because he had to, it was his job as an actor on "Guiding Light." Ironically, his declarations only made him sound that much more like one of our students, albeit the more conflicted ones, who love the excuse that they are brought here not by choice but by force of circumstance. Methinks, these ladies doth protest too much.

From Herr to Herren

The noted German actor Helmut Zierl arrived here with his entourage from Phoenix Film in Berlin. These included his producer Karl "Charlie" Schappers, a big, bald, worldly fellow who loved thoroughbreds and cigars; Helmut's personal business partner, who had a camera always at the ready; and their costume designer, who was eager to explore New York. It felt as if we were under siege. Never had so much male energy been in the academy at one time. Before arriving in New York, the group had stopped off in Hollywood to meet makeup artists and mold makers who might construct new faces and body suits for Helmut, who would spend five episodes of his series "Nobody Is Perfect" *en femme*. With the exchange rate in their favor, the Germans had plenty of money to spend but almost too many options. They were excited and confused and they did not know what to do first. As with any student who arrives for a Femme Intensive, I had prepared a schedule to make the most of our three days together. But Helmut was so tired by the first part of their trip that he thought he wanted to spend the first day in bed. Miss Deborah, our Dean of Cosmetology, deserves the credit for coaxing our reluctant debutante into the makeup chair that very afternoon. I supported her endeavors by sending the other three men on a field trip—in other words, getting them out of our hair while we put Helmut into his. Then Miss Dana,

our Dean of High Heels and Body Sculpting, arrived for padding and posing. When his associates returned to find Helmut transformed for the very first time, there was a collective sigh of relief. Standing before them was not Helmut but Kristiana and she was proof that this crazy idea could really work. Helmut, with twenty years experience and confidence as an actor, let go of his ego and became the part. By the time he was ready to graduate, he thought he was Princess Di.

Her Brilliant Career

I have said that any man, including one who does not identify as a cross-dresser, can still gain much from the academy. The experience of John White is the exception that proves the rule. John did not reach us through the normal application process. He was volunteered by Miss Viqui, who was then his girlfriend and has since become his wife. In spring of '94 I agreed to produce a class for the Learning Annex, the company that presents adult education seminars on subjects from Aerobics to Zen. At the same time, producers from HBO and the Playboy Network, as well as other media representatives, contacted us to do stories on the academy. I invited them all to come to the Learning Annex presentation, a sort of academy road show in which we would give information about our school and transform a candidate from the audience. Under normal circumstances, I knew there would be plenty of enthusiastic volunteers, but with so many cameras around our ladies-in-waiting might turn shy. So we needed a ringer, someone we could count on to raise his hand at the ap-

John White is Joan Hazelnut.

ad: Griffith/Lovering (photo: Jim Salzano)

propriate moment. This would also be helpful because if we knew in advance who our girl was going to be, we would not have to transport so many different-sized shoes, wigs, etc. Miss Viqui and I were in the academy office discussing the plan when she said, "John will do it."

John White had grown up in the Midwest, come to New York to become an actor, but after several years of small parts and restaurant jobs, enrolled in semi-nary school out west at the request of his family. They hoped he would continue the family tradition and become a Methodist minister. John had his doubts about whether the ministry was for him; after a year and a half, he was sure it was time for another career. He flew the coop, landing in New York with much exuberance and in a short time he began nesting with Miss Viqui. He returned to being a waiter and he was excellent at it. He also kept his eyes and ears open for other freelance work. When time constraints made it necessary for me to give up the column that I'd written for a dozen years covering New York's erotic life in *Adam* magazine, John jumped and asked to be given the opportunity to write it. He was excellent and after a year in religious training, very enthusiastic. John White was ready for anything.

We told John of our plan and he agreed to help. The night of the program, we actually had a legitimate volunteer whom we put into a corset. I was not going to let such courage go unrewarded, but it was John, or rather Joan, who was our star. The experience brought out the actress in him. He ad-libbed marvelously, telling me as I asked the audience to decide whether we should give him a D cup or

B cup, "Large breasts don't run in my family." The producers from HBO and Playboy almost came to blows trying to get more time with him. John had so much fun that he continued to explore the character of Joan, becoming one of our academy ad campaign supermodels and even allowing Joan to make a cameo appearance the next Halloween at a friend's gourmet coffee store located across from Beth Israel Hospital. Sales increased by $200 that morning. John became more aware of Joan's effect on the general public and of her dating opportunities among the doctors. Later he wrote of his transformation:

> *Bending gender, for me, allows me the freedom to approach a deeper sense of human sexuality, to stop labeling sexuality in tight little boxes . . . Cross-dressing is a way to free me from my conservative Republican, Midwestern background . . .*

John, Viqui, and Joan went to bed together when they returned home on the night of the Learning Annex. His report can be studied in Sex Education class (Chapter 14).

Co-Education

Many women have told me that they would like to attend our school and learn the same things as the men: how to walk in high heels, how to do their makeup . . . I envision a day when Miss Vera's Finishing School will be co-educational with women as students and some of our more successful male to female candidates as assistant professors. In some areas of the country, such as the South, the concept of the finishing school still exists, but for the most part this idea has become an anachronism, especially since the rise of feminism in the seventies. But the lessons of the finishing schools and the feminine ideals that they celebrate are worth reconsideration, particularly in light of our school's popularity. We are filling a gap in higher-heeled education.

Chapter 4

Herstory

*I*n the previous chapter, you have read the fascinating herstories of a number of academy alumni. Now you are invited to recreate your own. Let's start with a name.

The Name Game

What's in a name? At the academy, a Rose is a Rose or a Robert. Most of our students arrive with names for their alter egos that are the feminization of their male names. Presumably so that they get full value from one set of monogrammed his and her towels. Joseph becomes JoAnn, Steve becomes Stephanie, Don becomes Danielle. If a girl has some familiarity with her name, she is more likely to come when called. Our students' choices also reflect the popularity of certain names from their boyhoods. The most popular girl's name of the past thirty years, by this count, has been Jennifer. We have had so many enrolled at one time that I thought I might call this academy the School for Jennifers. Of course, that also means that the "J" names—James, Joe, John—have been popular boys' names. I guess in years to come, we can look for lots more Samanthas and Katies and Chers among the academy's ranks.

The choice of a name is important. It is the reference point. It is a way to be free. It is a way to connect with a role model or an idea. A student is encouraged to put some thought into the choice of his *nom de femme*. Names have a powerful allure. They are invested with magic.

When I entered the world of sexually explicit media as a writer and then as a performer, I felt the need to choose another name. My new name would help me to maintain my independence—I was named Mary for my mother and she was named for her mother and we were all named for Mary the Mother of God. The new name must also be easy to remember and pronounce. I had already chosen a new first name. "Veronica" was the name I took at age twelve when I was confirmed. My acquaintance with "Veronica" came from the *Archie* comic books. She was the girl who got the hero; she was rich, though a bit spoiled by Daddy. "Veronica" had it all. The name also satisfied the requirements of the Catholic Church, which demanded that all confirmation names must be the names of saints. Veronica was she of the famed Veil, who wiped the sweat from Christ's brow as he carried his cross up to Calvary. So I dropped my given name, "Mary" (God, how could a

blue movie star be named Mary—), and used Veronica. I planned to carry my new name for a long time, so I wanted it to be a reminder to me and to others too, of what I considered important. Truth is important to me, telling the truth as I understand it. My family surname is Antonakos, and we come from a proud Greek heritage that can be traced back to the warriors of Sparta, to Helen of Troy, even Leda and the Swan. The Greek word for truth is *"Alethea"* but I had grown up with one tongue twister last name and that was enough. My friends, sex magazine pioneer Max Leblovic and Fluxus artist Willem de Ridder, suggested the Italian word for true or real, which is *vera*. "Veronica Vera." I liked the sound of it. V.V. The name seemed to fit like a glove, which Veronica Vera enjoys wearing.

Choosing a new name is a lot of fun, no matter what the reason for doing so. Names given at birth are often burdened with unwanted significance. Many a student found himself in the predicament of being named after his father when he felt more like his mother. This became a cross to bear and in the true spirit of Veronica, I have helped many bear it, wiping the sweat from their brows with the swish of a powder puff.

Pick a name that you fantasize yourself to be and, little by little, you begin to see ways in which you have become that fantasy. Change your outfit, change your name, change your life—here we do it all. Sometimes a student will arrive whose femmeself has no name, poor darling. I might refer to him as "Bill soon to be Barbara," or the generic "Missy" or "Dolly." After the student is transformed with makeup, the naming process becomes easy. If she has not completed the her-story assignment, we will ask questions for a clue into our girl's personality. We also rely on whom she resembles. We might name her after a movie star or celebrity. We have named girls after Debra Winger, Meg Ryan, Loretta Young . . . I told one student that he looked like a Jacqueline to me (in this case, I meant a tough gum-chewing Jackie, like the Rizzo character in *Grease,* a Jackie more Stallone than Kennedy Onassis). The student looked at me in amazement and told me that was his mother's name. *How did I know that?*

We named one dark, voluptuous student Erica Fellini because she looked like an Italian movie star, especially around the eyeliner. Student Ed was creative and cal-culating when he chose the name June G. Edwards. Since Ed's first visit to the acad-emy coincided with his birthday, he cele-brated his femmeself by naming her after that month in which he had been born and was now reborn. The name also alerted friends when it was time to send cards and presents. Jack aka Sally Sissyribbons took his last name from the cult magazine the *Sissy Times,* published by male to female cross-dresser Sharon Stuart aka Susie Sissyribbons. Jack chose Sally in honor of the family pa-triarch, his grandfather, big Sal. As Sally's personality evolved, this sobriquet, which began as an attempt at self-mockery, be-came more and more a method of self-ac-ceptance, a reclamation of the word *sissy* as the international organizations of sex workers who call themselves the Whores' movement or gays and lesbians who have organized as Queer Nation.

A student needs a name, and that name needs a personality. By answering the questions in the homework assign-ment "Create a Herstory" the student is encouraged to see his femmeself not sim-ply as his own Barbie, but as a human with talents, characteristics, and poten-tial. Our girls sometimes have difficulty answering these questions—but some answers they know by heart. They may not know one perfume from another, but our ladies-in-waiting all know what kind of car they drive. Most of the time it's a cherry red Mustang convertible.

Create a Herstory

Dear Lady-in-Waiting,
Thank you for your dedication to fun and femininity. In order to further your progress, I have designed this homework assignment. Use the follow-ing questions to help you discover the personality of your femmeself. Use de-tails that describe not only who you are but who you would like to be. In other words, your responses can be based on fact or fantasy. Let your femmeself choose the answers. Your responses will be used in planning your classes. Have fun and, of course . . .

Cherchez la femme,
Miss Vera, Dean of Students

What is your age?

How do you support yourself?

How do you spend most of your time? Hobbies? Work?

What are your favorite colors?

Which fashion designers are your favorite? (If you cannot think of designers, try looking at *Harper's Bazaar, Elle, W,* and *Vogue.*)

Which is your favorite perfume? (Sample them in department stores.)

Do you have any galpals? What are they like?

Do you date? Men? Women?

Are you a virgin?

If not, what is your sexual experience?

Is there someone special in your life?

What kinds of music do you prefer?

What sort of entertainment do you like?

Do you read? What?

Which season of the year is your favorite and why?

If you could live anywhere in the world, where would you choose?

If you could live during any period in history, which would it be?

Do you participate in sports? Which ones?

What is your favorite style of home decoration? Ex: Early American, fifties retro, French Provincial, Louis XIV, Japanese modern, etc.

Do you live alone?

Do you own a car? If so, what kind?

What do you like to eat?

Do you cook?

Are there other skills often associated with females that you want to nourish in your femmeself? Ex: sewing, housekeeping, child care, hostessing, dancing, sexiness, making art, feminist activism, gardening . . .

Which female movie stars most appeal to you and why?

Who are your favorite famous male hunks?

Who are your female role models? Which other, well-known or known only to you, women, living or dead, do you admire, and why?

Chapter 5

Hair Dressing

To create Eve from Adam, we treat the student's body like a sculpture. We mold, we squeeze, we add, we subtract. The first thing we subtract is any unwanted body hair. I have learned from my students that most men hate the daily ritual of shaving their faces. Ironically, a student feels different when it comes to hair on other parts of his anatomy. Prior to his first visit to the academy, the student may be eager to get a headstart by shaving his legs, arms, chest, and any other area he can reach without winding up in a chiropractor's office. It just won't do to have that tuft of fur protruding from the neckline of his Christian Dior. Besides its aesthetic appeal, removal of body hair is an important step because it is a rite of passage, a ritual that marks a leap from the male world into the feminine.

In our culture's perception, men are hairy, women are smooth. Smooth, hairless skin is more sensitive. Shaved, the student can feel the silken fabric of his clothes unimpeded. When dressed in these clothes, he feels more open to the world. He feels different—and that difference is marked. The hair that is removed will take a while to return, so he feels committed.

Shaving is convenient but very hard on the skin and hairs grow back quickly. The Art of Shaving, a new store in Manhattan, opened with an in-store promotion in which Ian Mathews, the Royal Barber of England, performed shaving demonstrations. The store was besieged with men eager for the promise of this new dawn and a release from their five o'clock shadows. Whether they are shaving their faces, legs, buttocks, or bikini lines, I encourage our girls to use the best products for their skin types—to try different soaps, cremes, gels—to experiment and to spend a little more if need be, in order to pamper themselves. And never, ever use a dull blade.

No one need start each day with an experience he hates. Why not build some rewards into the shaving process? My dad simply compliments himself at the mirror: "Gee, Pete, you're handsome." A man could pay himself a quarter after each grooming ritual and buy himself a specific present with the funds from his shavings bank. Or the payoff could be in points, a sort of trading stamp policy. For every three shaves, he would earn an hour's worth of self-gratification. And if most men hate to shave, why shave so often? The process could be much more optional. Companies that presently look askance at unshaved employees could adopt a much more relaxed policy. Swarthy—as actor Alec Baldwin has proved—can be sexy and fashionable as men learn to be kinder to their skin.

Waxing is a popular method for temporary removal of body hair. It's quick, thorough, relatively inexpensive, and it lasts for a couple of weeks. It can be a bit painful—but this is one of the reasons girls learn early, "You have to be willing to suffer to be beautiful."

Student David, on becoming Susan Sargent, surprised me with his method of triumph over adversity. As he lay on the table and the Dean of Depilation applied the warm wax, to be followed by strips of paper which would rip the hair from his body, David whispered softly, "I am thinking of a place that is calm . . . the lake glistens in the moonlight and I am on the porch of a big house, looking off through the pines. The air is sweet and a cool breeze rustles through my skirts . . ."

It was a self-hypnosis technique he had perfected to withstand long hours, packed like a sardine, in troop transports over Vietnam. It was particularly ironic that our dedicated depilator, My Tran, was from Vietnam. Susan Sargent endured her waxing like a good little soldier. But had she needed to shed a tear, I was right there holding her hand, as I am with all students. Waxing is not always painful; however, sometimes certain areas, particularly the bikini line—can smart, and it helps to have a big sister standing by. A note of caution: Never attempt to wax yourself. I did once, only once, and I strongly suggest students learn from my mistake. Waxing salons are quick, clean, efficient, and often accustomed to a male clientele—lots of bodybuilders do it. So they do not raise eyebrows . . . unless requested.

Some students prefer not to remove body hair. In those cases, we camouflage with scarves, tights, and gloves. I can respect a student's limitations, except when it comes to mustaches. He may do what he chooses on his own time; however, no applicant is ready for the freewheeling life of an academy deb if he is not ready to let go of a handlebar. Yet there are exceptions to every rule, even this. I relaxed my rule once when a Hassidic Jewish man applied for entrance. I knew that his long beard and sidecurls were part of his religious observance and thus not to be removed. Under all of that hair, his long-lashed eyes emanated sincerity and earnestness, so I took pity on him. We used a veil and turned him into an Arabian princess, not only accomplishing his transformation but doing our bit to heal Mideast relations.

To alleviate the trauma of removing a beard or mustache after some years, I recommend making a party of it. When André and his wife Heidi arrived at the academy for our initial consultation I was surprised that André had a full beard and mustache. "I think you know what my first question will be," I said to the two of them, as I looked askance at André's chin. "The answer is 'yes,'" said André. They told me that André had worn his beard for sixteen years and that they wanted to include shaving the beard as part of the transformation. Heidi wanted to participate. Miss Deborah, our Dean of Cosmetology, accomplished most of the beard removal, but Heidi and I both got in a few licks. We completed the transformation, turning André into Julia. While Deborah and I worked on Julia, Heidi, who was very fun-loving and beautiful, began to put on her own makeup. The dress Julia chose was a long flowing silk outfit decorated with suns, moons, and stars, borrowed from Heidi with her permission. Julia looked like a sorceress. We were not scheduled to take Julia out, so we were all very surprised when Heidi announced that she wanted Julia to accompany her to the concert of New Age music they had planned to attend.

"I love to wear makeup and knew how much time and effort would go into this transformation," said Heidi. "I made up my mind, when we decided to do this, that I would take Julia out."

At Miss Vera's Finishing School, we encourage each of our girls to integrate the lessons of her femmeself into her male persona. If she takes pleasure in having smooth arms and legs, why not stay that way, no matter what his fashion statement. I would not be surprised to see the students of the academy at the forefront of a new trend. Every Samson can still feel like Delilah.

Crowning Glory

No items in the academy's inventory have more personality than our wigs. We have even given them names: Tina Turner, Bernadette Peters, Molly Ringwald, Rachel (from "Friends"), Amy Fisher (The Long Island Lolita) . . . the list goes on. The wigs take up an entire wall of the academy. Each one sits comfortably on a Styrofoam head with a painted face and smiles down on us beatifically like a holy icon. During the winter of '93, in which one snowstorm followed another, our Professor Emeritus of Cosmetology, Anthony McAulay, used the time he was snowbound to paint those faces, so that we now call the wall collectively,

Abe Frajndlich

Joan's crowning glory. Left to right, standing: Miss Mishell, Miss V, Patti Harrington, Jennifer James; seated: Joan Hazelnut.

"The most beautiful girls in the world." They represent many different makeup styles and time periods and the multicolors of the human spectrum: red, yellow, black, brown, and white. Every wig has a story, most have more than one and with every student who wears it, that wig's story continues. Sometimes a wig seems destined for a particular student so we give it to him as a gift. Sometimes it is the student who gives the wig to us. One of our Deans of Cosmetology, Miss Mishell, referred to them as party hats. The name is appropriate

because at the conclusion of the makeup session, when the student is crowned with her new do, the party truly begins.

Hair Picks

After the student has been transformed with makeup, it is time to choose her wig. We always offer our girl the first pick, but she usually asks us to decide. Countless times I have heard the phrase, "Whatever you think." The deans of cosmetology have an idea what will look good on the student. If our girl has strong masculine features, we go with curls to soften. If her face is lined and heading downward, a long hairstyle will only make her sag farther, so a short updo works better. If our lucky lady has finer features, she has more options. The best and most fun way to decide is through trial and error. We put the possible options on her head, take a Polaroid, and then we all vote. The Polaroids are a tremendous help, especially for the student, because she has a chance to study her captured image, and not judge simply from the fleeting reflection in the mirror. Our girls usually prefer long hair, but every would-be Rapunzel will go with a bob if she can see that it is more flattering. Sometimes a student will really show an affinity for a wig that the deans and I might not think is the best. Unless that wig really looks terrible, we tend to go with the student's feeling, because if a girl really believes in her look, even if others do not, it can be the right look for her. The confidence, pleasure, and comfort she feels when she wears that do will be revealed in her face and transform it from a hair don't.

We might give a student a wig from our collection or we might take her shopping. Lee's Mardi Gras, the world's premier transvestite boutique, just a short block from the academy, has a wide variety of choices. Recently, we have given our girls a more customized treatment by taking them to Barry Hendrickson's Bitz-N-Pieces, a wig boutique where the hair can be cut to the face. Barry and his assistants Gwen and Ed appreciate the unique problems of our students. When New York's hard-nosed Mayor Rudolph Giuliani decided to soften his image and become "Cutie Rudee" for a political bash, he got his inspiration from Marilyn Monroe and his wig from Bitz-N-Pieces. The next day the papers were filled with the story, pointing out that Rudy was not the first New York politician to dress in drag. Edward Hyde, who governed New York and New Jersey from 1702 to 1708, was an avid cross-dresser, a fact noted by Marjorie Garber in *Vested Interests,* as well as by other authors.

Bewigging bigwigs is no big deal to us. We had had another mayor in just the week before Rudee made news, though our girl preferred not to give a press conference. Our student was afraid the revelation of his femmeself might not be popular with his constituents. I sent him the clipping, in hopes it might put a bee in his bonnet. Another student, who visited us a few weeks after the mayor's metamorphosis, reminded me that a year before she had, in a way, foreseen the act. Our novice, Kelli, was in advertising and a very clever girl.

"Remember, Miss Vera, I suggested that you have a television interview program, during which the subject would go through an academy transformation. I said it would be fun to have the most challenging "girls" as guests and on the top of our list was Rudy Giuliani!"

Kelli had given the mayor a much better name: Julie Annie. There was a second part to her prediction which still could prove true. Why stop at a mayor? We've got our styling combs ready for Governor Pat Tacky.

Outfitting our girls in their wigs has inspired me to add a few new do's to my personal collection. Wigs are such fun and offer such freedom, especially for the girl on the go. It is not true that wearing a wig harms the natural hair. It can actually be more of a protection from the ill effects of dirt and the sun. A wig can keep the head warm in winter, though it is best to stay in air-conditioned rooms in the summer. (Summer is the season when our girls tend to melt.)

Hair Care

The same instruction that was given to every child before going to sleep is one to remember when caring for a wig. "Don't forget to brush." I have seen too many ratty wigs. Girls come to the academy, unpack their clothes, and there in the bottom of the suitcase is this tangled, ratty mess that the student presents as his crowning glory. I don't think so.

Brushing a wig is a very simple matter. The student holds the wig in her hand and brushes the bottom strands to remove all of those hidden tangles. When the bottom is smooth, the wig can be brushed from the top. A stable wig base that is attached to a table is a big help for brushing and styling but if this is not available, the wig is pinned to a Styrofoam head and brushed or back-combed.

Sometimes our girl will be wearing her wig when it's time to brush. She can't very well take her party hat off in the

Reporter Chet wigged-out as Chloe.

Marty Fishman

ladies' room with all those other girls around, so she had better learn to brush in place. Here her goal is not a complete new hairdo, she only wants to put the wild strands back into place. Most wigs have elasticized bands in the crown to help the wig fit securely, but still she needs to brush with care.

I have seen a wig fall off a student head only once. Student Jennifer James and I ran into a gentleman friend of mine who offered to take us for a ride in his convertible. As Shirley MacLaine said in *Terms of Endearment* when she took that convertible ride with Jack Nicholson, "a grown-up girl is prepared in any emergency," then she whipped out her scarf. The scarf really did not help Shirley and our Jennifer was only a simply-dressed ingenue, so she did not even have a scarf. Plus she was so excited to be going off in a convertible that she did not even think about it, and I must admit, neither did I . . . Jennifer was chattering away when all of a sudden she gasped and her hands flew up to her bare head. Fortunately, the wig only fell into the backseat. Jennifer was also lucky because we were riding at night on the West Side Highway and not through the center of Times Square, so the only witnesses were my gentleman friend, who being a gentleman kept the story to himself, and me and, of course, I'll never tell. Wigs usually do not need to be pinned but when in doubt, better to be safe than unexpectedly bald. A scarf is good to carry not only for those moonlight cruises but also to protect the wig from the glaring rays of the sun.

Keeping a wig fresh and clean is really very simple. At the academy most of our wigs are made of strong but soft, easy-care modacrylic fibers such as Kanekalon. These can be washed just like real hair and usually spring back to shape without setting. A shorter curly do is the easiest to care for. The wig is washed with shampoo, rinsed with conditioner, shaken out or combed through with a wire brush or a wide-toothed comb or pick, then placed on a wig head to dry. Electric hair dryers and curling irons can be used on wigs, but the heat must be kept at a very low level. Many of these appliances have specific settings for wigs. The best hair spray is light and water soluble. Lacquer is overkill. It will hold a set but attract so much dirt that the wig will need to be cleaned each time it is set. Hair care for our student is like playing with the Barbie doll he may have always wanted but probably never owned—until now. However, for most of our girls, such a hair plan is very ambitious. Most prefer to send their wigs out to be done. Wig care is offered at most beauty parlors and there are wig salons in all major cities. In New York, we recommend Bitz-N-Pieces and Miss Shannon at Perfidia's wig salon in Patricia Field's trendy unisex boutique. Most shops love to show off their more famous clientele. Bitz-N-Pieces boasts photos of RuPaul, Madonna, Diana Ross, Cher. Perfidia's most famous hair hopper is Howard Stern.

Hair hopper is the term made famous by John Waters and Ricki Lake in *Hairspray,* a movie that holds an exalted place in our academy library. Hair hopper usually refers to big do's. Most academy girls, even the ones from Dallas, prefer a more conservative coiffure, figuring they are already tall enough without another foot of hair—though we have had a few budding Las Vegas showgirls come to class. There was also one student who just loved the short Wedge.

The Beauty Parlor

By far, the most popular excursion for our girls is a trip to a ladies' beauty parlor. June G. Edwards was the first student to make this request. Most of our students can take advantage only of the manicure and pedicure facilities at these salons, but Ed's hair was long enough to wrap around rollers. Ed had visited us for the four-hour Miracle Miss class and was so enthused that he decided to return for a two-day femme intensive. The beauty parlor trip would be part of that schedule.

I set off to find an accommodating salon and found the perfect place in the West Village. The shop had been in business for forty-five years. The two owners were not fazed by our type of girl and neither was their regular clientele. Some of the female patrons had been coming to the salon since its inception, others were the granddaughters or great-granddaughters of clients.

June leaned back in the shampoo chair, an expression of bliss under her long soapy locks as the beautician massaged her very large head. It is the pampering and the attention, students tell me, that make this a thrilling experience. June was receiving lots of both. The staff enjoyed working on her and she loved every minute she was being *done.*

June's hair was set in rollers. There is something about the look of a woman in rollers, or in this case, a lady-in-waiting— the rollers make a statement about bondage to beauty. They wrap around the brain as a sort of mind control. The woman in rollers is caught at an intimate moment, at a time when she is really not supposed to be seen, but a time when her femininity is exposed. If she is covered with a hair net or scarf, that femininity peeks out from under wraps. For our girls, the idea of their femmeselves laid bare, especially in a room full of women, is enough to curl their hair. June was moved to the drying area and joined the row of women under the big heat machines. She sat next to a tiny redhead who was unmoved, only glancing up momentarily to smile before looking back to her copy of *Cosmo.* The manicurist sat in front of June and applied the nail extensions that turned her bruiser's mitts into elegant painted talons. June carried her crown of curlers with pride as she was led back to the stylist to be combed out and teased. And teased she was.

There have been other occasions when we have set students' hair either at a salon or here, at the academy. Sometimes, I do the setting personally and I enjoy every moment of the process.

Wigstock

In New York, Labor Day has come to mean one thing, "Wigstock"—that celebration of freedom marked by fake hair that began in 1985 when a handful of club kids, budding drag queens, performance artists, and assorted exhibitionists—the regular irregulars of a punk club called the Pyramid—decided to show off their talents in the light of day. One Sunday afternoon in 1985 they threw a party in Tompkins Square Park, the emerald green epicenter of the East Village, a part of town known for its drugs, Day-Glo and kosher delis. Nine

Stephanie

Jennifer James interviews Consuela Cosmetic.

years later, at Wigstock '93, the participants numbered in the thousands.

The day was sunny and beautiful, reflecting the moods of the many wigged-out participants. On assignment to bring back a report of the festivities was the intrepid team of junior high-heeled journalists from Miss Vera's Finishing School for Boys Who Want to Be Girls: my students, Stephanie, womanning the camera, and reporters Jennifer James and Susan Sargent. The girls would make it possible for me to come up with a column for the one magazine that I still held

on to, and still get to the hospital to visit my friend Thomas Williams, the beautiful black erotic model. In honor of the day, I wore a blond wig, which made me feel like Charo. I knew Thomas, who had once transformed himself into a big-bottomed mama in wig hat and heels for a Village Halloween parade could appreciate it. Before setting off on Angel of Mercy duties, I dressed my boys in their girl frocks, patted their ruffled panties, and sent them out on assignment. "Come back with the story," I instructed and in the best tradition of all for one and one for

Lady Bunny.

Wigstock. "I'm sure you won't mind this extra stop." I smiled as I imagined the delight of this threesome as they stepped into the tiny boutique, a cocoon of sexy shoes.

Jennifer took her writing assignment very seriously and asked me for a notepad to take with her. I handed her a real collector's item, one that bore the logo "The School of High-Heel Journalism," the name created by me, Annie, and our writer friend Jennifer Blowdryer to describe our glamorous gonzo-style of reportage. Our cub reporter carried it with pride.

The academy girls had managed a successful pump pickup but now ran into a snag at the drop-off location. Tompkins Square Park was so crowded, their taxi could not get closer than one block away. Susan Sargent was left holding the bag to watch for Ms. Patricia, while Jennifer and Stephanie hurried on to phase two of their assignment, the festival itself, Wigstock. In her best tomboy fashion, Jennifer scaled a fence and landed right in the midst of the "backstage" area where performers awaited their turns.

Lady Bunny was the star of the show. Beneath her platinum blond vinyl tresses is the brilliant mind that helped create the first Wigstock and has kept it alive ever since, at least in spirit. Lady Bunny has always displayed a kind of realness that speaks from the heart and to the community. And quite a community it was.

Jennifer's pick for the best of show

all, off went the team of missketeers in somewhat sensible pumps.

To add challenge to their assignment, I told them to make a stop at Joseph's Imports, a stiletto shoe shop—once an Eighth Street institution, popular, especially, among performers, drag queens, and dominatrixes, some of whose pictures lined the walls—to pick up a pair of six-inch pumps which they would deliver to my friend Ms. Patricia Marsh, the academy's honorary Dean of Discipline, who was in town from Toronto and would be at

was the group who claimed to be from the House of Pancakes, a takeoff on the drag houses like the House of La Beija, the House of Extravaganza, and the House of Corey, which ran Harlem balls and competitions that were the subject of Jennie Livingston's *Paris Is Burning*. The houses were home and family to many young gay men who came to New York and followed a transsexual lifestyle. One member of the House of Pancakes wore five feet of wig designed to be the Eiffel Tower; another sported a meticulously detailed and multicolored planet Saturn; a third wore a very blue blueberry pancake; and there were eggs Benedict in a frying pan, all made of wig hair. In this as in many of the cases, the wigs were bigger than the rest of the outfits.

The genders bent as tall boys wore long hair that covered their mini-skirts, and genetic girls, g.g.'s, who were in the minority, either flaunted their breasts or sat back in Gap drag and watched from the park benches. Wigs practically floated in the trees as platform shoes elevated audience members to star status.

The towering singer/ model RuPaul not only performed but provided inspiration to the multitudes with comments such as "We are all born naked, the rest is drag." That day, dozens of hair-o-ween addicts could be seen wearing skimpier versions of the American flag costume that Ru had cavorted in on stage earlier in the year when Gays and Lesbians had marched on Washington in a symbol of pride.

Some attendees chose to shave their heads and wear wigs on their genitals. Even the dogs put on the wigs. One bulldog sported a mop o' red fringe and a toy poodle was happily blue.

A sign that this dizzy festival had gained prominence were the numbers of city bigwigs on hand to salute the event. Ruth Messinger—who at that time was president of the City Council with definite mayoral ambitions—declared it Wig-

Marty Fishman

RuPaul.

stock Day and saluted Lady Bunny as "the hair spray that keeps Wigstock in place." Councilwoman Liz Holtzman came out to make friends and Marty Ralph of then-Mayor Dinkins' office was quick to take credit for helping Wigstock organizers to cut through a new ruling which imposed a four-hour time limit on the park's gatherings to let Wigstock run for eight. In the past, other gatherings in Tompkins Square, sometimes with police help, escalated into riots and, because of these incidents, each year the festival had to fight for its right to exist. But Wigstock was a celebration of peace and love and freedom, not unlike the Woodstock celebration of 1969 that inspired its name. The city officials did provide good material for the comedienne Linda Simpson whose job it was to roast Lady Bunny. When in the middle of her lines, the microphone quit (with a secret assist from Lady Bunny), the lippy comedienne deadpanned, "Why couldn't this have happened when the politicians were up here?"

Knowing Jennifer's propensity to chattiness, I suggested that she prepare herself with a single question to ask interviewees in order to get right down to business. "Where did you get your wig?" Most said they made theirs, some "borrowed" theirs but promised to return it that night. Some bought theirs from wig vendors in the park for three to five dollars. One enterprising hair hustler displayed her wigs on a parasol.

The team had started off in different directions but soon Jennifer and Stephanie were working together as efficiently as garters and stockings. For the first hour the girls had felt imperiled because of their failure to deliver the con-

signed pumps. When they finally found Ms. Patricia of Toronto they breathed a collective sigh of relief.

Over dinner, the girls, now back in their male drag, filed their report on the day. Steve was still agog. He'd spent the day as Stephanie, getting doubly turned on—by the g.g.'s who danced for Stephanie's camera, their big fleshy breasts shaking like maracas, and by the bare-assed boys dressed as girls who let it all hang out. David, who had traveled the world with the army, was still filled with wonder when it came to the exotic taste of the Big Apple. He waved his arms in the air as he described Susan's experiences that day. I knew James would have pages of notes for me, for Jennifer James had really become my protégée. The School of High-Heel Journalism was alive and well, and not even I could have imagined this wild metamorphosis. But that is what Wigstock and the academy are all about: accepting the impossible as totally real and making the dream come true.

In 1994, Wigstock was moved to the West Village, where it was held on the piers bordering the West Side Highway. Then in 1996, there was no Wigstock. It was overcome by the bureacracy and red tape, but not before a documentary was made that would preserve the meaning of Wigstock, its fabulous performers, and the hairdos it celebrates forever.

Chapter 6

Bodybuilding

The Tender Trap

*W*e could not hope to teach a student about womanhood unless we also dealt with his manhood. In this lesson, I refer not to the concept of manhood but to that constant reminder that sits between our girl's legs, his penis. Occasionally, I receive calls from prospective students who ask me how to deal with this problem. (If that is the right word.) Personally, I think a penis is a delight rather than a problem. But it can get in the way if it causes a suspicious bulge or if it makes our lady-in-waiting's pinafore pitch like a pup tent. Sometimes these inquiries are made by those who really do not want to lick this problem. They are just men acting like naughty little boys who are excited to hear about penis restraint. But most of our girls are really conscien-

Everyone who cross dresses has something to hide.

Not to worry.

You simply need "cheater's panties." Now you see it. Now you don't.

At Miss Vera's Finishing School, we'll teach you all the basics of cross-dressing. In fact, we'll teach you every trick in the book. That's what makes us America's foremost cross dressing academy.

Our experienced faculty will work with you in one-on-one classes at our Manhattan campus. From courses in dressing to depilation to diction, we'll make sure you know how to bring out your best.

Even THE SIMPLEST EVENING GOWN CAN BE RUINED BY A PENIS.

And conceal the rest.

You can enroll for a day, a weekend or a week. You may even feel ready for us to take you out on the town. Because at Miss Vera's, you'll always look outstanding.

But you won't stand out.

MISS VERA'S
FINISHING SCHOOL
For Boys Who Want To Be Girls.
212-242-6449

ad: Griffith/Lovering (photo: Jim Salzano; dress: Frances Colon; Wearable Energy, NYC)

Our penis ad won Madison Avenue's prestigious Andy.
Today Andy, tomorrow Oscar and Tony (Patti).

tious about their appearance and want to look as convincing as possible. As we say in our award-winning academy ad, "Even the simplest evening gown can be ruined by a penis."

At the academy, we use minimalist panties called "gaffs." The dictionary cites several disparate meanings for the word "gaff." A "gaff" is defined as a "hook" or a "spear" used for lifting a heavy item such as a log or a fish; it is a "gimmick" or "trick"; and is also an "ordeal." These meanings all apply. The penis will not be as hefty as a prize trout but it is a weighty matter. The objective of the gaff is subterfuge, hence the name "cheater's panties." Unfortunately, gaffs are ordeals. We rod-tested many different kinds of gaffs, from panties with elephant trunk–like sheaths that employ Velcro fastenings to surgical tape, which should *never* be allowed in any proximity to pubic hair. A tight pantie girdle held down the penis but also confined the hips and made them smaller, and hip reduction is a no-no. Afer much experimentation, we rely on two different kinds of gaffs, neither of which is very comfortable. One version consists of two flat triangles of satin fabric held together by thin elastic—the whole thing looks like a slingshot and with this tiny slingshot we bring down many a Goliath. The other model is a tight pantie made entirely of power net Lycra. Both have thong backs that rest between the buttocks, sometimes digging pretty deep, and always making quite an impression.

When a student arrives at the academy, immediately following the dedication ritual, he is instructed to strip naked so that we can inspect his male body before resculpting it. Is he hairy—or, clean-shaven from nose to toe? Will we need to camouflage with tights and turtlenecks? Does he have a curvy rump or a flat backside? All of these things and more are taken into account. Not one man has ever hesitated to comply with my request that he present himself naked. Our expectation is that he will follow through with this necessary part of the transformation process, and he does. Rather than feel embarrassed, I hope he feels a sense of relief to be rid of his male costume and that he feels excitement for what is to come. Sometimes we have to wait a few minutes before proceeding because standing naked in front of me can call our lady-in-waiting's manhood to attention. When he is at ease, we tuck. The student is instructed to gently pull his penis down and back, so that the shaft rests between his testicles. The gaff is used to hold the penis in the tucked position. He must make sure that his jewels are totally encased in the satin codpiece because any skin hanging out from the sides will eventually pinch and distract him from her lessons.

Experience has caused me to rethink my original position on the penis. Initially, if our student was going to remain on campus during class, and no field trip was scheduled, we gave him the option to gaff or not to gaff. Gaffs are uncomfortable contraptions, and I assumed that anyone who chose to wear one, either really needed or wanted to be flat, or really liked the confinement. What I did not consider was that many students are tucking virgins with no idea, literally, of what they are getting into. They opt for the gaff because they want to experience *the full treatment,* and then suffer in silence because they think they might displease me if they whimper.

A Cockeyed View

This was not the case with reporter Roberto Santiago, who became Roberta on the trail of a story for *Time Out New York*. I have Roberto to thank for making me more aware of the true nature of the tucking experience. Roberto, who described himself as "a macho Puerto Rican man," proposed the story to his editors because, he told me, he wanted to do "something no one would ever expect me to do." He opted for the gaff in the interest of good journalism. At his first glimpse in the mirror after his transformation, Roberta exclaimed, "I look like my sister!" and "I'd date me." He produced a delightful, though cockeyed account that said less about his feelings when faced with his femmeself and much, much more about his relationship to his penis.

"The most important thing I learned while being Roberta is that I am glad I was born Roberto. I like my penis. It enables me to stand while going to the bathroom, wear pants all the time and sit with my legs spread and crossed any old way I want."

It was not unusual that Roberto used the experience to remind everyone, including himself, that this chick had a dick. One motivation behind the act of cross-dressing is to assure the lady in question of her virility. In *Observing the Erotic Imagination,* Robert Stoller, M.D., who until his death a few years ago was a professor of psychiatry at UCLA, quoting his words to a patient, wrote: "No matter how many feminine clothes you put on, you did not lose that ultimate insignia of your maleness, your penis." There can be no more glaring reminder that she is a he than the salute of a penis from beneath a skirt.

As I wanted the academy experience to be one of pleasure rather than pain, Roberto's candor regarding the tuck made me more careful to explain the rigors of the gaff and the discomfort that might follow. A survey of students informed me that the only ones who seemed to actually *enjoy* rather than simply endure the gaff were those few who really did not like their penises or who enjoyed discomfort. Our new rule is that gaffs are worn only when requested after careful explanation of the risk to reward ratio, or when absolutely necessary for modesty's sake. Girls who stay indoors can usually rest their genitals in a pair of silk panties. We can also proceed with makeup application first, prior to body sculpting. That way the student will be seated for less time. Standing while gaffed is only a bit uncomfortable, but our gaffed girls must sit down very, very carefully. If we are going out and the student would like to avoid the gaff, we can put her in a loose skirt or tuck *him* under a crinoline. As Rich Cohen, who became "Rachel" on an undercover assignment from the *New York Observer,* helped us to see, you may have to suffer a bit to be beautiful, but we don't have to endanger future generations.

Glam Gams

If our girl does not feel at liberty to shave her legs, we camouflage with tights. We use Danskin "glimmer" tights in shades called "champagne" and "golden toast." The trick of flesh-colored tights under sheer stockings is often used by stage performers to

Joan with pads, panties, and prosthetics.

Abe Frajndlich

ensure that their legs appear picture perfect under all kinds of light. The "glimmer" of the tights produces a shimmery effect under the panty hose or stockings, which come later. Danskin tights are widely available and come in large sizes. Lee's Mardi Gras, the world's premiere transvestite department store (which is happily located just a short stroll from our campus) carries these in sizes from L to XL on up to 3X, but extra large will easily fit a size-forty-two suit. While these tights do the trick, I prefer not to use them because I like our girls to wear as few layers as possible and I know that for many of them, the feel of sheer stockings against naked flesh is very pleasurable. A student who is scheduled for a field trip has no option—she must shave or wear tights. We will not be gallivanting about town with a girl who is not well groomed and our girls trust us to make sure they pass inspection. But a student whose classes take place indoors only and whose legs are not particularly hairy may get away simply by wearing dark stockings.

What Is Hip

Padding the buttocks and all aspects of sculpting a female form from the male is a challenge. Here, we rely heavily on the expertise of Miss Dana, our Dean of High Heels, who is also the Dean of Body Sculpting and Pygmalion to our Galateas. She explains to the student that the male form, which in its ideal is what we see in Greek art, has a longer torso than that of the female, with the distance from waist to hips shorter than that of the female. That is why the student's new femme waist needs to be about two inches higher. Men as a breed are taller than women because the extra height is in the legs, a fact that our girls never let us forget. They are very, very proud of their legs.

The difference between a woman's hip measurement and her waist measurement is usually about ten inches, while a man's waist could measure the same as his hips. We have a drawer full of padded panties, the kind with oval pocket slits on the sides and the back to accommodate foam inserts. These padded panties are sold as "enhancers" most commonly in mail-order catalogs such as those from Frederick's of Hollywood and J. C. Penney. (Both of these catalogs—the first from America's avatar of bedroom naughtiness; the second from this country's most white-bread mall-and-mail-order paragon of wholesomeness—are "musts" for the library of any fledgling femme fatale.) Miss Dana makes sure that the hip pads are placed in the correct position: not too high, not too low, and undetectable under clothes. The choice of outfit directly dictates the degree of difficulty. Prom queens in bouffant skirts have no worries, but our spandex sluts demand perfection. The padded panties are not the easiest things to work with and even Miss Dana has experienced frustration. The good news is that now that cross-dressing has come out of the closet, improvements are made more rapidly to accommodate this newly recognized market. On my most recent visit to Lee's Mardi Gras, proprietor Lee Brewster showed me a new model padded pantie with only one, more realistically designed, pad. Our students can also be counted on to come up with ingenious solutions. Ashley is one of our girls who is well connected. She is a member of several cross-dressing social clubs. This girl *networks*. She is also a very successful businessman who appreciated creative problem solving. Ashley custom-designed and built her own bottom from foam and plastic and tape. She also told us about another cross-dresser who offers a service in customized curves. The portable buttocks is called, I am pleased to say, "Veronica" and it was created by Espy Lopez as a result of a feeling of frustration. Espy had sent $100 for a hip-enhancement product from a company she saw advertised. What she received was very disappointing. "There were two pieces of yellow foam that I could have cut out in my garage." The company refused to give Espy her money back. "You don't know who you are dealing with," she told them. "I am a design engineer." Espy sat down at her computer and created what she calls "The best rear ends bar none." Sales are in the thousands and that other company has since gone out of business.

From the brochure:

Classic Curves presents the "Veronica." Aerospace design comes to the aid of crossdressers! The Veronica is the first foundation garment designed by computer to make your hips and rear perfectly female . . . Each washable Veronica is custom-padded to feminize your proportions. Simply return the measurement form we'll send you, and Classic Curves will create a custom garment just for you!

Really passing used to be impossible. Now I can go to the beach with Classic Curves!
—Sarah Claire

Of course, padding the derriere is not de rigueur. Some of our more voluptuous girls have more than an adequate supply of flesh. A student whose hips are as large or larger than his shoulders begins with a shape that is quite feminine. Some even have bubble butts. There is no need to gild the lily.

The Truth About Falsies

I was surprised to discover that not all men want big breasts—at least when they are wearing them. Initially, I thought that our girls would all want to look like Dolly Parton, and some do, but more often a student must be encouraged to go up a cup rather than down. Most students prefer a smaller cup size for fear that humongous breasts might cause them to be inspected a little too closely and lessen their chances to pass as real girls. Real girls have less to lose by being fake. For most of our students, B and C cups are better fits. We have many, many, many breast forms—our drawers runneth over: large silicone-filled D, C, and B cups that jiggle and warm to the temperature of the body; oval pillows stuffed with polyfiber; small simple rubber disks. But while we've come a long way, baby, from stuffing bras with sox or Kleenex, there is still something to be said for the homemade versions. One of the best breast ideas that I have seen was a student invention that had come down through the years via the grapevine. The student had cut the feet from a pair of stockings, filled the feet with birdseed, and tied off the ends. The knots at the tied-off ends made perfect nipples. The birdseed inside the nylon jiggled provocatively. I admired the practicality of the idea. Our girl could easily accomplish a breast reduction or enhancement, to accommodate her mood or her outfit. And if stranded on a desert island, she would be less likely to starve.

Ready to bust (Miss V and Patti).

Eric Kroll

How to Choose a Bra

At Digby and Peller, the London shop that bills itself "corsetiers to the Queen," women of all ages stand in line to be properly fitted for their bras. For about $300 U.S. a pattern is made and for her entire life, or until her size changes, the client's bras can be custom-made from her pattern. It is possible to go to great lengths for a great fit. Is it any wonder that the average student, who drops into a department store, and without trying it on, snaps up a bra from the rack because a) it looks pretty; b) it feels pretty; and c) it is available, might wind up with a bra that does not fit? And what of the man who relies on his wife's lingerie drawer for his wardrobe? Chances are better than good that they are not the same size.

In bra sizes—34C, 36D, 38B, etc.—the number refers to the chest measurement; the letter refers to the size of the cup which holds the breast, or a reasonable facsimile. Cup size is relative in proportion to chest size; in other words, the B cup in a 42 will be larger than the B cup in a size 40 by the same manufacturer, and considerably larger than the 36B. In one style, our girl may take a 38C, in another 40B. Bras are elasticized, so there is some leeway regarding the chest measurement. For instance, a man who wears a size 40 suit could fit into a size 38 bra. But if our girl has a 42-inch chest, that 38 magnum could be overloaded.

Bra styles change. In the fifties, the cone-shaped "torpedo bra" was very popular. The torpedo brought the breasts in toward the breastbone, so that the nipples were presented front and center. Today's bras emphasize the natural form of the body. Many bra styles incorporate a strip of fabric to separate the breasts. One of the first to do this was Vanity Fair in its Satin Smoothie, an academy favorite. Instead of up and in, the breasts are lifted up and out. This style is much more flattering across an academy girl's broad chest. Another aspect of the Satin Smoothie that we applaud is the wide strap, which is so much more comfortable than a strap that is narrow, particularly for any girl who is carrying a hefty handful. There needs to be plenty of room for strap adjustment and the SS satisfies also on that score. We usually open the bra straps all the way, so that the female nipple will be lower than that of the male. Firm upright breasts look too high. We don't want our girl to hit herself in the nose.

A bra is a foundation garment, part of the base on which we build our girl's body. Bras have their own mystique. If a student has only one female garment, it will most likely be a bra because a bra is the most significantly female piece of clothing he can own. A bra that does not fit properly can ruin the most gorgeous outfit—under a sheer blouse, especially, there is no margin for error.

Diane Gets Malled

Bras do get tired and need to be replaced. Such was the case of Richard, who flew in from the Lone Star State to spend a day with us as "Diane," a girl on the go. Diane Richards' dream was to go shopping at a mall. Malls can be a family experience—there is something for everyone. But it is female territory. A woman enters any mall confident in the knowledge that she will

Annie Sprinkle

We like our girls with muscles!

soon get the lay of the land. Men understand this and submit to female expertise in this area. A man who invades a mall in female camouflage is a tourist who seeks fun, relaxation, and pleasure. Also, like a spy in a foreign land, he is there to gather goods and information. A not so innocent. A broad.

Before Diane left for the mall, we inspected her wardrobe. While the two dresses Richard brought with him showed that he had excellent taste, Diane's underwear was in a sorry state: one old worn-out white bra and a pair of stretched-out panties. As the first acquisitions in Diane's wardrobe, they were of sentimental value but they just would not do for an academy deb. Goddess forbid she wound up in an auto accident. (Emergency room statistics reveal that 2 percent of males arrive in female undergarments. A girl can't be too careful.) Off we went, Miss Deborah at the wheel of her BMW, through the Lincoln Tunnel to New Jersey and the Garden State Mall—our destination, Nordstrom's. In the depths of the lingerie department, we picked out several bras for Diane and one for me. Then all three of us piled into our spacious dressing room. I took off my blouse and Diane looked a bit nervous. "It's just us girls," I teased.

Then it was Diane's turn. Off came the dress, leaving Richard to stand in his bra, panty hose, padded panties, corset, and half slip. Each time we removed one bra, we had him hold on to her breast forms to continue the illusion that these were really Diane's breasts. From an adjoining dressing room, we heard a woman complain to her friend, "I almost don't want to try things on, it's such an effort to get dressed and undressed." Balancing a boob

in each hand, Diane Richards said, "She doesn't know the half of it."

Of Corset

Of all the garments we have in our closet, the item that I consider the most effective in changing boys to girls is the old-fashioned lace-up corset. Not only does the corset transform a man's straight lines into a woman's sexy curves, but the very experience of wearing a corset can be quite erotic. The metal stays envelop the body within a tight squeeze, a strong caress. A corset can turn each breath into an orgasm. Kathy (a genetic female) and her husband Dr. Bob, frequent revelers at the Dressing for Pleasure Ball, are an attractive couple who use corsetry as an exotic form of sex play. Through years of diet and exercise, at times even sleeping in her corset, Kathy reduced her waist to sixteen inches. To see Kathy in a beautiful low-cut ball gown, her creamy breasts raised and proudly displayed over her tiny, tiny waist and round hips, is a mesmerizing sight.

We do not advocate such extremes for our students (please do not try this at home), but we do appreciate the effect a tight-lacing corset can have in changing a student's figure from even a beer barrel to an hourglass. Once we have added curves to his top and bottom, it is time to pull our girl together in the middle and go from virile to voluptuous.

Corsets are sized according to waist measurement and busk length (the distance from top to bottom). A good corset can bring the waist in about three to four inches, but even a two-inch reduction is a cinch to produce a visible difference. In fitting a student with a corset, we measure his normal waist and give him a corset that measures three or four inches smaller, to allow for ambition. Initially, all of our corsets featured twelve-inch busks. The garments came up right under the breasts and ended at mid-tummy. But Miss Dana discovered that these inhibited the girls' freedom of movement when learning to walk, sit, and pose. So we switched to corsets with seven- or nine-inch busks. The shorter corsets allow more freedom of movement, and they do not squash the hips, which need to be bigger, not smaller. Of course, some girls love to be caressed by a very long corset that confines as much of the body as possible, and we are attentive to that desire. Student Jennifer James purchased a corset that was really a bodysuit. It came down to mid-thigh and included torpedo-shaped breast cups. She quickly learned the difference between fantasy and reality as this lovely number proved great for photo sessions but definitely restricted the movements of our girl on the go.

Some girls need help in staying erect and a corset provides encouragement to sit up nice and straight, while keeping the student on the edge of her seat. It is also a good idea to get out of that corset, into pink spandex workout togs, and concentrate on the abdominal muscles, the body's internal corset. Additional help in posture is accomplished during ballet class.

When wearing a corset, a girl must cut down on the amount that she eats. Our students do not need to be reminded of this—the corset is all the inspiration they need to opt for light meals and nutritious juices.

Corsets come in a multitude of colors and fashions, many with evocative names. My friend Mistress Antoinette supplies corsets via mail order. There is the twelve-inch "Majesty," the nine-inch "Suzette," and many, many more. We have some at the academy that are so frilly and beautiful they cry to be seen, like the one in virginal white with white lace trim and a band of pink flowers around the waist. The "Valentine" is scarlet satin with scarlet lace trim with scoops at the top to fit around the bosom. The most versatile corsets are plain black satin. Most girls wear lots of black bras and panties to coordinate with black cocktail dresses, so a black corset is the most useful choice, as well as sexy.

It is always preferable to have help when getting into a corset. Four hands are definitely better than two and a strong knee in the back can prove useful when our Scarlett needs to be squeezed to the max. A perk of marital bliss, especially for women, is to have help getting into our clothes, as well as out of them. And what about those garters? It is a lot easier, more fun, and more effective to be laced in by a partner than to snap up solo. Some of our girls take pride in being quite proficient at corseting themselves, but it does cause additional wear and tear on the garment. Corsets with seven-inch busks make the task of lacing a lot easier.

Corset enthusiasts have many resources to explore. Entire books have been written on the subject. There is even a publication called the *Corset Newsletter* published by the corsetiers at B&R Creations in San Francisco. Corsets date back to the Egyptians and despite their controversial reputation it is likely they will be around for centuries to come.

Wearing a corset does not mean that

In corset and Mommie Dearest's pearls.

the student can forget about the internal girdle provided to each of us by Mother Nature. Our lady-in-waiting needs to do some form of abdominal exercises. Down on the floor, lying on his back with knees bent, he can do crunches, but since this action is best taken without a wig, she needs other options. Yoga is a great discipline and energy revitalizer. Our girl can build strength, learn to breathe most effectively, and increase her agility. But yoga garb is not much of a training incentive and for academy girls, the outfit counts. Ballet, as we will discuss in Chapter 9, offers all of the benefits of yoga or gym exercise, and the compelling inspiration of the tutu.

After seeing himself transformed, particularly for the very first time, a student may be inspired to go on a diet. One student, Denise, used to complain often about her male persona, constantly speaking of him in the third person. "I told Fred he cannot eat at McDonald's every day . . . He tells me it's because he likes the salad bar, but he's sneaking in those Chicken Mc-Nuggets . . ." I made some simple suggestions to Denise—like putting some healthy snacks, like apples and oranges, in Fred's car so he would not get so hungry. Perhaps the student could participate in a support program for weight loss and nutritional guidance. Some apples and oranges and positive action would do more to quell Fred's chicken compunction than all of Denise's henpecking. I am all for our girls learning to eat healthy, but it makes me sad if they act as if they just want their male selves to disappear. I like the men—but we all have room for improvement.

Chapter 7

Makeup Test

$\mathcal{M}$ akeup is magic. When he learns to create with creams, powders, and paints, the student steps through the looking glass, from reality to fantasy. What might at first seem impossible becomes real. That is why makeup is such an important element in transformation.

As our envious Venus fumbles with powders, puffs, and pencils he might suppose that every genetic girl is born with the knowledge of how to apply makeup, but not one of us is. Many women have begged for admission to our academy to learn the same things our faux femmes need to know. Until I created Miss Vera's Finishing School, I knew only the barest minimum when it came to the art of cosmetology. Oh, I had managed to coast on my natural beauty—and some lipstick and blush, but when it came to using makeup to create an illusion, or transforming boys to girls, I was at a loss. So I got help.

At first, I used the services of various friends who were a lot less timid about creating with powders and blush than I. Most were struggling artists or performers or both. Whenever I visited a beauty salon for a personal treatment, I looked to enlist the services of practitioners who might be willing to moonlight, like Miss Penny from a salon in the Village. Another makeup artist went from the Red Door to our pink door, working at the academy on her days off from Elizabeth Arden. Our Deans of Cosmetology are now all experts in their field. I wanted only the best for our girls and as our students learned, so did I.

Not every student chooses to learn to do his own makeup, some prefer the luxury of being done. To surrender to the soft touch and deft strokes of our Deans of Cosmetology is a very sensual experience. Also, makeup class takes a bit more time; the student might prefer to use that time in other ways, such as trying on more outfits. Sometimes our neophyte has just taken her first baby steps out of the closet and the idea of actually doing her own makeup is too premature a commitment. The student might lack confidence or be afraid she'll make a mess.

My friend and neighbor Ingrid Pascual, an executive in Manhattan's (and now California's) Cosmetics Plus chain, has watched the growth of our academy like a proud big sister. She has occasionally gifted us with no longer needed displays and promotional materials from these stores, which are true makeup paradises, stating, "Anything for your girls, Miss Vera." Through her column each week in the *New York Times* Miss Ingrid of-

fers makeup tips and advice such as, "Experiment, don't be afraid, it's only makeup." It is a good thought for our girls to remember.

Each student must, at the very least, learn to properly apply lipstick. We encourage complete makeup lessons so that our girls can be more independent.

Makeup is an art, not a science, so there is lots of room for creativity. There are some basic concepts, but there are different approaches. Each of the academy deans has her own style. The Professor Emeritus of this department is Anthony McAulay, my adviser and cosmetic confidant. Anthony likes to joke, "Too much is never enough," but his basic approach is that makeup must be clean, never messy. His makeup mantra: "Big eyes, big lips!" and in some situations, "Big hair!"

Anthony is handsome and sexy. When he visits from his home in London, he often stays with me, which means I have my own live-in makeup artist, every girl's dream. For him, makeup is foreplay. He just can't keep his hands off my face. I love having my role reversed and being Barbie, for a change. The experience brings me that much closer to our students.

Another makeup artist who left an indelible impression is Mishell Chandler. Mishell was an expert before she got her license. She got on-the-job training in the drag clubs, which prepared her for live TV, as in "Saturday Night Live." Mishell is both an artist and performer. Makeup artists must learn to work quickly and Mishell combined talent and speed. She also brought with her the trade secrets and colorful language of the drag world. Among other things, Mishell taught us that a wig is a "party hat." She now lives in Hollywood where she continues to spread beauty as a television makeup artist and she drives a white Cadillac. You go, girl!

At the head of our makeup department today is Miss Deborah, with Miss Maria. Deborah Raposa is a flaxen-haired blonde with a sunny, upbeat personality and a wry sense of humor. She applies makeup with the lightest touch, as if a feather brushed over the face. "You can always add more," says Miss Deborah, as she instructs our girls, many of whom are accustomed to using their hands in a more two-fisted approach. Miss Deborah is also the queen of tweeze in her crusade to remove stray brow hairs. "Just a few and no one will know the difference. You will just look well rested."

Facials and moisturizers are the pet projects of Miss Maria and our girls certainly need them. Maria Giorgio grew up in New York's Little Italy. Her own complexion is alabaster and flawless. Her eyes and hair the color of espresso.

All of the academy's Deans of Cosmetology have done work for movies, magazines, stage, and television. But all would agree with Miss Deborah, who says that to transform an academy student is most rewarding. A real girl, especially a model, expects to be beautiful, but an academy girl is always grateful, his makeover is a constant source of awe and wonder. The energy of our cosmetologists, their talent, opinions, and artistry add to the rich palette from which our student draws to add color to her life. Before we are through, our lady-in-waiting understands

Viqui Maggio

Miss V, Peach, and Miss Deborah, dean of cosmetology.

that she too has choices, not only in how she looks, but in how to achieve it.

Tools of the Trade

Makeup, as our girls know better than most, is not only about the sight of it, but also the feel and the smell. Here at the academy, we enjoy every aspect. Of course, before each student begins makeup class, we put him in uniform: a silken peignoir, garter belt, stockings, feather-covered satin mules, and a generous spritz of perfume can be very inspiring. The right tools are a big help to any fledgling femme fatale and choosing the right tools is essential. The tools a student uses, like puffs or brushes, depend on the area to be transformed and on personal preference. Powder and blush can be applied with brushes or puffs. Brushes can be easier to work with, but I have seen Miss Mishell squeeze her puffs into submission and send them into every nook and cranny of a complexion. Brush tips can be squeezed together to make the brush easier to control. These tools will be dancing lightly over the face, so we want to find the ones that feel most delightful on the skin.

Anthony encouraged our use of velvety puffs by Shisheido. These cost a pretty penny, but they last longer—they can be washed in mild soap without falling apart—and they feel extraordinary.

I used to make a total mess of my brows until Miss Deborah recommended eyebrow powder applied with its own tiny

Abe Frajndlich

Mishell begins John's transformation.

brush instead of eyebrow pencil. It is so much easier to control. And she is really ecstatic about the Form-a-Brow kit available from Senna Cosmetics (1-800-537-3662) which she learned about from student Renée. The kit comes with three stencils and powders. Our students are a great source of information. Many of the girls really keep their eyes peeled for valuable products. To keep those brows in shape Miss Deborah recommends tweezers from Tweezerman. I find it easier to use a scissor-handled tweezer. In any case, says Miss Deborah, remove only one hair at a time.

Liquid eyeliner often comes with its own built-in booby trap—a thick scraggly brush that should bear a warning label. A thin, pointy brush can lead to eyeliner artistry.

Some lip pencils, like those by Mac and Lancôme, work better than others, though these brands are more expensive. Pencils that are kept in the fridge are easier to sharpen. A girl can get very frustrated, plus ruin her manicure, sharpening a pencil that keeps falling apart down to a stub.

The Transformation

Step One. An hour before makeup application, the student gives himself a very close shave, leaving his face smooth, hairless, and totally clean. Miss Maria likes our girls soft and moist and usually advises moisturizers at this point. Jane Ellen Fairfax, M.D., a cross-dressing dermatologist who contributes to the *Femme Mirror,* the magazine published by Tri-Ess, the Society for the Second Self, a national cross-dressing organization, recommends the application of a vitamin E mask about one hour before shaving and we concur. This will help remove any excess of skin cells that might cause a rough complexion.

Step Two. No matter how closely our lady-in-waiting has shaved and exfoliated, there may still be a bluish tinge left by her beard. To remove that bluish tinge, he applies a red-orange camouflage creme. Covermark and Joe Blasco are excellent brands. An old trick from the drag world, preferred by Miss Mishell, is the use of a red-orange lipstick for this purpose. Beard cover is lightly applied with a sponge, over the beard only, not over the entire face. With beard control under his garter belt, the student is ready for skin color foundation or base.

Step Three. Forget about liquid makeups. These are not for academy debs. Our girls need plenty of extra coverage and that means an oil-based creme foundation. These are made by many companies. The most widely available are Max Factor pan sticks, the kind that come in a long hard, plastic tube, with a color sample on the outside of the package. Our academy foundations are from the studio line by Mac Cosmetics. During makeup class, the student learns which color foundation most closely matches her overall complexion. When shopping on his own, perhaps still in his overalls from the construction site or uniform from the precinct, a shy student can match his foundation to the skin on the inside of his wrist. I would love it if every prospective student could visit our campus for a consultation and transformation, but I know for some that is impossible. Still there is plenty of expertise available. Representatives from companies such as Merle Norman and Mary Kay in communities large and small across the United States are usually quite willing to advise a girl with something extra. A fellow can find plenty of help in becoming a lady, provided he acts like a gentleman when he makes that initial request.

Since men have been encouraged to be rugged rather than refined, their complexions can sometimes resemble old orange peels. Our girls do present a challenge, especially the sailors. When our dames at sea are off duty, they and all men must moisturize, moisturize, moisturize and use sunblock to protect them from those harmful rays that can also cause premature aging. In order to get in between each hair follicle and into every nook and crease in the face, the student will use a wedge-shaped makeup sponge, the best tool for applying foundation. He pats foundation over his entire face and under his chin. He is instructed to apply foundation to his neck only if the beard really makes that camouflage absolutely necessary. A clean neck saves his blouse from greasy smears and his pocketbook from too many dry cleaning bills. The proper stroke for applying foundation, especially over the area that is already covered by the reddish-tinged beard cover, is to pat it, gently but firmly, one layer on top of another. We don't want our girls to smudge the two colors together and wind up with a red face. When I say, "Think pink," I am talking about a state of mind, not the color of a debutante's nose.

Step Four. A powder puff or rounded makeup brush is used to apply translucent powder and seal the foundation.

Step Five. Our student's face canvas is ready to be sculpted with light and dark powders that create highlights and contours. Base is an appropriate term for foundation, because the highlight must be lighter than the foundation and the contour powder must be darker than this base. Using these three shades—highlight, contour, and base—the student is transformed from he to she. The dark contour makes things that are big appear smaller, and the light powder or highlight makes a desirable feature more outstanding.

Every face has its own shape and peculiarities that are determined by bone structure, but there are some areas that are common places for highlights. Highlights under the eyes make those dark circles disappear. A highlight down the center of the nose will narrow and shorten it, and make it seem to end where the highlight

ends. Noses are really fun to reshape and it is amazing what can be done with powders. It is usually a good idea to highlight the area just above each eyebrow—not the entire forehead—but just about a half inch to an inch above the brow. With highlight above and below the eyes, we surround the eyes with light—in other words, frame them.

The two basic areas for contours are the nose and the cheeks. Unless our student is blessed with one of those petite perky noses, and we have had a few who are so blessed, he will want to apply the dark powder to the ridge of his nose on each side to slenderize it, and maybe some contour at the bottom, if he wants to shorten his nose. Another prime contour area is just under the cheekbone, so that the cheekbones themselves appear more prominent. To help the student to find the right spot for this particular contour, we ask him to suck in his cheeks so that the contour powder can be applied to the indentations. I am amazed at the difficulty some girls have in learning to suck.

As our student continues the highlight and contour process, all of the strokes will go from the front of his face to the back. A highlight or contour is not a little dab, but a bold stroke. By the time he is finished, our girl will resemble Pocahontas in war paint.

Learning the secrets of makeup application helps the student to see as well as to be seen in new ways. He learns that the parts of his face that are really seen are the light places rather than the dark, like those optical illusion black-and-white drawings. Look at the black space and you see two profiles, look at the white space and you see a vase. Here we look on the bright side. The white spaces dominate, so when dark colors are applied, the student must be sure to use upward strokes so that the white, highlighted skin appears to move up into a smile and *voilà!* Instant face-lift! The femmeself usually looks ten years younger than her male counterpart and she's got plenty to smile about.

Step Six. When highlights and contours are complete, a large puff or brush with sheer finishing powder is used to blend everything together. He now uses light strokes. If he uses a large puff, he dips the puff into translucent powder that is the same or one tone lighter than his foundation. Excess powder must be shook from the puff before patting. Our girl must be careful not to get powder in his eyebrows, or he must brush it out with his fingers. A big smile will help him find the apples of his cheeks, the place where he applies his pretty pink or bronze blush as he prepares to face the world.

Subtle is not in our cosmetic vocabulary. The same principles apply to our girls as to Cindy Crawford. Academy girls need makeup that can be seen ten rows back from the catwalk. Too much is never enough for our glamour puss. The face a student sees up close in the mirror is different from the face that the world standing a few feet back from her sees. It is the same effect as looking at a painting in a museum. Who would stand nose to nose with the Mona Lisa?

One picture is worth 1,000 words and so we document every step of the makeup process with Polaroid photos that the student can use for future reference. We also suggest she look at full-face portraits of women, in the pages of fashion or movie magazines, and try to determine how their makeup was applied. The artists who create the makeup

Miss Vera

New eyes and eyelashes.

Viqui Maggio

Blushing Patti.

the center of the lid, darker shadow is brushed in the crease of the lid on the brow bone and the darkest shadow is used at the outer corners of the lid. The light shadow can also be brushed just under the brow. This pattern brings depth and mystery to the eye of any girl, and also directs the eye of the viewer up and to the center where the iris, the most lively part of the eye, awaits.

Eyelashes Forever

Miss Maria went to a very strict high school where students were permitted no makeup. (Unlike our school where such shenanigans are rewarded.) Within her breast beat the heart of a painted lady and future makeup maven. There was no way she could deny her nature. Miss Maria chose the one cosmetic that would be subtly dramatic—in other words she'd look glam and the nuns would never catch on. She wore false eyelashes every single day. With very rare exceptions, false eyelashes are a must for all of our students. They soften the face and also help to complete the total makeup look. Learning to apply them takes practice but they are worth it. As Miss Maria understood, false eyelashes make a big difference. If our girl has only limited time to practice her makeup, she can concentrate on her eyelashes, mascara, and lipstick. Mascara is easy, as we will discuss, provided the student does not pinch her lid in the contraption

for the photos use the same method of highlights and contours that we do. An educated observer will discern the spot on the model's cheek where a darker powder was used to enhance that cheekbone and create the illusion of a deeper plane, just as we do with our little TV stars.

The Eyes Have It

The same principles of highlight and contour apply to eye shadow. Light and dark lines and shadows are used to sculpt the eye. Most often, we use a combination of three shades. Light shadow is brushed onto

that resembles a medieval torture device, the eyelash curler.

Using the Eyelash Curler

Way Bandy, in his book *Designing Your Face,* advised positioning the eyelash curler at the base of the lash, then squeezing and keeping the curler in one place. Kevyn Aucoin, in *The Art of Make-Up,* says the curler should be moved along the lash every few seconds as it is squeezed, thus avoiding a bent-lash look. I say, the most important thing to consider is not how many seconds you squeeze, or where you place the curler along the lash—just make sure not to grab your tender eyelid in the curler. Squeeze gently and slowly, making sure of exactly what you are squeezing before you add pressure. I do not imagine pinching a lid is as memorable as having a penis caught in a zipper, but it is no picnic. Once the eyelashes are curled, false eyelashes are applied. Eyelashes can be cut and applied in short strips or applied as one long strip. We apply the lashes as one strip. The lash is removed from its box, then wrapped around a pencil or makeup brush to curl the band. This will make it fit better across the curve of the eyelid. Use a tweezer to hold the eyelash as you apply clear drying eyelash glue. A pin can be dipped in the glue then used to spread the glue on the band of the false lash. It is very important to let the glue set for about 15 seconds until it is tacky. Using the tweezer, place the false lash at the edge of the lid. Use lashes that are graduated with longer hairs at the far corners and shorter ones near the nose. Shorter, thicker lashes, rather than super long ones, work best for our girls, who usually are opting for that sophisticated career woman look. Tap the lash down at the inner and outer edges to secure it. With lashes in place, use liquid or pencil to line the eye on top and bottom, being careful to draw lines out and up rather than down. Apply mascara to the lashes, including lower lashes. Give the mascara a few seconds to dry, then flirt and flutter. False lashes are easy to remove; just lift off, being careful not to pull the natural lashes. Unless lashes are very expensive, like the mink lashes I once wore for a photo shoot, it is better for hygienic purposes to toss them and use a new pair the next time. On busy weeks at the academy, our bathroom shelf can look like a caterpillar graveyard with dead lashes left behind after our butterflies have disappeared.

A quick word about eyeglasses. Among my favorite excursions is taking a student for new frames. The very first time I did this was at the request of Susan Sargent. We were fortunate because the shop that we walked into, which unfortunately is no longer there, was staffed by a young woman who really understood frames. She helped us to see that there are frames that make a statement and frames that disappear. Frames must be the right size for the face. For Susan, we chose a pewter frame by Jean Paul Gaultier. What a difference a more hip, feminine frame made in her face. Rather than thinking of eyeglasses as something to detract from their beauty, our girls who need glasses understand that the right frames can be a great prop and very sexy. That's why I own a whole collection.

Lipstick Kisses

Ah, lipstick! What wonders are held in the tiny little tube. I think that no other cos-

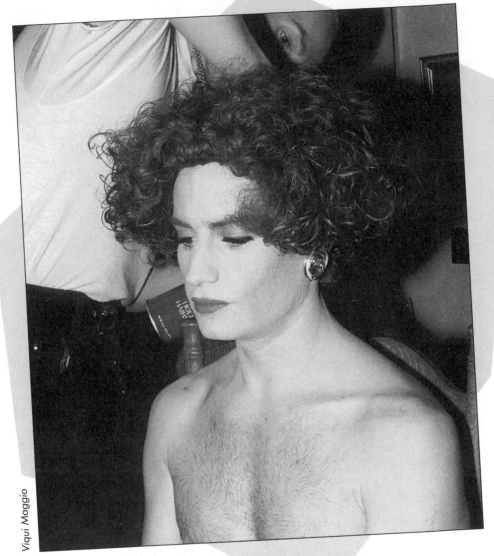

Viqui Maggio

Lady-in-waiting Stefania gets ready for the ball.

metic stimulates the imagination with the same degree of erotic power. We see a lady's face marked with creamy red lips and we are inspired to think of another set nestled far below.

At Miss Vera's Finishing School lipstick

application is one of the most important lessons. With the right tools, it is really simple. Lipstick is the one cosmetic that even if worn by itself, can make a man feel feminine and desirable and yes, oh so kissable.

Once, long before I created the academy, I had a lover who enjoyed cross-dressing. One evening, I decided to transform him. He slipped into his favorite garter belt, bra, black nylons and panties and I proceeded for the very first time to apply makeup to his handsome face. I did not have all of the cosmetics and brushes available to me at that time in my lover's bathroom, just a few basic items from my personal makeup case. I patted on the silky powder with a soft, gentle puff, then some eye shadow and mascara. But it was when I applied the color to his eager lips that everything changed. "Open your mouth, just a little," I told him, and when he dropped that lower lip, he looked so vulnerable. His lip quivered with anticipation. It was the same movement that Marilyn Monroe understood so well, that little quivering mouth that made her so irresistible. And so I kissed him, mouth to mouth, sigh to sigh, lipstick to lipstick.

Lip Service

Since men have drier lips than women, a good first step is to moisturize the lips with vitamin E. The student then learns to draw his mouth, using a lipstick pencil to outline his lips. In the beginning, it is best that he follows the lip line exactly. As he becomes more sure-handed he can add fullness. Often the upper lip needs to be enhanced—sometimes considerably—as with student Giselle, whose lips, after years of playing the trumpet, had relocated to the inside of her mouth. When applying lip liner, it is best to close the mouth and smile so the result will be a happy face and not a droopy mouth. Once lips are outlined, lipstick is applied with a lip brush instead of directly from the stick because without the

lip brush there is little hope of staying within the lines. The student blots his lips by pressing a tissue against the luscious mouth of his femmeself. He can stop now or he can get long-lasting coverage by patting his lips with a tiny bit of powder, brushing on a second coat of lipstick, blotting again. He can also try any of the new colorfast lipsticks on the market, such as Revlon's Color Stay.

Lipstick tends to wear away during a day of shopping or a night on the town, making touch-ups necessary. I think it is perfectly appropriate for a lady to touch up her lips at the table after she has finished a meal. In fact, I think this is very provocative and sexy and I do it all the time. Our girls get demerits if they do not have their compacts with them. However, this advice is only for light touch-ups applied from the tube to the center of the lips. If the student needs to repair the lip line with the lip brush or pencil, he steps into the ladies' room, but of course only if dressed entirely *en femme*. I say that because I do envision a time in the not too distant future when we will all feel free to wear lipstick, women and men, no matter what the fashion statement.

As with all cosmetics and related equipment, I advise our girls to buy the best, which does not necessarily mean the most expensive. A soft lip pencil is easier to use than a hard one. They can be sharpened more easily if chilled in the fridge. A lip brush must be free of straggly hairs. Choosing lipsticks is lots of fun. They can be sampled at cosmetic counters, discreetly on the inside of the wrist, or not so discreetly smack dab on the lips. Then get ready for lots of kisses.

Men use a gun. Women are the

shrewder more subtle sex. We prefer the lipstick wand. Ready, aim, fire: With it we can change the world.

Makeup class would not be complete without a lesson in removal. This is a big concern for all of our girls. Each one presents himself to me for inspection before he leaves. Most have scrubbed themselves to a bright blush, but sometimes I discover foundation at the temples or glue near the lashes. Max Factor makes a good one-step makeup remover that just swishes on and wipes off. Revlon's Going, Going, Gone is great. Andrea's eye-makeup remover pads are good for stubborn eyelash glue. After using these products, the student uses a gentle facial soap to get that fresh clean feeling. Then he is ready to step back out into the world, no one the wiser, except him.

Chapter 8

Fashion Assignment

"Do you have a favorite article of female clothing? (Please describe color and fabric.)"

The overwhelming favorite item cited by students in response to this question on their enrollment applications is "lingerie," and the particular items of lingerie that rank highest are stockings and panty hose, though panties give nylons a run for first place. Actually, while stocking enthusiasts are most intense, the panty fanciers are more numerous. This erotic association with clothing is not something reserved for academy students, nor something reserved only for men. I remember a scene in a preview for a Joan Crawford movie that I saw as a child. When Joan lifted her nylon-clad leg to her boudoir bench in order to fasten the ankle strap of her shoe, wolf whistles resounded throughout the theater as hundreds of young boys who'd not expected this perk to accompany the Saturday afternoon western voiced their appreciation. I don't remember if I whistled, but I was affected. Miss Crawford raised her leg only once, but I stored the image and sound effects in my mind in continuous replay.

Another clothing memory I have is more directly sexual. It did not involve an actual dress, but one that I created from the quilt on my bed. At age nine, I would spend

Eric Kroll

From Hose to Clothes (Miss V, John, and Miss Tiger).

hours alone in my room wearing nothing but my quilt wrapped around me like a strapless gown, held together with a stretch belt that I found in my mother's drawer. I loved looking at myself in my bedroom mirror, much the same way as our girls ogle their reflections here at the academy. I could look past the blanket and see a designer creation, just as our student can look past his maleness and see the female within. I would stand there and pretend I was a movie star receiving her Oscar. After making my acceptance speech, I would throw myself on my bed and kiss my pillow the way I'd seen movie stars kiss and as I rolled, my gown would slip down from my nipples, whose sensitivity I was just beginning to appreciate. When it is connected with early erotic feelings, clothing exudes a powerful allure. Why do these memories leave such an impression? Because they are usually accompanied by feelings of sensuality and security—pleasure, excitement, love, or all of the above. In the case of our students, that connection of the clothing with those feelings of pleasure has been reinforced many times over through the years. Even though our girl's attachment to her outfit might not seem logical, if we trace back through her evolution, it all makes sense.

In 1984 I testified in Washington before a Senate Judiciary Committee chaired by Senator Arlen Specter. The purpose of the hearings was to determine if additional laws needed to be enacted to restrict sexually explicit expression. I recounted my experiences in adult media and advocated for freedom of expression. Testifying on the same day was Dr. John Money, a world-renowned psychologist and expert in what he defined as "paraphelias" or fetishes. Immediately following my testimony and just before his own, Dr. Money came up to thank me, saying, "I am very glad you were here today." I was very impressed with Dr. Money's brief testimony but I did not realize how much more his research would mean to me later. Not long after, while creating a fetish resource directory for *Penthouse Forum* magazine, I read Dr. Money's book *Lovemaps,* in which he states that children often deal with emotional traumas by eroticizing them, thus creating fetishes, which represent "triumphs over traumas." The trauma does not have to be something as physically dangerous as the beating described by Loretta, the student who remembered dressing to save himself from getting hit. The trauma can be fear, humiliation, or confusion around sex. This goes a long way to explain our students' feelings of being "relaxed yet excited" when they are *en femme.* Dr. Money's "lovemaps" support my theory of sexual evolution and now it is my turn to be grateful to this dedicated man.

The clothes in our academy closet are not simply things to wear, they are fetishes, objects charged with sexual significance. In the case of some garments such as bras, panties, corsets, stockings, stiletto heels, and tight mini-skirts this is more obvious because these items have historically sexual reputations or blatant tease qualities. But even when our girl is dressing as a conservative career woman, conservative librarian, or harried hausfrau,

he is turned on. Most students admit this; some are more inhibited about claiming the sexual aspect. A main difference between transvestites and transsexuals is, as John Money would say, "the orgasm," or as Stan Bernstein, a former sex magazine editor I worked with, would describe it, "the horny angle." For a transsexual a dress helps define her identity; for a transvestite the dress is sexually exciting. Some students are not sure where they fit in. They have imagined themselves living full time as women for so long, they think perhaps that is their destiny. We give them the opportunity to live out their dreams, to make their fantasies reality and to learn the difference.

Many times people ask why is it that men wear fetishistic clothing, while women do not. Venus Envy or the desire to share more in the female experience, especially that of the desired lust object is one part of the explanation. Many a baby boomer corporate mogul, who watched his mother fasten garters to the tops of her hose, can't wait to slip out of his pinstripes and wing tips and into seamed stockings and stiletto pumps. A man may be a six foot plus construction worker who values brawn over brains, but there can be a part of him that is still three feet small, and sitting just about skirt level in awe of the world.

Another reason is that we women have had more freedom of dress than men in the last two centuries. But the scale was not always so disproportionately tipped in our favor. Henry VIII was the first person to wear stockings . . . and men have been trying to show off their legs ever since. I do not think that our students, as men, are alone in this pride and enthusiasm, but merely represent a desire shared by many men to be less regimented in dress and to use outerwear as more of an expression of their inner selves or their psychic *infra-apparel*. The term infra-apparel was coined by Richard Martin and Harold Koda, who took over curatorship of the Metropolitan Museum's Costume Institute immediately following the reign of Diana Vreeland, one of my personal role models. The Costume Institute has been the site of many of our student field trips. In the exhibit of the same name, Infra-Apparel was defined as *structure disclosed* or *inside appearing on the outside* and was a show of underwear-inspired dresses. For our students, every dress is an item of psycho-sexual infra-apparel. No matter how conservative a dress he might choose the student is an exhibitionist who wears his heart on her sleeve.

Men's desire for variety in clothing far outdistances the choices currently offered to them by the fashion industry. In recent years fashion designers, among them Jean Paul Gaultier and Donna Karan, have featured skirts and sarongs in their collections for men. I think one overlooked reason these fashions have not caught on is because the look was not "finished." Why should a man wear a skirt if only to show off hairy legs in oxfords and argyles. The look is as jolting as an otherwise nude man wearing black socks in a skin flick. The man who goes all the way and shows off his pins to the utmost may just score a strike every time!

The Silk Stocking Club

Carla is a notorious transvestite and Manhattan lady of the night who created what he called the silk stocking club, by decorating his apartment with nylons that hung from the ceiling like jungle vines and inviting footwear fetishists and cross-dressers of all manner to slip into stockings and socialize. Virginia Prince aka Charles Prince, a pioneer of the organized cross-dresser's movement, tells the story of how sheer stockings gave new meaning to the term support hose. When Virginia and friends began their early meetings in secret, cross-dressing was against the law and police would sometimes infiltrate the group and make arrests. The girls found that they could weed out police and maintain security by requiring that the first order of business was for everyone to put on nylons and high heels. Anyone who hesitated was given the boot.

Dangerous Dress

There is a danger in focusing too much on the frock, if what our girl really wants is a friend. By putting a student into the garments of his dreams, by helping her to experience life in the raw silk, our goal is to open her up to the world, not isolate her from it.

Sometimes the smallest change can make a big difference. After spending a weekend with us in a Femme Intensive, student Melanie Frances decided that she would, at long last, allow her male persona Frank, to switch from a cravat to bow tie. As harmless as a bow tie may seem, to Frank, a staid banker, it had represented a part of himself that he felt he needed to hide. When Melanie finally went out in a dress, the bow tie became far less threatening. Frank reported that after he started to wear bow ties, he seemed to be more intriguing to acquaintances old and new. In loosening the hangman's noose, the phallic cravat that was a means by which he kept himself in check and a constant reminder of the man he was supposed to be—Frank offered himself as a new package all tied up in a bow.

In the Closet

A stroll through the academy's closet reveals clothing ranging from kinky to conservative. There are skirted suits and sheath dresses. Maids' uniforms, little girl's rompers and pinafores, tight spandex minis. The list goes on and on. The feel of the clothing is very important. Silk, satin, or nylon—any fabric that glides over the skin—can bring a flood of subconscious memories. The most popular dress in the academy wardrobe is—surprise! surprise!—the wedding gown. Yes, "the happiest day of a woman's life" is the day that many boys dream about too, dressed to thrill. The feel of layers and layers of satin skirts, ruffles, and lace are a tactile reminder of childhood pampering, real or imagined. The bride is the center of attention. Most big boys still crave attention and find all kinds of ways to get it. Wearing a dress is one. Being perfectly groomed and accessorized—with hair, makeup, and husband—are also part of the magnetic appeal of playing bride. The hair and makeup reflect a desire to be pampered, a desire to be touched. Little boys are weaned of caresses, little girls are not. A gentleman need not be gay to fantasize about having a groom, he may just miss his dad and many, many men do. In fact, I think there are more men who miss their dads than those who do not. After a boy reaches a certain age, the physical con-

tact he has with his father is often limited. Physical signs of affection between man and boy are curtailed at an early age, while the need for this affection endures. We're not talking lust, here, we're talking love. Many big strong men would like to be swept up into the arms of another big strong man; and a dress can make it all okay. Not every male bride wants a male groom. There have been double bride ceremonies in which both partners wore gowns, such as the one pictured in a recent issue of *Femme Mirror,* the magazine published by the Tri-Ess organization, or where the sexes switched their genders, the man wore the dress and the woman the tux, as Mariette Pathy Allen documents in her extraordinary book of portraits and interviews, *Transformations: Crossdressers and Those Who Love Them.* A most memorable sight occurred at a bridal fashion show hosted by the cross-dresser's social group, Long Island Feminine Expression (LIFE). Student June G. Edwards, one of our most masculine-looking girls, had joined the group and invited us to attend. June, as the newest member of the LIFE sorority, was relegated to mother-of-the bride status in a burgundy gown while the other eight models wore white. At the finale, the girls were so excited, one rambunctious bride tossed her bouquet. The bridal gown epitomizes Venus Envy.

Here Comes the *Dead Bride*

The most memorable bride to visit our academy was the dead bride. Ned, a Wall Street financier, had been a football player in college, a tight end, and one of our more macho girls. It is not unusual for our acad-

Bride of Wigstock.

ter we transformed him we dress Nadine in a bridal outfit. He also requested that Nadine wear a girdle. Though the academy collection now boasts several lovely high-necked, long-sleeved bridal gowns, at that early stage we owned not a single one. The deans and I just had to wing it. Using white slips and tulle we spun fabric around Nadine's corseted figure until we'd created a bridal gown, much like the birds and the mice did when they created Cinderella's dress in the Disney version of the story. "I would like to lie in a coffin," Nadine whispered. No problem. After our success with the wedding dress, a coffin would be easy. We outfitted a futon with a white satin sheet and a pillow and surrounded our coffin with some of the many candles that other students had brought to class. We led our glamorous corpse to her final resting place. Then lit the candles around her. Nadine had already coached us in what to say. "Isn't she beautiful . . . So dead but still so sexy . . . Look at her breasts, boy, she was really voluptuous . . . I almost want to climb on top of her, she looks so delicious . . . she'll never know . . ." The deans and I could not help but giggle as we commented over our desirable departed, yet there was something more going on. We all felt it. I was reminded of my own mother's funeral. Ned told us later that the death of his mother had a great effect on him. We had walked

emy girls to be super jocks, either from a love of a sport or from a desire to prove themselves more "manly" than they actually feel. Ned arrived at the academy during our first year. Like many of our girls, he was very nervous when he arrived. Ned was about to reveal a part of himself that he considered pretty bizarre. He asked that af-

through the looking glass into a very primal part of the mind. Ned's erection strained against the confines of his girdle. "It is a very relaxing and very sexual feeling," he told us. We had dressed his body and walked into his soul—and our own, as well.

Clothes Remake the Man

What does a man's choice of clothing say about him? There are two kinds of students who visit the academy. Those who think about their clothes and those who do not. Those whose clothing keeps pace with the times and those who have been wearing the same style for years. One such student was Don/Dolly. Dolly traveled with a very expensive wardrobe. He described himself as "the executive secretary type," very poised, confident, and particular about her wardrobe—only the best would do for "Dolly." It was Don, however, who arrived at the academy. Creamy white skin, a sort of droopy do, wearing khaki slacks and the same button-down-styled shirt he'd been wearing since college. Don was the sort of fellow who fades into the woodwork (should I say closet?). Yet, he seemed to have the entire contents of Dolly's closet with him, stuffed into several big suitcases and garment bags: fine satin teddies, frilly panties and nylons, a half dozen pairs of pumps from vamp to conservative, and a makeup kit filled with the very best products, much of it a gift from a former girlfriend. I encouraged Don to let Dolly take him shopping in order to integrate these aspects of his personality or invite a fashion-minded friend to help him reshape his image.

Our student council president Jennifer James and I have purchased clothes for James as well as Jennifer. Of course, Jennifer's wardrobe came first. We took Jennifer to Wearable Energy, a shop in Soho, at which the accommodating designer Frances Colon agreed to custom-fit Jennifer and any other of our girls who were interested. After Jennifer had acquired an enviable wardrobe and her tastes for things like velvet and tapestry patterns became apparent, I decided that I was tired of seeing James arrive in the same old L. L. Bean sweaters and worn-out jeans, not to mention oxfords that reeked. In Chelsea, where the academy is located, there is a very fashionable men's store called Camouflage. Off James and I went to find a new look for him. How he loved marching in and out of the dressing room as we put him in shirts by Calvin Klein, Italian knit slacks, a fine suede windbreaker to replace the nylon parka he'd been wearing forever. On another trip, we got more adventuresome and visited Raymond Dragon, a designer who became popular with designs that held tight to the male body, displaying the form to the max. James bought a shirt made of brown stretch velvet with a mock turtleneck. When he wears this shirt, he accessorizes it with a brocade vest and a crystal pendant which we found the same day. It is his seventies' London look and it brings out his personality more than any other outfit. With a new pair of shoes, those offending oxfords were put to rest and James' new wardrobe was complete.

From the Fashion Police Files

When fantasy meets reality a whole new set of challenges must be faced, particularly when it comes to clothing. What

Abe Frajndlich

Jennifer, all dolled up.

member that all of the male joints are larger than those of genetic females. Knees can be a dead giveaway, so it is best to keep them covered.

It's All There in Black and White

Another basic rule—whether the student is dressing or applying makeup—is the rule of black and white. An area that is white is more prominent than an area that is black. A man's chest is broader than his hips. To transform him, we will make his hips appear larger and his chest appear smaller, our goal, most often, being an hourglass figure. Rather than wearing a black skirt and a white top as a bottom-conscious female might choose to do, our girl needs to do just the opposite. She will downplay her chest by wearing the darker color on top and the light one below to accentuate her hips.

Stay as Real as Possible

We prefer to work with the figure we have before resorting to padding, pinching, and prosthetics. This rule applies particularly to our more voluptuous students. At five eight with a forty-two-inch waist, Ken could be described as rotund. When we transformed Ken to Carole, the extra pounds worked to our advantage. It softened his face, which was already quite pretty but after makeup was gorgeous. In a record-breaking one-hour shopping spree we whisked Carole to Macy's large woman shop and found loose-fitting satin tops that draped over her skirts and allowed her to be much more mobile than any restrictive

looks good in our student's imagination might not translate when the woman of his dreams becomes a material girl. Miss Dana, our Dean of High Heels, has a strict set of rules and recommendations.

Avoid the Tight Mini Mistake

Our girls love to show off their legs, but there is that third leg to consider and it is a lot easier to camouflage with a skirt that is more modest. Even if a girl is tightly gaffed and displays no bulge, she must re-corset. With her pretty face and figure-flattering clothing, she looked much more authentic than she would have in a tight-waisted corset, and there was much less chance of fainting.

No Padded Shoulders

Remove all shoulder pads from femme clothes. Academy girls just do not need them. Though shoulder pads may seem to improve posture, ballet class can have the same effect, is far longer lasting, and gives our girl the chance to wear a tutu.

Soften the Look

Certain styles enhance the femme illusion. Football shoulders can hide under more softly draped tops. An Empire waist hides the fact there may not be one. A sassy peplum or ruffle at the waist such as the one on Patrick Swayze's outfit in the movie and publicity photos for *To Wong Foo . . .* add an extra dimension to the derriere.

Mirror, Mirror

I always advise our girls when they look in the mirror to make sure they actually see. Some take a look, confirm they are wearing a dress, but forget to really make an inspection.

Shopping Sprees

Here is advice for students who dream of going out shopping and I know that includes very many because shopping sprees are very popular field trips.

Merchants are in business to make sales. If our girl looks good and behaves accordingly, she will have success. If she walks into a store looking scared or guilty, casting furtive glances to left and right, this will only provoke fear and suspicion in others and she will feel less than welcome. To assure herself the best service, a girl must look her best. The student will take time with her appearance, learn to do her makeup properly, and carry her femmeself proud, but with a casual air. Shopping is fun. It is very helpful to go with a friend. A sister by our student's side can make all the difference. To have some genetic girlfriends as chaperones can help defuse what might otherwise be a volatile situation, sort of like having an interpreter in a foreign land. Slowly but surely, we are all learning to understand one another.

When Like Meets Like

Charlene was a cowgirl who flew into the academy from her ranch out West. Charlie's earliest memories of his femme feelings had been through his sister's rubber raincoat, but that was many years ago and now, "Charlene needs a new wardrobe," said Charlie. He added that his real goal was to just be Charlene as much as possible. Charlie was scheduled for a two-day Femme Intensive, which consisted of makeup and walking classes among others and lots of time spent going out. Our first excursion was to the nail salon. Charlene explained that long red fingernails not only looked exciting but felt exciting, especially when she used them to touch her lingerie and other silky fabrics. Charlene looked beautiful and very real. Part of the reason that she passed so well was because she did not forget to smile. A smile immediately softens the face. Charlene had a lot to smile about. "I've been thinking about this for months," she confided. It is a big responsibility to me to be in charge of making a student's dreams

Eric Kroll

Shopping at Lingerie Olé.

broad shoulders and long arms. The area of the Lower East Side around Orchard Street is a known bargain center where many of the shops are owned by Orthodox Jewish business-women and men. I had never taken a student shopping there and was a little apprehensive. Would the shopkeepers be more conservative and therefore be uncomfortable with our type of girl? What I forgot was that many Orthodox Jewish women choose to follow custom and wear wigs. We entered shop after shop, meeting women in wigs. Charlene fit in perfectly. It was like wearing a camouflage helmet in the jungle. In one lingerie shop, Miss Dana and I chose some items for Charlene. There was no dressing room and a no-returns policy so we had Charlene remove her coat and we held the bras and corselettes up to her body against her dress. We made sure the cup size fit her breasts perfectly. We fastened each garment at the back so that she was now wearing a bra over her dress. Charlene tried to remain cool, calm, and collected but she quivered with excitement. There she was, the center of attention, as Miss Dana and I along with about six female employees and customers checked her over to make sure that the lacy black bra was just the right size. Beneath that stuffed B cup beat a heart that recalled being in his

come true, but fortunately, I just seem to have a genius for it.

On the second afternoon of Charlene's visit, I planned a long shopping spree. Miss Dana, our Dean of High Heels would accompany us. I had seen a shop on the Lower East Side of Manhattan where designer clothes were sold in sizes for larger women. Charlene was very slim, but like many of our girls, she had

sister's bedroom, raiding her drawers, and being hugged by that raincoat.

Next we visited a plus-size dress shop, to accommodate Charlene's long arms. All of the saleswomen wore wigs. The lady who helped us complimented Charlene on her lovely figure and even suggested we also try the shop next door where the smaller sizes were sold. At first, Charlene left the choices entirely up to me and Miss Dana, but as she grew more at ease, she began to voice her opinions. We picked out dress after dress, eight at least. (None of our girls has ever complained that she had too many dresses to try.) In the end, we chose a black dress with gold buttons that had an oriental motif and a burgundy coat dress. The color was beautiful with Charlene's chestnut blond hair. When it was time to pay the bill, I took care of the financial transaction while Miss Dana led Charlene outside for a much needed cigarette and a lesson in how to smoke like a lady.

That night we took Charlene to a Broadway show in her new black sheath. She had become the girl of her dreams. As a thank you, our final meal together was prepared by Charlene: antelope steaks that she'd brought from her home on the range and which she cooked up on ours. Then she flew off into the sunset a new man and with the new information and acceptance she found, definitely no longer a lonesome cowgirl. A few weeks later, along with a thank-you note, Charlene enclosed as a gift a shiny pink raincoat.

Don't Leave Home Without It

Many of our students find that using a credit card in their femme name makes

them more comfortable, but while advisable this is not essential. When I take a student on a shopping spree, I often handle the payments. I present the student's card and sign the receipt with his male name, and have never had a problem. As long as the card is not over the limit and has not been reported lost or stolen, merchants will accept a man's card from a lady. If there is any problem, I advise our students to stay cool. It is not illegal to go shopping in female clothes. Our girl can always own up to her male identity and present more proof or make some other arrangement like paying cash, the universal problem solver. If the store is not accommodating, the student is advised to cross it off her shopping list. Remember, the customer is always right and most store policy advises that personnel treat patrons that way from the tiniest boutiques to the largest department stores.

Break the Ice

From the moment we met Laura, we knew she was a Saks Fifth Avenue girl. She arrived with a dress and jacket ensemble that looked very Chanel, though we did have to make a few alterations for a proper fit. Her dress was a little too tight across the chest, so, rather than give her a breast reduction, we added a long-sleeved black blouse from the academy wardrobe over the dress, cinched it with a narrow leather belt, and put her jacket on top. The long sleeves of the blouse extended below the cuffs of her jacket, which meant her sleeves were the right length. Laura was booked for a Ladies' Day course, a day of classes within the academy followed by a shopping spree and tea at the Plaza. "Do you think I will pass?" she asked, as so many girls have. One look at her after her transformation and I blurted out, "You look like Sandra Bernhard." She was Sandra down to a tee, though our Laura was even prettier. (But then I am slightly prejudiced.) "If anyone comes up and asks for your autograph, just sign Sandra's name," I instructed. "Why burst anyone's bubble?"

As we walked past the perfume counters on the first floor of Saks Fifth Avenue, I asked Laura if she had a favorite scent. When she replied, "No," I suggested that we set about finding one. We went from counter to counter, salesperson to salesperson, sampling scents until Laura, Miss Deborah, and I smelled like three high-class whores. Laura decided on a scent from Hermès and made her very first purchase. "Even if I just wear it home on the train, it will be well worth it," she said. "I'm glad you encouraged me to buy something. If we were alone, I don't think I would have ever had the nerve."

Now that we had loosened her purse strings, we were not to be stopped. Miss Deborah suggested that we find a blouse for Laura with long sleeves so that she could use it with her outfit the way we had the academy blouse. In the dressing rooms of Saks we tried a number of blouses and suits on Laura. We took Polaroids of each outfit to help with our decisions and so that Laura would have some great souvenirs. (A Polaroid camera is essential to any serious shopping spree.) There was a red suit that Laura was very tempted to buy. "Ask them to hold it for you," I suggested, "then you will have three days to make up your mind. You can always have it sent."

I knew it would be a challenge for Laura to give her name to the saleswoman and ask her to hold the suit. Laura had a naturally soft voice and we encouraged her to use it. "Did you get a thrill when you heard yourself speak Laura's name to the salesperson?"

"Oh yes," she sighed, "it was music to my ears."

We walked the eight blocks up Manhattan's most fashionable avenue from Saks to the Plaza, where Laura would learn teatime etiquette from Miss Viqui. Just outside of Saks, near St. Patrick's Cathedral, while Miss Deborah was taking a photo of Laura and me, a gentleman offered to take a picture of the three of us. It was a thrill for Laura to see how easily she could be accepted into the world's ebb and flow.

"You have the best job in the world, Miss Vera," said Laura, as she expressed her thanks. Just before we had left to go shopping, a big bouquet of pink roses had arrived in appreciation from another student, Carole. The gift proved to be inspirational for Laura, who sent us a fruit basket as her personal *merci*. "Gosh, maybe we're in for an avalanche," said Miss Deborah as we sat smelling the roses and licking our fingers from the treats. It was just another reason to enjoy being a girl.

Chapter 9

Best High Heel Forward

*L*earning to walk in high heels is the most challenging course in the academy's curriculum. It encompasses both the physical and mental aspects of femininity. No other item of female attire puts our student more in the femme mode than high-heeled pumps. One reason is that the shoes make a powerful physical change in his appearance. They lift him right off the ground. They throw him off balance. High

Estate of Robert Mapplethorpe. Collection Dana Greene.

Roger in fishnets.

and unfortunately women's shoe manufacturers still do not appear to have a realistic impression of the human foot. Some shoes are not made for walking, but posing, preferably with legs in the air. As night club queen and real girl Diane Brill advised in her book *Boobs, Boys and High Heels*—another from our list of recommended readings—"All birds need to perch."

There is a basic difference between the way women walk and the way men walk. Men take control of the earth. Their feet are planted firmly on the ground. Women go with the flow. We dance through life. High heels are designed to complement that dancing, light-footed movement. In the days before sidewalks, the entire base of the shoe was often elevated. These early platform shoes made it possible to rise above the muck. Men wore them as well as ladies. But while men have toppled from their pedestals, we ladies remain there, usually being admired. High heels show off the calves and other parts of the anatomy to advantage. The higher the pump, the higher the rump. In high heels the buttocks are raised to provocative heights, inviting admiring glances. Just as some women choose not to wear high heels because they do not want to invite those glances, many men are starved for that attention. In high heels, our students'

heels demand attention. At the same time, they are easy to put on and take off. This is important for girls who are still in the closet about their dressing and need to wear and remove their garments quickly and discreetly.

To better grasp the physical lessons of high heels, it is helpful to understand the philosophy behind the shoes. High heels, like the corset, have a controversial reputation. Both have been regarded as instruments of female power as well as female oppression and arguments exist to support both sides. But like everything else in life, the secret is in the balance, and no more so than when teeter-tottering in pumps. High heels can be uncomfortable,

legs appear longer and, though our girl may be concerned with her height, her legs can never be too long.

Miss Dana is our academy's Dean of high heels, a position she acquired during our very first class pajama party. Sally Sissyribbons had come to town, and I wanted him to meet some of his sorority sisters. My concept for an academy, with a curriculum of classes, had just come into focus. I invited a few of the other cross-dressers with whom I had been working as well as a few of my girlfriends to serve as female role models for the students. We all dressed in heels and lingerie. Sally was the spoiled princess in poufy baby doll pj's. Jennifer James was the good girl, offering assistance in a lacy mini-dress. Stephanie in a floor-length silk gown was the confident big sister, the most relaxed in her femininity. And Giselle was the gawky newcomer in a borrowed kimono. She was so happy just to have been invited to be one of the girls. All were on their best behavior, as they clomped to the buffet table and then tried to eat in little bites and sit with their legs together. Jennifer and Sally couldn't get to the sink fast enough, each one trying to outdo the other scoring brownie points in the dishwashing department. Suddenly, Miss Dana sprang to her feet. "Miss Vera," she said, "do you mind if I give these girls a lesson in how to walk in high heels?" "Be my guest," I responded.

I knew that Miss Dana, as a sculptor, had a clear understanding of the human body, how we are built and how we move. She understood the physical and physiological differences between women and men and had used her knowledge in her art. In creations like her design for the Ms. Olympia medal that is presented to female bodybuilders, Dana Greene knew that the female figure on the medal must not only look different

Miss Dana (left) with friend, circa 1968—perfect even then.

but must be posed differently from a male, and she incorporated those differences into the finished piece. What I did not know was that Miss Dana had once dreamed of being a dancer and though she would not become a professional dancer she would always walk like one. It is that respect and love for grace, movement, and design that she imparts to our students.

Until now, walking classes, like all classes at the academy have been taught one-on-one, a private lesson for each student. But there is such a demand for instruction in how to walk, sit, and pose in high heels—including requests from genetic or perma girls—that I envision co-educational group classes. We could initiate a co-educational lunch hour lesson: forgo the total cosmetology makeover in the interest of expediency. Our ladies-in-waiting need only apply their own lipstick, then don a class uniform—a jumper or skirt and blouse. They might even wear their own shirts and ties. Panty hose or stockings, garters, and panties would still be required and, if necessary, a tight-fitting gaff for those girls who showed signs that this lesson in femininity might call their manhood to attention.

How is high-heel class taught at the academy? I invite faux femmes, as well as biological females, to follow along, step by step.

Getting In

Are you wearing your high heels right now? If not I suggest that you slip into a pair. Uh, oh. Be careful there, miss. The proper way to put on your shoes is, while sitting down, hold the shoe in your hand, point your toes, and place your foot in the shoe—a shoehorn will help. Don't be a lazy Susan. I know this can be a difficult move, particularly for a girl who is on the edge of her seat, trying not to crush her gaffed penis. The corset or waist cincher that encourages you to sit up straight may make it difficult for you to bend but it is much better to put your shoes on correctly than ruin them by trying to shove your tootsies into your shoes while standing. Reaching down with your right hand to your right foot and vice versa can make this move easier. Not sure of your size? Your female shoe size is usually one number higher than your male shoe size. If you are a size-nine man, you are probably a size-ten lady.

Getting Up

Stay on your toes. Walk on the balls of your feet, not on your heels. Your goal is to raise your buttocks and make your legs appear longer. The heels of your shoes are there to lift you up but offer little real support. Normal walking for both sexes begins with the heel of the foot. It is just as unnatural for a female to walk in pumps as it is for a male—that is why so many women do not know how to do it. However, from boyhood, you copied the walk of the men in your life, which means you must have most likely been bending your knees, resulting in a lumbering, bouncing gait. You also learned that it was okay to walk and sit with your legs spread wide apart, an obvious accommodation to those elements of your structure that we are trying to camouflage, so the legs must stay closer together. Instead of letting the body sink to the ground with each step, the student must learn to carry her torso with her legs, so the upper body floats smoothly. As a female, your weight is on your balls.

Here is an exercise to help you understand this concept: Imagine yourself in your pumps trying to cross a busy intersection. Cars approach more quickly than you thought and you must get to the other side quickly or be flattened like a pancake. There is no time to remove your shoes, you have only to run. How would you do it? I have seen student after student go through this exercise with Miss Dana. When faced with this dilemma, a little lightbulb seems to appear over the student's head and before you can say Wilma Rudolph or Gail Devers our girl is up on her toes, with wings on her heels, as she scurries to safety. Sometimes a girl needs a little extra motivation to grasp a concept. One summer evening after a full day of excursions, Jennifer James and I were having dinner at a restaurant when she realized that she had left her purse behind. I made it a policy to never let a student walk the streets unchaperoned but as we were just a few blocks from the academy and as I was tired and a bit irritated with Jennifer for being so forgetful, I agreed when she immediately volunteered to scoot back on her own. It was a Saturday night and some yahoos who were out joyriding spotted Jennifer hustling down the block in what probably was not her most ladylike mode. They pulled over and opened the car's doors to begin pursuit. Jennifer, who until that time was known for dragging her heels only when it came to walking class, suddenly got it. She rose to her toes and flew like Mercury to the safety of our campus.

Go ahead. Try it. Up on your toes like a prancing pony. Now you will understand the proper way to shift your weight when wearing high heels.

Getting Straight

Don't buckle at the knees. As you step forward, toes pointed, keep ankles locked and knees straight. If you find it impossible to keep your knees straight, then the heels of your shoes are probably too high. In the high-heel department, bigger is not always better, so student JoAnn learned. JoAnn's style was that of fetish pinup: leather mini-skirt and matching jacket; seamed stockings and a tight corset; dark red nails that curved like parrots claws; and red patent leather platform ankle straps with six-inch heels. When Eric wore these shoes at home and looked at his legs in the mirror, he thought he looked fabulous. And he did, as long as he stood absolutely still. But when fantasy met reality and Erica actually tried to walk in her stilettos, her arch was not good enough to accommodate the challenge of those heels. She would have had to have been a prima ballerina. JoAnn was forced to bend her knees and even she acknowledged that this was not attractive, or safe, and not even close to comfortable. So she wore her three- to three and a half-inch heels on the street, four-inch spikes if she only needed to make it into a taxi or the ladies' room, and she reserved the six-inch stilettos as posing pumps.

Getting Around

Sometimes our lady-in-waiting will think that she has to walk with one foot directly in front of another. She might have heard somewhere that this is how models walk or she may have had her eyes glued to

Fashion TV and thought this is what she saw. Runway models cross one foot in front of the other, this is how they keep their balance. If you walk as if you're on a tightrope, you will soon topple over. For a graceful, female walk, imagine that your feet are coming down on either side of a straight line. Your toes are pointed slightly out. Your torso does not follow your toes, but moves straight ahead. Now, take smaller steps. Remember, part of the pleasure of high heels is that they slow you down, invite you to step out of the rat race. Notice the women around you. Notice the size of their steps. Have you, as a man, ever walked with a woman and found that you had to slow down to keep pace with her? Well, now that slower, delicate creature is you. Cut your male step by more than half, so there is less than the length of your foot between each step, and you will achieve a more elegant walk. You will also find it a lot easier to walk in high heels if you do not take such big steps. You would have to stoop down and bend the knees to take large steps or strides—not a pretty picture. Remember, as a femme you are not looking to take up lots of space; your goal is to float *within* space. Though you take smaller steps, you will be amazed at how far you can go.

Getting Smaller

Squeeze your shoulder blades together. This will give you a narrower torso. It will also push out your chest. Be careful not to lift your shoulders as if you were at attention military-style. When you pull your shoulder blades together in the center of your back, your shoulders will follow, as will your arms. Take a look in the

mirror as you do this and you will see a remarkable difference in your upper chest. You will suddenly appear smaller and narrower up top, with your breasts naturally uplifted, something every girl wants. To avoid that Neanderthal hang, make sure that your thumb, rather than the back of your hand, is facing front and your elbow is facing back instead of out to the side. These rules apply whether you're standing or seated.

Getting Happy

I know while trying to balance in those perilous pumps there is a great temptation to keep your eyes glued to the ground. But this is not attractive. You want to present your beautiful self to the world, so look up. You may glance down every now and then, to make sure that there are no banana peels or sidewalk grates in your path, but never, never lower your chin. Give a quick downward glance, but hold your head high and smile, smile, smile. And you, my pumped up beauty, have plenty to smile about.

Taxi Maneuvers

It is a great thrill to walk down the street *en femme,* but you also deserve to ride in style and that means another lesson, which is part of Miss Dana's class prior to going out: how to enter and exit a taxi or other automobile. First of all, if you are with a gentleman, let him open the door and precede you into the taxi. This may look to the world as if he is being less than gallant, or as one swarthy male chauvinist driver once remarked to me and my escort, it may appear that you are showing proper deference to the superior male. In reality, he has saved you from having to slide across the often cramped backseat. As it is, you will still have to fold like an accordion to make a successful entry. Enter backside first. Turn your backside to the seat. Sit down sideways, with your feet still on the ground outside the door of the cab. Now, keeping your knees together, and I cannot emphasize that too strongly, hoist your legs up over the bottom edge of the door frame, into the vehicle. You can lift both legs together or one foot at a time, but for modesty's sake, keep those knees together. Use Princess Di as your role model. She has this procedure down perfectly, as well she must for she never knows when the camera and the eyes of the world will be watching her. (There was that awful moment when the *National Enquirer* caught her with her legs apart, but they must have been snooping very vigilantly.) Just as a princess must be on guard, so must every queen.

Sitting Pretty

The first thing to do is sit intelligently. That sofa may look nice and cushy and comfy, but you won't look so fetching if you have to almost crawl out of it. Pick a firm chair, instead. When sitting, keep your knees together, your toes turned out. "When in doubt, turn them out," says Miss Dana. Let one foot point to one o'clock and the other to eleven and be sure to pull your feet out from under your chair. All this will elongate your legs. Another sit-

ting position and one that is helpful for girls who have spent many years with their thighs open is to sit with your weight on one hip and let gravity help your knees come together. Again your feet will be out from under the chair and one foot will be next to the other with the toes of both feet pointed down. Sitting with legs crossed is a challenge, particularly for our gaffed and corseted girls. As a man, you have been used to lifting your leg at the ankle and resting it on the opposite knee. Now you must lift your leg at the knee and lower it not quite all the way down on top of the other knee. Keeping that top knee slightly raised will keep the top calf from bulging out at the side as it rests against the bottom leg. If this cross-legged position sounds difficult, you are right, and

Abe Frajndlich

Sitting pretty (Joan, Patti, and Jennifer with Miss V).

any chiropractor will agree, it is also not the best position for your body. Now that we have given you other lovely sitting poses you may keep this one for special occasions, like photo-ops. Look for role models. TV commentator Mary Hart, host of "Entertainment Tonight," has a reputation for a great pair of legs because she knows how to show them off most effectively in positions that flatter her attributes. Sophia Loren reflects beauty in every movement and RuPaul is an expert when it comes to displaying her charms and staying every inch a lady.

Standing Poses

Don't make the mistake of thinking that every woman can be your role model or even that every model can be your role model. Models make mistakes, especially when they are coaxed into positions by male photographers. Jennifer James, who likes to think of herself as a tomboy, attempted to emulate the saucy deb in the Virginia Slims ad. Jennifer thought that she'd come a long way, baby, but she quickly learned from Miss Dana that she still had a long way to go. Until walking class, Jennifer's favorite stance was to put her weight on one leg and bend the second knee in— toes in, thinking herself a saucy vixen, but looking more like an awkward three-year-old. We asked Jennifer if her goal was to look like a real girl and she answered yes. Her posture was corrected by keeping that second knee in, but turning the toes out. Here are some popular positions and how we rate them: knee in and toe in, wrong; knee out and toe out, wrong; knee in and toe out, right! Toes of the unbent leg are at eleven o'clock, toes

of the bent leg are at one o'clock. As our Dean of High Heels explains, if you want to appear as feminine as possible, you have to try harder than a real girl. You are creating an illusion, so you must eliminate everything that does not contribute to that illusion.

Ballet One and Tutu

With more and more students enrolling for our two-day Femme Intensive course, more ladies-in-waiting are taking advantage of that seemingly frivolous but actually very essential course, ballet one and tutu, which is taught by Irene Clark aka Miss Tiger. Miss Tiger's early studies were with George Milenoff. Her talent and love of dance have won her professional placements and prizes. And when the academy is on summer sabbatical, Miss Tiger vacations at Noyes Rhythm Camp. She has the training and the pointy stick that encourage our girls to stretch their limbs and their limits. The course title refers to the costume, a hot pink tutu worn over a black leotard and the classic pink tights. Miss Tiger makes sure that our ladies-in-waiting position their tutus at the proper hip level, thus accentuating the buttocks and giving many of our girls a lithe and willowy appearance. Corsets are not permitted in ballet class since corsets inhibit movement, so if our student's figure is closer to a beer barrel than an hourglass, he might not be quite so willowy as the next girl. Have no fear, Miss Tiger has a movement routine worked out for every physique and figure type. Even girls who have been bruised and battle-scarred benefit from her instruction. Former Green Beret Melissa managed to stretch and bend her grenade-shattered leg at the barre. With an extra pair of tights we camouflaged her scars so that even in the sheerest of hose, her legs looked perfectly smooth.

I have been shocked, at times, by a student's lack of limberness. Some of our girls have difficulty raising their arms above their heads to take off their dresses. Ballet class encourages suppleness and strength. Learning to plié helps a girl to stay on her toes when in her heels.

Your Turn

To plié in first position, stand facing the ballet barre—at home you can use the back of a sturdy chair. Put your heels together and let your toes point to opposite sides. Keeping your back straight, clench your buttocks and lift yourself onto the balls of your feet, then allow your knees to bend and lower yourself straight down. Uh, oh . . . no need to go too far down. You don't have to wind up in a squat to reap the benefits of this exercise, especially for girls who are out of practice. Follow the same path all the way back up onto the balls of your feet. As you hold gingerly to the barre, your abdomen is tight and your buttocks are clenched. Lower your heels and rest and try again.

Miss Tiger recommends a simple exercise to keep your calf muscles limber for walking in heels is to hold on to a railing, stand on a step with your heels hanging over the edge, and put your weight into

Miss Vera

Beginning ballerinas (Jennifer and Joan).

your heels. Do this one barefoot or in ballet slippers, please.

Though corsets are not part of the traditional ballet outfit, and thus are not allowed, we do relax some rules. Miss Tiger, who was a soloist with the Florida West Coast Dance Company and later ran ballet studios, says that in a traditional ballet class, dancers do not wear jewelry, but she gives our girls special dispensation when it comes to earrings.

In a typical academy ballet class, the student, *en femme,* is at the ballet barre in his pink tutu, black leotard, pink tights, and pink slippers; the lush piano and violins of music by Vivaldi echo through our rosy studio. He is surrounded by statues of women, photographs of women, and before him stands Miss Tiger, her long brunette tresses pulled back in a tight bun, her dark eyes sparkling with excitement as she guides our ballerina through each move, expecting him to do his best and be the best she can be. He is usually surprised at exactly how good that is.

Our first ballet class was a group class, organized at the request of Susan Sargent, who was spending her first Femme Intensive with us. Jennifer James, who loves ballet (or the outfit), begged to be enrolled. June G. Edwards, who is a second-degree black belt karate master, wanted to see how ballet compared. Anthony McAulay is always ready for a music class. He was just back from Bali, so he wore a sarong. I, too, was not going to miss the opportunity for a lesson from Miss Tiger. I rented a studio for us, since the academy could not accommodate so many ballerinas in one room and we danced to our hearts content.

One of my favorite classes took place as part of a television piece on the academy that was to be shown on French television. Jennifer and Joan were at the barre, Miss Tiger was at the head of the class, while Miss Viqui, Miss Deborah, me, and the programs hostess watched. Jennifer James was in ecstasy: she was in her outfit, in her favorite class, and all eyes were on her, plus she would get to see herself on videotape. Miss Tiger gave instructions but Jennifer seemed not to hear. She was dancing to an idea in her mind and unaware that her overly broad gestures were hitting Joan Hazelnut—who was bending and creaking next to her—smack in the hairdo. Poor Joan's job in the restaurant re-

quired him to do a lot of standing, and while the ballet stretches were beneficial, they produced lots of sound effects. But at least she groaned in time with the music.

At first, ballet class started off slowly. It seemed that though students often inquired about the class, not many actually chose this elective and those who did were embarrassed at what they feared might be seen as a course for sissies. Fortunately all that has changed. By actively promoting the ballet class and treating it as a required course, many more of our on-campus students have learned to be more graceful much faster. I have seen luscious red lips lift in a smile of pride as our padded Pavlova pliés and pirouettes, feeling his body move in ways he thought possible only in his dreams.

I am constantly amazed at the barbaric rigors of the male world. From war to boxing to football. Men are constantly encouraged to beat themselves or others. Many of our girls have participated in such combat while hating every moment, or at least feeling that something was wrong. Through the gentle, fluid movements of ballet—which nonetheless require and inspire strength and concentration—we not only give the student another way to express his body but to express his heart, and a great way to show off his legs.

As a good antidote to an afternoon in pumps and the perfect treatment *après* ballet, the student needs to soothe her muscles in a bubble bath laced with epsom salts. For many a problem, a long soak in a tub piled high with suds—some candlelight, music, incense, a cup of tea—is my favorite prescription.

Chapter 10

Home Ec

Though most of our students state in their enrollment applications that they identify their femmeselves as sophisticated career women, many choose to identify as young wives, and we also have a very strong sissy maid contingent. The sissy maid—a man in a short frilly dress—is prevalent in commercial fantasy literature, as is his female counterpart, the French maid. The maid fantasy harkens back to the idea that servants, because of their position, must not only perform their tasks but submit to the lustful cravings of their employers. Until recently, women as wives were in this vulnerable position. We were the property of our husbands, expected to have sex at their bidding. In the real world of fantasy, a person who chooses any submissive sexual position does so to relieve himself of the responsibility of owning his desires and actually putting those into practice. The sissy maid has more than dust on his mind.

The sissy maid is often the first image with which a prospective student identifies when he begins to comb through adult bookstores or other reading sources in order to discover more about this feeling inside of him. He has already connected female clothing to his sexuality. He feels guilty about wanting to dress as a female and guilty or unsure about what sexual actions to take, so the maid looks for a mistress or master to serve who will accept him and take him further. We accept our sissy maids and every student into the curriculum in order that they accept themselves. What we do not accept is the idea that this is a humiliating position. That is why we teach our maids to have pride in their work, pride in their appearance, and pride in themselves.

The role of the maid or housewife is also popular because of the unstated agreement that in return for service, the domestic diva is protected. Many of our students grew up in the fifties, that other TV era, when prevalent female images were June Cleaver, the Beaver's mom; Harriet Nelson, Ricky's and David's mom; and Mrs. Anderson, the wife to the father who knew best. These women were the queens of their castles. Dressed in pretty flowered dresses, they lived in a perpetual springtime, taking care of the home and the children while being taken care of themselves by men who were actually present. Mom represented beauty and security and even in those wholesome years of the fifties, she was the sexy one. It was a role that many boys envied then and still do now.

I once gave a party in honor of Xaviera Hollander, who is perhaps better known as the Happy Hooker. To make sure the party flowed smoothly, I had hired a bartender, requesting that he be young and handsome, two traits that the infamous Dutch authoress is known to appreciate, and I allowed one of our students to serve as our French maid. Jennifer James had proven himself many times. As a maid, he was still a little rough around the edges, in terms of refinement, but

Viqui Maggio

Sally Sissyribbons lights a fire.

120

Maid Jennifer bottoms up.

Annie Sprinkle

he was full of energy and enthusiasm. His uniform was a traditional style for fantasy maids, the kind named Fifi who wear high heels and short skirts and tend to bend over a lot when they dust. Jennifer's outfit was a pink satin dress that ended at mid-thigh. The collar was high, the sleeves were long, and both collar and sleeves were trimmed in white lace. He wore white-patterned stockings attached to garters just under his ruffled rubber bloomers, which warmed his bottom and recalled those safe, early days in the playpen. His pink ruffled crinoline caused his skirt to flare so wide it dusted the furniture and his white pumps were not quite so high as he would have liked but high enough for him to feel good and still accomplish his duties. After Xaviera and her entourage (which included a Dutch television crew) had departed, I was confronted with an image that has stayed in

my mind and caused me to think many times over about the many-layered role of the ruffled sissy maid. Near the end of the party the guests had dwindled down to just a half dozen close friends, male and female. We sat in a cluster and continued to chat. Looking to be of service, Jennifer James entered our circle with a tray of strawberries. Jennifer bent at the waist to offer the tray to a guest seated directly in front of me. This brought our serving girl's ruffled derriere, panty bottom, slips, garters, and stocking tops right up to my face. The image arrested my attention. It was at once rude and provocative. Sexy, yet immature; subtle, yet blatant. I recognized that I was nose to pose with Venus Envy.

Feminist scholars have argued that the academy reinforces the same female stereotypes that women have fought so hard to put to rest. What such critics overlook is that the segment of the population who choose to explore these roles are not women but men for whom this endeavor represents a new direction and a striving toward balance. Is the student who chooses to identify as a sissy maid or the young wife that far removed from the house husband? The phenomenal success of Martha Stewart both raises public consciousness to the joys of home work and attests to its popularity. I know from my students that some of them watch her programs, as well as other similar shows, and I am sure that other men do, too. Just as women have proven themselves in the sports world, the corporate world, and other arenas of men, so are men equal to the task of taking care of a home and children. In the early seventies a movement arose called "Wages for Housework." It reappeared recently in San Francisco. In a way, it is the basis for community property laws. There is no doubt in my mind that if more men did their home work, this idea would be implemented pretty quick, thus making housework even more attractive to both sexes. More men would go into housework, thus leaving other employment opportunities open to women and making it easier for women to leave the home, if we choose. The wage differential would close. As genetic girls spend more time in the workplace, it only makes sense that men be encouraged to pursue their dreams of domestic bliss. In encouraging our male students to explore their inner feelings and see them as options and choices, not only to cross-dress but to cross over into the territories formerly reserved for the other gender, we chip away at those barricades that have already begun to crumble.

At Miss Vera's Finishing School, we don't fall for a man just because he's in uniform. We teach him to look good and be of service. There is a certain sense of calm and tranquillity that accompanies housecleaning. Any good domestic can attest, a clean house gives back. The rewards are immediate. It is a job rich in instant gratification, and little conflict. In an Inauguration Day interview on CNN, First Lady Hillary Clinton stated that one of her and the President's favorite pastimes when they have a rare free moment is to clean out the closets. "Housecleaning is a great way to relax," she said. "It is a job with a beginning, a middle and an end." Cleaning can be a meditation. It is also a way to express love without words. A home that is neat and clean reveals that there is a caring person within. But many students who come to the academy have to be educated to this understanding. Their first thought is to put on the uniform and sashay around the parlor getting lots of attention. They have been taught, we have all been taught, to belittle "women's work." At the academy we reinforce its value because it is valuable work, and it's man's work, too.

John R. enrolled for the "Maid to Order" course because he said that he hoped if he learned to be useful that his wife, who knew that he cross-dressed on his own, might be more inclined to enjoy his cross-dressing with him. Immediately after John's transformation in which we created Janet and put her in uniform, the deans and I decided it was time for lunch. Janet Johnston had no idea how to set a table, so we gave her a lesson—nothing too complicated—just your basic knife, fork, napkin, plate, and drinking glass. As a captain of industry, John was called on to use lots of brain power, but when it came to remembering on which side to place the napkin (the left), our girl was stumped, even after a demonstration. We ate our meal; Janet ate at a separate table, which required a separate place setting, which required still more concentration. After the meal, when it was time to do the dishes, Janet seemed more inclined to give lip service than domestic service. "How about if we skip the dishes and, instead, I give you all massages?" John, for it was clearly John speaking now, suggested. "And just who do you think will do the dishes?" I asked. It took less than a minute for Janet to learn to clean a plate properly and less than five for her to clean up after our lunch.

Basic Table Setting 101

Table settings can get very complicated. They can involve many courses and many changes along the way. The French have made an art of this confusion. Americans usually eat very simply, often with all of the food, except for soup and dessert, served at the same time. Since we want our girls to learn quickly and pleasantly without too much frustration, we start off with the simplest table setting: plate at the center, fork on the left, knife on the right, and glass at the top, right. The napkin can be on the plate or under the fork. For a meal that includes soup, entree, salad, bread and butter, and dessert the table setting is more elaborate and our girl will open her copy of *Amy Vanderbilt*. One general rule is that items of flatware are placed on the table in their order of use, forks to the left of the plate, knives and spoons to the right. For example, the salad fork is placed to the outside of the

dinner fork because in American style, the salad is eaten first. At the academy we guide the student though a labyrinth of tableware as need be, but not then or now do I want to confuse anyone's pretty little head.

Some of our more exuberant girls would love to jump up and clear away the plate as each guest is finished, thus giving the student the opportunity to strut her stuff more often, but this kind of speed is incorrect. It is a food faux pas also committed in restaurants. My friend Lisa Sohmer, a well-brought-up young woman whose significant other Michael Rakosi loves to linger over his plate, spearheads a movement to educate the staffs in eateries from coast to coast. No plates should be cleared until all guests have finished dining. Plates are cleared from the right and served from the left.

Dishwashing Made Easy

Except for very large meals, I recommend washing dishes by hand rather than machine. It is usually just as fast and sometimes even faster, plus this too can be a very relaxing process. Our girls must first attire themselves with aprons and those all-important rubber gloves, preferably pink. Hands must be protected at all times. The maid never knows when she might be called upon to give her mistress a massage and she would not want to do that with sandpaper hands. Use a multipurpose dish and pot scrubber (a Dobie, for example); squeeze liquid dish detergent onto the scrubber; swirl the scrubber over the item to be washed; With these simple instructions Janet Johnston accomplished her dishwashing duties in just a few minutes.

At Miss Vera's Finishing School, the Maid Training course offers one of the sharpest encounters of fantasy meeting with reality. Men who are used to mothers and wives who clean up after them want to be maids when they can't even remember to put the lids back on cosmetic jars or close the closet doors. At the academy, we often must start at a very basic level of reeducation, but we have achieved great results.

The Scullery Maid

There are two types of maids: personal maids and scullery maids. Personal maids are those whose duties revolve around the clothing of the mistress; scullery maids do the heavy cleaning. The work of the personal maid centers around the bedroom and dressing room. Headquarters of the scullery maid is the kitchen or scullery. You might think that the personal maid is the more popular choice, but many prospective students like the idea of heavy cleaning.

An experience that proved very educational for me and helped formulate the academy's domestic policy occurred shortly after I had begun working with cross-dressers. I decided to take on a maid based on the recommendation of my friend Rachel, a dominatrix who was ending her business and about to get married. "Jessica is the best maid I've ever had," she told me. "He really does the work. He even irons!"

My field research in the realms of fantasy had already made me aware that there are maids and there are maids. And when a sissy maid is trading services—bartering cleanup in exchange for dress-up—very often the house is left a mess. Frequently a man claims he wants to serve as a maid, then goes around making lots of mistakes, in a sneaky effort to get attention. It's true what they say: There is a servant problem.

But I felt that Rachel would only be impressed with true devotion to drudgery. She had intimated that Jim, "Jessica," did not have much money, hence the decision to trade services. This barter arrangement would have been fine with me, except that in our preliminary conversations Jim portrayed himself as a wheeler dealer, with lots of references to big bucks. He may have wanted to put himself in a subservient position, but his manner was overbearing.

"So you know I'll do the ironing and cleaning, but besides helping me dress, what exactly will I get from you?"

Logically, I could have just asked him what he wanted, but his belligerent tone put me on guard. Instead, I told him that I did not like his attitude. I informed him that he had far more to learn from me than I had to gain from him and if he hoped to be allowed to do my cleaning, he must pay a token fee. This would be a sign of respect in a language he clearly understood. He apologized and quickly agreed. This was my first encounter with the dueling natures of Jim who was Jessica.

Had I asked him that question about his motives, I wonder if he would even have known what to answer. I learned later that what he wanted was a girlfriend. Before all that became clear, a lot of housework got done.

Jessica reported for work and I dressed him in a uniform, which on that first day consisted mostly of lingerie from my closet. Then I put him to work. The name "Missy" popped out of my mouth and stuck. Missy loved to hate dirt. He got into every nook and cranny and since my apartment had never been cleaned with such thoroughness, Missy found quite a lot to do. I rewarded him by covering him with depilatory and removing all of the hair from his legs, arms, and chest. Miss was in heaven.

On the next cleaning day, after several hours of diligent work, Missy told me that doing my cleaning made him very sexually excited. What a great quality in a maid! I was delighted and amused. The task that excited him the most was washing the windows, because of the chance that he could be seen.

As a reward for a good day of service, and to make sure that Missy looked fine, I left the apartment and headed for Macy's lingerie department, where I bought him the girdle he wanted and needed. I enjoyed going through the racks at Macy's, finding just the right garment to hold his tummy firm and reduce the size of his waist. I felt like a society dame. After all, I was shopping to uniform my maid. I also appreciated the fact that while I was doing my job, in this case browsing through the department store, there was someone at home devotedly making the house beautiful. An agreement not unlike that of the traditional husband and wife. The security seemed to work both ways.

Before he left one day, Jim asked if he could make a business call. He told his associate that he had had "a wild night." His tone implied an evening of drinking and debauchery. Our night had been "wild" but not in the sense his friend might assume. Missy had lit the bathroom with candles, drawn my bubble bath, given me a massage, and left, as planned.

Jim's female side proved to be sweet and accommodating; his male side could be an obstreperous bore. Could it be I was meant to bring together the natures of this man and his maid? Before long, I understood that Jim hoped that ours would become a romantic relationship. I did not share those feelings. What I wanted was a person to clean the house, so I hired a professional maid, one whose only strings were attached to an apron. Cleaning is cleaning and courting is courting, I explained to Jim, and if he wanted a girlfriend, he could try a more straightforward approach. There was no reason to think he might not combine the two acts, but he would likely be frustrated if he thought that one could be a total substitute for the other.

Students enrolled in our Maid Training program want both. They get tremendous satisfaction from being of service, so we teach them the skills that can help them to really be of service and encourage them to take pride in their work. Putting on the costume helps get them there. But putting on a costume, physically or psychically, can make it more difficult with another person. To get close they will need to remove the veneer.

Jacqueline was a student who sent photos of his sparkling clean toilet and bidet from Switzerland. Jacqueline's female role model was Cinderella, pre-fairy godmother. His uniform, which was laid out oh-so-neatly on the bed, consisted of a housecoat and head scarf and sensible wedged mules. He called me for a few weeks to discuss his proposed visit. His voice was low and gruff, made even more so by the difficulty he had speaking English. He talked of being taken out in his cleaning ensemble, especially his housecleaning shoes. He wanted it to be obvious that he was a servant. Though he said he wanted to be transformed, it became clear that what he really craved was humiliation. Having such a maid around would make me very, very tired. Application not accepted.

Deborah Rose, who edits the *Sissy Maid Quarterly,* likes to perform his duties as a sissy maid in sneakers, bicycle shorts, and a very tight-fitting gaff. Many students identify their desire to do "women's work" as their "sissy" side. At the academy we believe in sissy power.

It was the students as sissy maids, who stood boldly at the forefront in their aprons and lace and served the party, that brought the academy our first media attention and cleared the path for a multitude of cross-dressers to follow in their high heels. Jennifer James, who was then a nuclear engineer working in a city full of men . . . June G. Edwards, who was a second-degree black belt as well as the proud owner of a garter belt, and Raquel, pretty but shy . . . these were our standard bearers. They were dressed in outfits that seemed ridiculous for men to be wearing, and in so doing, they embraced that part of themselves, and the world embraced them too. Had they been wearing olive drab instead of Barbie pink, they could not have shown more grace under fire.

What Every Pretty Maid Needs to Know

Our academy library is filled with books on every subject within the curriculum, including housekeeping. Our girls can supplement their education with additional reading and extra-credit assignments. There is no need for me to try to reinvent the wheel and cover every do-mestic problem our lady-in-waiting may encounter, I prefer to point her in the direction of a book such as *Hints from Heloise* or the *Readers Digest Guide to Household Hints.* However, there are some home-making fundamentals that cannot be overemphasized, particularly when I see that our girls are uniform in their mistakes. These are often the most common, everyday tasks, things that books don't even bother to cover, assuming that all the world knows how to do them. Making the bed is one such task.

I remember very clearly the day my mother showed me how to make my own bed. It was as if she was entrusting to me some secret of the ages. We were bonding. Perhaps, that is why I take such pleasure in making my bed, first thing each morning. It is as if by setting my bed in order, I am setting my life in order, or at least on my way there. Our military girls usually have had some experience in this area. A bed is made with a bottom sheet that is usually fitted and thus very easy to place snugly over the mattress. Next, a top sheet, which should be tucked in at the corners, followed by a blanket or quilt and the bedspread. The spread is turned back to make room for the pillows, then lifted over the pillows. The finished bed should be neat and tidy, which means a nice even fold under the pillows and the spread hanging evenly all around. Then place your dolly or teddy at center of pillows (optional).

How to Wash Lingerie

Director Mike Nichols quipped in an interview that one of his joys when spending a holiday in a hotel with his wife, Diane

Sawyer, is to use the opportunity to wash her lingerie. For genetic girls, washing lingerie is a chore, but to some men, especially our boys who want to be girls, this is sheer ecstasy and a great way to score points with their wives or lovers. But, of course, they must learn how to do it right. Lingerie is usually washed in the bathroom sink with dishwashing liquid or liquid lingerie soap, such as Woolite. The water should be lukewarm and sudsy. Frillies can soak in the bubbles for twenty minutes and then be rinsed in cool water. One of the most important steps in the process is drying the garments. These delicate fabrics must not be squeezed, but instead,

wrapped in a towel. The towel is then rolled up so that the water from the garment is soaked up by the towel. The garment can then be hung to dry, either on a special rack or on a towel placed over the shower rod. But remember, gentlemen, don't wear your ladies' lingerie without permission.

Geisha Training

The skin is the largest sensory organ and our students love to be touched. In our years thus far, only one student was germ phobic. He did consent to let us apply his makeup, but when it came to blotting his lipstick, he drew the line. He told us that he did not even like to touch his lips with *his own* hands and made an elaborate ritual of holding the tissue to his ruby red mouth without getting his fingers too near.

The rest of our girls feel quite the opposite. I think being dressed by me or one of the deans is exciting not only because of the thrill of wearing the clothing but also because we are dressing the student, putting our hands on his skin, touching her shoulders as we adjust her bra straps, holding his hand as we slip it through the long sleeve of a satin blouse, encircling his waist with our fingers as we feel the effects of a tightly laced corset, brushing against her nipples as we slip the breast form into her bra. I always encourage our girls to touch themselves as well, to close their eyes and just feel their new curves.

Massage is a more direct way for our students to experience

Eric Kroll (uniform: Versatile Fashions)

Boudoir girl hard at work.

touch. It goes beyond the subtle tease of dressing and helps the student reach a new level of intimacy beyond clothes. One of the best ways to learn how to give a good massage is to receive one. It is the first step in learning to be a geisha.

When you are receiving a massage, you will want to stay as relaxed as possible. Empty your mind and surrender your body to the person who is treating you to this delicious experience. Try not to talk too much. I know some of you like to chatter when you are excited or nervous, both of which you might be during a massage, particularly if this is your first. But try to remain silent, concentrate on your breathing, and just let yourself feel. This will help you have some idea of the differences in hand pressure and the variety of strokes that are possible. Of course speak up if you are in any way uncomfortable—if your tootsies are cold, ask for a towel.

In the next step in geisha training, the student gives the massage. The first thing to remember is to concentrate. Don't get distracted. If you were giving me a massage, I would want you to burn some incense, light some candles, or set the lights low. Use a good olive oil to which you have added a scent, or a good massage oil like Aura Glow. Make sure the oil is room temperature or slightly warmer. All during the time that you rub, it is important that you pay attention to the reactions of the person whose body is in your hands. A sigh usually means pleasure, a gasp denotes discomfort or pain. If you are in doubt about the effect you are having, ask. When you massage another person, you almost become that other person, your bodies become linked. You give energy and get energy in return.

Pay attention to what you are doing; vary your strokes and the pressure of your strokes. You might press with your fingertips and make circles, or make your hand into a fist and knead the recipient's muscles. Maybe you want to treat her to a fingernail massage. Be careful not to let your routine get monotonous. And don't be afraid. Massage is a beautiful, safe way to get physically closer to someone without the pressures of sex. Perhaps you have not had much sexual experience, or maybe you have had a lot of experience, but you want to get back to the basics. Massage is a great way to learn to give and receive pleasure all over again.

Are any areas of the body off limits? When I give a massage, I think of the body as my playground. I also think that a good way to feel balanced is to massage every area of the body, including the pubic mound, but I am careful to pay attention to the reactions of the other person, be they spoken in body language or with words. When in doubt, just ask if she would like your stroke to be more soft or more firm, ask if there is a particular area of her body that needs special attention. Really try to let yourself go. You will be amazed at how creative you can be if you let your fingers do the talking. And, of course, wear something sensuous, like a silk kimona to help you feel like the geisha that you were born to be.

Chapter 11

Girl Talk

*H*aving a new voice that complements our student's new look is not about speaking in falsetto. Even brand-new students understand that a mousy little squeak emanating from a mammoth femme fatale will turn her into a cartoon. As role models, the student is encouraged to think of examples like Lauren Bacall, Marlene Dietrich, Tallulah Bankhead, Debra Winger, and Demi Moore, women noted for speaking in very low-pitched tones. There is no doubt about the femininity of any of these voices. Granted all of these women are very female in appearance, but then, so is our student once we have gotten our hands on him. The sooner our student begins to accept the image of herself she sees reflected in the mirror, the sooner she can give voice to that image.

Miss V and Grand Duchess Swana, tête à tête.

Even before the first official Voice class, new students at Miss Vera's Finishing School receive some instruction on girl talk. I don't know how many times I have asked a student to say "yes" instead of "yeah." There she is, all dressed up in the sheerest nylons and sexy pumps, seated in the makeup chair, wearing a lovely, soft negligee or perhaps a silk slip, bra, garter belt, and stockings while being transformed by the Dean of Cosmetology, who uses the finest powders, lipsticks, and blush. Inside she feels all relaxed and excited at the same time . . . all lush and juicy. Then I ask a question and she an-

swers, "Yup," in a voice like John Wayne. This won't do. We start by refining speech in small, simple ways. Say, "Yes." The phrase "Yes, Miss Vera" is music to my ears. It is not so much how high she speaks her words that counts, but how deeply she feels what she says and how much of that feeling she lets pass through her ruby red lips.

It is a great challenge to our student to have her voice sound as soft and sensual as she feels. Many girls clam up rather than be jarred back to reality by the sound of their own voice. In her initial outing, student Sandra Peters sat in the back of the taxi as we went for a brief tour around Manhattan. Sandra had been quite the little chatterbox in the safe confines of the academy, and while a respite from her patter was certainly welcome, it was quite strange during our hour's drive off campus to watch her eyes dart back and forth excitedly while her lips stayed mummy tight.

Voice class, despite its presumed difficulty, has been very popular because of deans such as Miss Dorothy Chansky, Ph. D., a beautiful, dynamic teacher whose own voice sounds like music. Our girls dress in pink warm-up suits for class, no corsets allowed, because voice class, when taught by Miss Dorothy, is very physical and very dynamic. Skilled in, among others, the Kirstin Linklater method of "freeing the natural voice," Miss Dorothy begins by getting our girls down on the floor to do breathing exercises; later they will stand and stretch their arms to the ceiling. She rests her palm on their tummies to make sure

130

they are breathing properly and they are putty in her hands. Breathing is very important.

As Miss Dorothy explains, we as humans have a whole range of tones available to us, three or four octaves. (Yma Sumac, the amazing singer who recorded in the thirties and forties in Argentina and became well known in the United States in the fifties, has claimed five.) But most people use only one octave. The student learns to let her voice rise and fall as she speaks. If she is excited, she must not be afraid to let the world know it. A man might say, in a near monotone, "That's a nice dress," but a woman, allowing her vocal pitch to soar, would say, "You look gorgeous!"

"I give the student the opportunity to describe herself to me," Miss Dorothy explains. "If she thinks she is a one-dimensional creature, we can reflect that in her voice. But all of the students tell me they have rich inner lives and they would like that to be evident when they speak."

Breath is the most powerful tool available for modulating sound. The student who is short of breath will eat her own words. Instead, she must feast on each vowel, stretch them out, for emotions luxuriate in the vowels.

I don't say changing the voice is easy, but it can be done. I've done it myself. Often it just takes awareness and persistence. When I arrived in Manhattan from New Jersey, I brought with me some obvious speech patterns from the glorious Garden State. It was very noticeable to my friend, art collector Stuart Pivar, who would one day create the New York Academy of Art, that I did not punch up my d's and t's. I could not hear myself say "dint" instead of "didn't" but Stuart certainly could and he tirelessly pointed this out to me, on this one point at least, playing Professor Higgins. I was not always receptive to this correction, but today I regard it as a generous gift.

An essential tool of Voice Class is the tape recorder. Most people will say they do not like the sound of their own voices, but our girls must learn to get over that because a tape recorder is the most valuable tool in improving the voice. Students are also encouraged to read from theater books that contain monologues for actresses. These are excerpts from plays in which the female character has a longish, compelling speech. For instance, Lady Macbeth's mad scene, the one that goes, "Out, damned spot! out, I say!" (Well, that may not be the cheeriest selection but it is well known) or Juliet's famous, "O Romeo, Romeo! wherefore art thou Romeo?" Many girls can identify with the latter. The plays of Tennessee Williams are another treasure trove for a budding femme fatale. It can be difficult for the student to make his femme voice sound different when she is not quite sure of who she is. Experimenting with dramatic speeches helps the student to let her imagination run wild as she plays different characters. As his tongue and his lips and his breath play with the speech of these make-believe women his femmeself becomes more real.

Voice Class is quite a challenge to all our ladies-in-waiting, but there are good reasons to try to develop a more feminine voice. Michelle Michaels visited the academy for a two-day Femme Intensive. As usual, she engaged in Voice Class. Since Miss Dorothy was on sabbatical in Calgary where she summers on a horse ranch with her artist husband, Michelle's teacher was

Sam Chwat, whose New York School of Speech is located near the academy. Sam has had many years of experience teaching actors, including Robert De Niro and Kathleen Turner, to lose or gain accents and change speech patterns to complement their roles. While Miss Dorothy likes to proceed at a more leisurely pace, letting the femme voice evolve over time for more long-lasting results, Mr. Sam is used to working with actors who must be ready on deadline. In Mr. Sam's class, the student sits upright in a high-backed chair, the perfect young lady, as she learns to engage in conversation. Mr. Sam, being new to the academy was amazed at how real our girls look. At first, I was not sure how our girls would react to a male teacher, since our deans are with rare exception always female, or at least, dressed that way. But the students sense Sam's admiration for their efforts and as they hear another man able to transform his voice and put forth a more feminine sound, they feel encouraged to believe in their own possibilities. I listened as Mr. Sam encouraged Michelle to speak with more breath in her voice. According to Sam, another thing our girls must remember is that as men they speak from a place that is deeper in the throat. As their femmeselves, each must try to start her words at the roof of her mouth. A good way to do that is to start each sentence with an "h" sound. This gives our girl more breath and brings her voice into the roof of her mouth. Michelle repeated the sentence, "Hello, my name is Michelle Michaels and I live in Chicago." Mr. Sam made comments. "Vowels are meant to be elongated and stretched, don't skim over your words." This leaves more opportunity for feelings to be re-

leased with sound. Another good tip is to end sentences on an up note, almost as a question. This can be difficult for men who are used to sealing each sentence with authority. Our Southern belles are a little ahead of the game because Southern accents often involve upturned endings.

Student Michelle made good progress during Voice Class. However, as soon as class was over, she reverted to her male voice. As I have often said, we can turn a student into a gorgeous femme with clothing and makeup, but many aspects of her training take practice, practice, practice. Now we were going to take Michelle shopping. One look at the wardrobe that Michelle had brought with her and I could see that she preferred not to spend a fortune on her clothes. She was not a Saks Fifth Avenue or Nordstrom's girl. Michelle liked a bargain. "Let's take her to T. J. Maxx," I suggested to Miss Deborah, our Dean of Cosmetology and a shopping maven. I had recently visited the new T. J. Maxx store in Manhattan and was pleasantly surprised to see that the place had individual dressing rooms, a must for academy girls. However, at the entrance to the dressing rooms was an attendant who asked each customer how many items she carried, counted them and passed her a plastic number. Miss Deborah went in first and I stood behind student Michelle, wondering how she would do in this first test of her femme voice, particularly since over the course of the afternoon she appeared to have forgotten Sam's lesson. The attendant questioned Michelle and suddenly from the roof of her mouth, but from a feeling far deeper, came a melodic, very feminine, "six." She took her tag and trotted proudly into the ladies' fitting room. Miss Deborah had already grabbed the larger room reserved for a handicapped person, "I figured we qualify," she laughed. Michelle's experience proved that in a pinch she could definitely speak up for her femmeself.

Girl talk includes learning to listen as well as to speak. An academy tea party is an excellent opportunity to learn the art of conversation. Danielle was one student who attended the academy for a two-day Femme Intensive. Included in her schedule was a tea party at which Dan would learn to be a good hostess. In her male life, Danielle was a lawyer who often found himself in court. I decided that Danielle and Dan might benefit from meeting my friend Mary Dorman, an attorney well known for protecting the rights of artists such as Karen Finley, women involved in sexual harassment suits, AIDS activists, and other provocative cases such as that of lap dancing pioneer Dominique and the belles of the Harmony Theater. The tea party began well, as Miss Viqui taught Danielle the fine points of tea service. But not long after we took our first sips, Danielle and Mary got into a heated discussion about trial law, to the exclusion of the rest of us at the table. I pointed out to Danielle that as the hostess at this tea party, it was her responsibility to make sure that everyone at the table felt comfortable and one aspect of that was to be included in the conversation, or at least, to be asked after once in a while. "Everyone here has something to contribute," I reminded her, "even if it is about a subject that you may not be so familiar." Danielle had fallen into two traps common to many students who try to navigate the sea of conversation. She stayed within territory that was familiar to her

male self, his job, and as is common in the male world, she felt a self-imposed pressure to perform. In conversation, women tend to have a greater willingness to listen, while men are more intent on being heard. Men are rewarded for dominant behavior. Tell a man that he has the responsibility to keep up the conversation in a social situation and his automatic response will be to keep talking, because he has not learned another option. Men and women have much to teach each other. The art of conversation is a valuable commodity, worth its weight in gold and worth considerably more than the cost of a meal.

A couple of years ago, I began a practice to help shift the economic scales and to validate my talents. I received a phone call from a well-known Broadway producer who had been referred to me by our mutual friend Jamie Gillis, the legendary star of adult films. The two men shared an interest in fillies, the four-legged kind, and had befriended each other at Saratoga Downs. The purpose of the producer's call was to find out the names of exotic night clubs where he might send some visitors. (Jamie had moved to San Francisco and so was not up to date on the New York scene.) Knowing that as a sex journalist, I had my finger on New York's G-spot, Jamie had recommended that he give me a call. The producer and I got along very well on the telephone. I so charmed him with my conversational skills that he invited me to lunch. But I held back because I thought, "Here is another high-powered businessman who is inviting me to spend two hours entertaining him in exchange for a meal." At the time I was working hard on a book about my personal sexual evolution, commuting each weekend to Kate Millett's art colony/slave farm for inspiration. I was working like a lesbian. I was busy. So I said, "I charge for lunch." He did not miss a beat. "That's okay, I'll pay." I was shocked at my own request, but the impresario said, "Never be afraid to ask to be paid for your talents." It was the start of a good friendship, and Mr. Broadway proved to be such a delightful table companion that I gave him a professional discount.

The goal of the academy goes beyond the individual student to shaking up the status quo. By putting economic value—since that is the easiest to understand—on the life experience of women and the expertise that comes from that experience, such as the ability to engage in social conversation, we give our students more reason to emulate that lifestyle and increase their options.

We all crave attention. Those few of us who don't are saints. Student Sally Sissyribbons needed lots of attention but he could not come right out and ask for it so he tended to dominate a conversation, not with facts but with requests. "Please, Miss Vera . . . please, please, please . . ." in a little squeak. Sally's pleas were actually the cries of a little child who needed assurance that he was loved and that he was not alone. It was important for Sally to acknowledge his need and to feel safe doing it. So as part of his Voice Class I taught him a little song. It had to be a simple song, because while Jack was brilliant, Sally was, by her own report, an airhead. The song was a version of the scales, but with just one word, "Me, me, me, me, me." Sally sang it loud and clear until he was tired. He began softly feeling a bit self-conscious, but then sang out joyously, "Me,

me, me, me, and finally danced around the room, *Me! Me! Me! Me! Me! Me!* Sally was finally able to laugh at himself and we were laughing not at him but with him. When he knew we accepted that needy, insecure part of him, he was able to communicate more clearly and succinctly.

It is only normal that when the femmeself finally takes her first steps out of the closet, she may run off at the mouth. So learning how to volley in conversation becomes a must. If our girl's jaw feels tired, she is probably talking too much.

When a student looks the most feminine is often the time when he feels threatened by a feared loss of identity. In an attempt to regain control by reasserting his masculinity we begin to hear about his accomplishments as a man, his business acumen, his sports prowess. If she looks sexy enough to stop traffic, blowing his own horn is a way to put on the brakes. It is quite tempting not to let his male persona impress us with big names or big numbers, but it is our responsibility to recognize such braggadocio, nip it in the bud, and lead our girl to new avenues of conversation. What would she like to do on a vacation? Does she have any unfulfilled dreams? How are things in the romance department? Sex is always a great topic and one in which I love to indulge. It is good for our girl to learn to let her hair down in conversation because then she can learn to trust herself.

Madame Antonia, our Dean of Divas, encourages the students to emulate the great artists and let out their passion in their voices. Antonia, my good friend opera singer Anthony McAulay, uses tapes and video versions of the lives and times of Maria Callas, Joan Sutherland, Kiri Te

Kanawa and more as audiovisual aids. But his greatest audiovisual aid is himself. To pursue his dreams of a singing career, Anthony had put aside a successful career as a makeup artist. Though his opera career was as a man, he cross-dressed when he visited us as Dean of Divas. His makeup, of course, was impeccable, very exotic; his breasts, big and heaving as he lectured student Susan Sargent in music appreciation. Susan, who had grown up in the harsh world of foster homes and orphanages only to graduate to the Army, was so moved by the depth of feeling in lush female voices that the hair on her arms stood on end. In another class I observed as Madame Antonia encouraged Southern belle Charlotte to sing a few bars of something. The student demurred. "Oh, I can't sing," she said. "I have never been able to sing. I don't know any songs."

"Surely you know something," I said. "How about 'Happy Birthday.' You must have sung 'Happy Birthday.' "

Charlotte confided, "I've never sung because the first times that I tried singing in school, I was told that I was so bad, I should just mouth the words."

He had been mouthing the words ever since. That day in class was the first time that Charlotte found her voice and for the very first time sang a song all the way through. No one told her that she was not good enough. To me and Madame Antonia the song was as rousing as the "Battle Hymn of the Republic." How fitting that it was "Happy Birthday."

Life on the Net

In cyberspace limits are transcended. There are no national borders, no age distinctions, no gender barriers. When chatting via e-mail our ladies-in-waiting always sound perfect. And they make much use of this mode of communication, sometimes going far beyond the reputations of genetic girls for gossiping on the telephone. A maiden's voyage on the gender link can be an extended cruise. Some of the most popular ports of call are listed in the Appendix.

Student Carole Kent told me she has racked up $400 monthly bills for on-line service, representing many hours of web browsing. She had the world at her fingertips. I became aware of the power of the web when new students began to tell me that they had learned of the academy via the internet. These girls were chatting up a storm about our service. The amazing power of the internet to link like-minded people together is felt by cross-dressers all over the globe. What begins as a way for members of a group to share fun, information, and beauty tips contributes to making that group a political force as its members find courage and strength in numbers.

After several months enmeshed in her e-mail pursuits, Carole Kent has decided to meet some of her sorority sisters in person at one of the many gatherings of cross-dressers that take place during the year. Her academic instructions have prepared her. She is accustomed to going out in public. Her walk and posture are much more ladylike and she is able do her own makeup. She is ready to expand her world.

The Fan

Before e-mail there was snail mail. It has long been possible to switch genders by post. Jamie Gillis comes to mind again as I recall a story he once related to me about the mash notes he has gotten over the years from prisoners. "They might read my name on some skin magazine's list of how to contact porn stars and think that 'Jamie' is a girl's name. Or they see a photo of me with a starlet and the only name that appears in the caption is Jamie Gillis, so they figure that the girl is Jamie." One letter read:

> Dear Jamie,
> I thought I would tell you how sexy you are and that I would love to suck you until you come. I want to meet you and marry you. I want to have sex with you until we die. I want to die on top of you . . . I love you!

Mr. Gillis told me that he was tempted to answer one of these fellows and see what it was like to go along with the fantasy. But he thought better of it. "I figured he might get released some day, be real pissed when he finds out I'm no bimbo, and come after me with a vengeance. Then again, I might get roses."

Homework #1

Our student is instructed to telephone the ladies' department of a local store and make inquiries in her femme voice about an item she has seen advertised. If the salesperson responds by calling him "ma'am," he earns a gold star, but if she inspires a "yes, sir," he must keep practicing. Of course no one should make a pest of herself with such calls. If she has no intention of buying, she must save her breath and the salesperson's time. She can always try it the next time she needs telephone information or, better yet, the next time a pesky unsolicited salesperson wants her to change her long distance carrier. A real exciting test would be to order an item from the television. There she would have the anonymity of mail-order shopping and maybe have the opportunity to hear her voice broadcast on the air, certainly a thrill.

Homework #2

Students are invited to turn on their tape recorders and look into their mirrors. Repeat the phrase "I love you" ten times, each time making it sound different from the last. Go ahead: I love you. I love you. I love you. That's what I like to hear.

Chapter 12

Field Trips

Academy girls go everywhere: shopping at Saks, tea at the Plaza, the Metropolitan Museum (especially the Costume Institute), restaurants, exotic night clubs and parties, and more. Field trips give students the opportunity to see and be seen through new eyes and new eyelashes. It is my responsibility, and that of the other deans, to make sure all goes smoothly. It takes a tremendous amount of courage to venture into the streets *en femme,* particularly after living a life of secrecy. To make sure that our students receive the maximum support from me, I know that I need to feel supported, so I make it a rule to take a student out in the company of another dean. A threesome feels better than a duo, as we say in our brochure, "three bombshells out on the town . . ." only a lot can happen on these outings, for we are making magic in the streets.

Passing

In our school, passing is not about an "A" or a "B." It is not even about passing vs. failing. When a student asks me, "Do you think I can pass?" he means, "Will my maleness be undetected?" This is quite a challenge, especially when our girl might tower over six feet and have correspondingly large appendages. All of our girls want to pass and almost all want to go out. If I waited until each one was perfect, she might never venture forth. I am not saying that it is impossible to fool the public, but it does take a combination of physical attributes and a lot more practice than most of our students are willing or able to devote to this endeavor. After all, each student, in terms of his femmeself, has spent many years perfecting mistakes. He would need to dedicate a lot of time that he usually does not have to unlearn his male mannerisms completely. So I encourage our girls to expand their ideas of passing. Rather than limiting his femmeself to who

June G. Edwards, Miss V, and Susan Sargent ride in style.

she "should" be, he can accept who she is. Let passing mean acceptance. He has spent years of his life confined in his male role, why subject his femmeself to a similar, though seemingly more tender trap? This is not to say that our girl need not practice and that with practice she might not accomplish amazing results. This is to say that life is a process. Academy students are part of a bold avant garde that is using the lessons of the past to break through gender barriers. While they are learning to walk neatly in their high heels, with every foot fall they get closer to kicking in the door of the establishment. Most of our students arrive with the fantasy that they want to live full time as women, but the reality is they are changing what it means to be a man, adding to what it means to be a woman, perhaps even helping to establish a third gender, and that reality is much more provocative and exciting.

Still, it is not impossible to pass in the traditional sense as female. One of our most successful students actually did accomplish this feat, but we may never know just how well, for she left in a shroud of mystery. Susan Sargent, the student whose self-hypnosis worked so well on My Tran's waxing table, had arrived for the "Cinderfella Experience," in Susan's case, a three-day Femme Intensive (see "How to Become an Academy Debutante"). During the course of her stay, we learned David's background, which included twenty years military service and the two tours of duty in Vietnam that inspired his expertise in self-hypnosis. Recounting his personal history, David told us that his second marriage had ended in a bitter divorce several years previously and he was the father of one grown child.

David had the physical attributes to make a transformation almost easy. He was five six and at the time of his enrollment he weighed 155 pounds, and measured thirty-six-thirty-two-thirty-eight (with hip pads). David, now Susan, took to her classes with enthusiasm. On her return for a second Femme Intensive, this former track runner had racewalked three inches off her waist and dropped 15 pounds. David was free to travel, and after his second visit, he decided to move from New Mexico to a New Jersey suburb where he would be closer to the academy. Susan became my personal aide de campus. The anal retentive qualities that had served her well in the military proved invaluable in this atmosphere of organized chaos and I must admit, though some of her stories seemed a bit exaggerated, I enjoyed having an assistant who claimed to have performed similar duties for General Westmoreland. Some of the other students who did not have the luxury of an early retirement were even a little jealous of the time Susan was able to devote to her studies. But Susan was so sweet and humble that she could not be disliked.

Then one day, she was gone. She had prepared us with a story about being called up again for military service on a secret mission and though the deans, the students, and I speculated that Susan's story sounded fishy, it was such a good story and she was such a "good girl," we were willing to believe her. Then came the letter.

"Dear Miss Vera . . . I am sorry that I lied . . ." She did not explain exactly how she had lied, which of her stories were true and which were not, so I sent her a return note:

November 29, 1993

Dear Susan,

Well, it was no surprise to hear that you lied. At different times, one or another of us here at the academy thought that your stories were too good to be true. But they were so good we were quite willing to believe them. You really know how to whip up a good tale and I guess that comes from having a lot of practice.

I am grateful that you wrote and told me that you lied. That took courage. I had begun to have my suspicions, particularly in the area of finances. So I did nothing that was dependent on any of the generous endowments that you volunteered. Still, it was wrong for you to dangle a carrot in front of me in the way of money, when you knew you could not come through. It is the kind of thing that men do to women all of the time, very ungentlemanly, certainly unladylike, and unnecessary to win my affections.

Your help to me has been invaluable. Just today, I put a new set of dishes into the cabinets that you trimmed so fastidiously with lace and the effect is beautiful. We use the jewel case you left behind for your sisters. I read by the lamp you put together. The drape that you hung in front of my desk makes a great difference in the academy's ambience. Most of all your sensitive, gentle, and steady helpful nature are things that I cherish. And you are certainly always welcome here. I know that I speak for everyone when I say that.

I am not angry that you lied. I felt kind of crummy when I read your letter. It was a mix of a lot of emotions. I was disappointed, of course. Lying is not something I encourage or support in anyone, especially a student. I felt vulnerable, realizing that in teaching students,

I might encounter people whose problems go very deep. Many of the events you described to us were serious: accidents, traumas, deaths of loved ones. I remember comforting you when you cried over these tragedies and I wonder were you lying then, too? Now that you have piqued my curiosity, not to mention that of all the other deans and your sorority sisters— (Needless to say, Jennifer James and June G. Edwards were pretty pleased that you were no longer Miss Perfect)—you must supply me with some facts. Inquiring minds want to know, Susan, what is true and what is false.

20 years in the army	T or F
Service in Vietnam	T or F
Wounded in battle	T or F
Aide to the generals	T or F
Death of first wife in fire	T or F
Divorced from second wife	T or F
Foster homes	T or F
Evil twin	T or F
Present active duty	T or F
Munitions expert	T or F
Bankrupt	T or F

Do your best to tell the truth.

I look forward to receiving the answers to my questions, and to just hearing from you. Also, if there is anything else that it would be good for me to know, please make a clean breast of it.

Take care and know that you have friends here at the academy.

Cherchez la femme,

It was not until later that I realized that David's affinity for cross-dressing might have helped him escape from some difficult situation. He had made a few visits to Atlantic City. Maybe he was a gambler with a mountain of debt? Whatever had been David's reasons for needing to drop out of sight, he could have done so successfully as Susan. She was that good.

Sunday in the Park with Jennifer

From experience with students, I have learned that the thrill of going out *en femme* far outweighs any tension inspired when a head turns and our girl is "read" as a man in drag. In one of our earliest excursions, with student Jennifer James, I was not the least bit concerned about our lady-in-waiting passing as a real girl, only about making the student's dream come true. So thirty-eight-year-old James became eight-year-old Jennifer wearing a gingham pinafore with stuffed dolly in tow. We ended our day at Rumplemayer's ice cream parlor over hot fudge sundaes. Of course we got lots of stares and one little girl asked her mom if she could have a dress like Jennifer's. But we were so obviously having fun, that people seemed only to want to join us. Crossing one of Central Park's many bridges, we met a woman with whom I had recently become acquainted through Feminists for Free Expression, the free speech group to which we both belonged. As she was introduced, with one hand Jennifer James lifted the hem of her petticoat, with the other she swung her dolly high in the air as she dipped in a respectful curtsy, demonstrating her own act of free expression. My colleague was most impressed.

Jennifer's experience in Central Park that first day demonstrated an important aspect of passing which I constantly stress to our students: attitude is everything.

Strawberry Fields forever (Jennifer and Dolly).

In our Easter bonnets at TOG.

Most of our students have kept their femmeselves secret for many, many years. Their first thought when faced with the prospect of going out is the fearful question "What will the world think of me, me, me?" Instead, ask how can I bring more happiness to the world? The answer is to share those good feelings that you have inside of you, then put a big smile on your face and go for it, girl. You will find that the world is much more ready for you than you ever imagined. You have guided them by your attitude. You can sell what you believe in, so believe in your right to be your femmeself and you will be empowered in all aspects of your life.

Take a Picture, It Will Last Longer

Some time later we returned to Central Park with Jennifer James. Having grown up during a photo shoot celebrating James' fortieth birthday, Jennifer was now an ingenue and after that first excursion, she had decided that she did not want to be quite so flamboyant. Jennifer wore a dress that came down to her knees (well, just about) and a stylish chapeau. It was Easter Sunday. Miss Viqui, Jennifer James, and I were having lunch at Tavern on the Green. TOG, as it is known in the press, is a big airy place that opens its windows on

Jennifer James as he sashayed through the crowd in her flowered gingham Easter frock, her high heels and swaying skirts, to be confronted by his femmeself returning his gaze.

We could not have picked a better place to view Easter bonnets. There were flowered hats and fantasy hats with fairy tale scenarios built into them. The restaurant was conducting a competition for the best bonnet and Jennifer took great pride in being asked to participate. She pranced over to the judges' table in her white high heels and posed for an entry Polaroid. We never did find out who came in first, but it really did not matter because the day was a winner.

We took more pictures with the Easter Bunny who went through the restaurant passing out chocolate eggs.

At Bethesda Fountain (Jennifer James).

Then the three of us decided that a walk through the park would help us keep our girlish figures. Jennifer had to be corrected a few times for swinging her purse like a lethal weapon. I guess the wind up her skirts got him so excited he could not remember what she was supposed to be doing. A cool breeze can be very distracting.

Central Park. It is surrounded by patios and topiary gardens, the most startling inhabitant of which is a giant green gorilla. There are special displays during holiday seasons to delight the many New Yorkers and tourists who make the place so popular. The decor is dominated by the lush, intense colors of Tiffany stained glass, crystal chandeliers, and mirrors galore. Visitors who walk through the restaurant's winding corridors from one dining room to the next constantly see themselves reflected. Imagine the excitement of

Central Park on any warm Sunday is alive with activity. There are strollers and skaters and cyclists. Music of all kinds floats on the wind: rappers and rock and roll, Peruvian flutes, Polish folk dancers . . . My favorite is the calliope of the Central Park carousel. The music lured us to the great old-fashioned ride. We picked our mounts, hitched up our skirts, locked our heels in the stirrups, and off we rode, round and round, up and down. Jennifer loves horses. As a boy he had a horse named Patches that he credited with teaching him loyalty and perseverance. As a girl, Jennifer seems to have snatched the brass ring. Jennifer James now rides tall in the saddle on a regular basis as part of his college polo team. The academy cannot take all of the credit for James' decision to quit a lucrative job in nuclear energy and enroll in another school to pursue a lifelong dream to become a veterinarian, but when you start making fantasies become reality, you never know where the trail may lead.

That day our trail led to Bethesda Fountain, another park landmark, where we took more photos. As there were three of us, we had to take turns, always leaving one of us out to take the photo. A young boy and his handsome dad out for a Sunday ride had parked their bicycles not far from where we posed. The curiosity of children is refreshingly indiscreet and I saw quickly that the young boy was really giving us the once-over. Sure enough I heard him whisper to his dad. "Pss-t, that's a *man.*" Much to his credit and my delight, Daddy replied, "I think that's great."

The father's response inspired me. I stepped over to the boy with my camera. "Would you take a picture of the three of us?" I asked sweetly. Why make him sneak a peek I thought when he could have a real good look? The boy glanced toward his father, who nodded approval, then he reached for the camera and with the greatest concentration, legs parted for balance, tongue inching toward his nose, he took a perfect shot of Miss Viqui, Jennifer

James, and me—an image I am sure that young photographer will long remember and one that we treasure.

Dining Debutantes

A restaurant is a great first-time excursion. New York, which normally has an exhaustive amount of dining experiences from which to choose, now offers some particularly suited to our type of girl. Drag restaurants, those that celebrate gender-bending in their wait staff and floor shows, such as current favorites Lucky Cheng's and Lips, are often seen as less intimidating to an academy debutante and, as evidenced by their extreme popularity, these places are a lot of fun. Still, I also enjoy visiting the more traditional eating establishments with our girls, like the Four Seasons, Sardi's, or a quick bite at Amy's Health Food in the Village. These places are better choices for the student who really wants to be assimilated into the everyday world.

Wherever we dine, once our girl makes it through the door, the hard part is over. She can sit on the banquette, look pretty, see and be seen, with one or two challenges remaining: ordering her food and visiting the ladies' room, for which she has hopefully had time to prepare in voice and etiquette classes. (Chapters 11 and 13.)

Kent was an impeccably dressed, blow-dried entrepreneur, who, like many of our girls, seemed very nervous about his first totally *en femme* experience. He had boldly opted for the Dining Debutante course, which meant his femmeself Carole, our Internet maven, would be going out for the very first time. "I don't know if I will have the nerve," he had told us on the phone. Kent had telephoned several times before class and had also dropped us a note. Each time, he mentioned that he might be too nervous actually to go out, but it was obvious that he wanted to try. Miss Maria Giorgio was our makeup artist that evening and by the time she got through, Carole Kent was a knockout. Maria used transparent surgical tape to raise Kent's eyebrows to new heights. Carole was one of the prettiest girls at school.

Miss Dana arrived for Walking and Posture class. Kent was slightly rotund, which worked to Carole's advantage. Rather than trying to squeeze Carole into a corset, Miss Dana suggested we use the more comfortable waist cincher and go with the figure we had. We transformed Carole into a smart and sophisticated full-figured femme who might have been a model for Delta Burke's fashion catalog.

Off we went into the night. It was raining, making it difficult to hail a taxi, so we decided to walk a block to a trendy restaurant called Kaffeehaus, which was owned by two women, Monique and Margo, and was decorated in the cozy wood and velvet Austrian tradition. On the way we photographed Carole taking her first steps outdoors. Every cloud has a silver lining, for while the rain put a crimp in our hairdos, as well as our plans to venture to more distant hot spots, it brought us an unexpected bonus. Carole's bright blue umbrella proved to be an excellent prop. Passersby would expect to find a woman under such a colorful parasol and it was just enough of a shield to give Carole that extra bit of confidence. The restaurant was very crowded and quite a few admiring glances were cast our way as

we snaked through the maze of tables to our banquette. From her perch against the wall, Carole could see and be seen, and enjoy every delicious moment. She confided that the academy was her birthday present to herself. (Quite a few students come here for their birthdays.) Carole also confided that he had almost not come. This did not surprise me, for she had arrived fifteen minutes late, while most students are early. I thought she might have been wrestling with himself. But now she was very glad that her femmeself had won this internal tug of war. Miss Dana entertained us with a sexy story about her reunion with a lover and we stayed at the restaurant until closing, enjoying every moment. A few days later Carole sent that huge bouquet of pink roses which proved so inspirational to Laura. Her thank-you note stated that she looked forward to her postgraduate courses.

Dressed to Thrill

Every field trip is a fun learning experience, but some events from the outset hold the promise of a more in-depth encounter. It is the difference between visiting the Egyptian exhibit at the Metropolitan Museum or riding on a camel through the Valley of Luxor. My good friend Jeanette Luther aka Mistress Antoinette and her husband Master Zorro announced they were adding another enterprise to their kinky conglomerate of fashion and media productions by inaugurating their first "Dressed to Thrill Ball," and I wanted to be there. The ball would celebrate their company, which was now sweet sixteen years old, and highlight Antoinette's fashion skills—she was known as

Dressed to thrill: Jennifer, Ms. Antoinette, and Miss V.

the Queen of p.v.c. or polyvinyl chloride, a patent-leather-looking fabric with a petroleum base that had been introduced in the world of fetish fashion and been incorporated into the mainstream, largely through Antoinette's success at the International Fashion Boutique shows.

I invited two students to accompany me. Jennifer James, whom I described as the academy's greatest asset and our greatest challenge, and Sally Sissyribbons, that determined self-described "little airhead" who was the rock on which I based my school. Jennifer, as usual, was quick to spot a good thing and needed very little coaxing. Sally took a couple days to decide,

though I never doubted his answer. I was sure Sally's sense of competition would not let Jennifer get this high-heeled step ahead of her. What I did not know was that while Jack was making his decision, he was being interrogated by the FBI regarding his cross-dressing activities. Sally was unexpectedly out of the closet. When the FBI confronted Jack, he brought up J. Edgar Hoover, who had recently been outed for enjoying black lace bouffant leisure gowns. Jack asked, "Well, what about your former boss. . . ." This made no impression on the fibbies. Jack, like many students, had always felt conflicted about his cross-dressing—loving it when he was

Sally; wondering whether it was all worth it when he was Jack. About a year after his first visit to the academy he began to see an excellent psychologist who was helping him work out his options, while Sally continued to come to New York for class. The shrink and I had never met, but we had a mutual respect for each other that was conveyed through Jack, who was growing in the process. In the midst of the FBI imbroglio, after giving it much thought, Jack decided to join us in Los Angeles for the Dressed to Thrill Ball.

I knew that to spend time with Antoinette, to be part of her milieu, would be a powerful experience for my students, just as it had been for me. She has that very rare ability to inspire flights of fantasy, while keeping her feet firmly planted on the ground. (It helps to wear super high heels.) She and her husband and partner Master Zorro have an appreciation for history and the efforts of those who have come before them, as well as a strong sense of community. These were all qualities that I wanted to instill in my brave students. Through their participation in the academy both Sally and Jennifer had chosen to put the clothes in the closet and let the "girls" out. Though Sally had not yet confided his problem with the FBI, I felt that more and more they would be faced with situations, in their social lives, and in the workplace, in which their pleasure in cross-dressing would be known. I knew it was important that they feel a strong sense of community.

So off we went—the three misske-teers, all for one and one for all. We were joined at the last moment by student Sandra. Sandra nee Peter, an art dealer, was a quick study. She was as fast to spot a rare opportunity as a valuable painting. A great fan of Antoinette, when Sandra learned of the party, she was smart enough to hike up her skirts and hop on the bandwagon. Sandra had made considerable progress since her previous class in which she rode wide-eyed and silent as we taxied around town.

"Will Jennifer be traveling *en femme?*" Sally had asked sweetly via telephone before our departure, a dollop of envy on the tip of her sugar-coated tongue. It was an interesting prospect, but our 6:30 A.M. flight put an early morning transformation out of the question. Still, the prospect of dressing unleashes tremendous surges of energy in my students and sets their imaginations soaring, so I figured that I had better let them know what was expected of them right away.

"You girls are being invited so that you may be of assistance to me and represent the academy in the best possible way. I do not intend to be your maid, but a princess. You will help each other to dress and I will supervise." I had lined up a great makeup artist for us all in Valerie Driscoll of Hair to Wear in L.A.

Jennifer, who always tries to be the good girl and a big sister, had no problem with my edict, but Sally, the little baby doll, needed some reassurance. She finally responded with that favored phrase, "Yes, Miss Vera." Peter had decided to travel independently, but I had a feeling that when we were all in Los Angeles, Sandra Peters would stick to us like nail glue.

Experienced academy girls like to be out and about, so with time on our hands on Saturday afternoon, the day of the ball, I shepherded my little lambs to an outdoor café in downtown Long Beach. We invited Sandra to join us, but I immediately regretted the invitation when she showed up as a bizarre interpretation of the lady in red, from head to toe. Peter did not think of himself as handsome, particularly since he was missing quite a few teeth, so he decided that his femme persona should look outrageous. Her hair was not Ann-Margret red, it was not even Lucille Ball's carrot top—this was red that could glow in the dark (which was exactly where it belonged). Sandra's wig and flashy outfit were Halloween material and I had my doubts about being out on the street in broad daylight with her. I put it to the other girls. "Oh, we don't mind. There is room for all kinds," cooed Sally in black patent leather short shorts, white heels, and gloves and Jennifer in pink country gingham. Bolstered by their support, I said, "Okay Sandra, your sorority sisters stuck up for you, so you can come."

Fortunately, it was just past lunchtime, so the posh terrace restaurant was not very crowded. This also meant that every member of the staff took a turn to serve us something. Some drifted past the table just to have a look. Sandra, despite her outrageous appearance, proved to be a wine connoisseur (not unusual for academy girls—one student has even gifted us with a bottle from his own vineyard). Sandra ordered a delicious Clos du Bois. At one point a handsome young man strolling past the restaurant stopped at our table on the terrace and complimented Sandra. "I like your red wig."

"See, Miss Vera," purred Sandra through a gap-toothed grin.

We returned to the hotel where Miss Valerie, our makeup artist, was waiting with powders, puffs, and paints. Jennifer, a blonde that night, donned her "firecracker dress," a sequined sheath in which swirls of brilliant color explode into a shiny black midnight. The dress punctuated our girl's sparkling personality. Sally's do was very big and very done, the look was ultra femme à la Dolly Parton. A sheer white lace peignoir, trimmed with feathers and pink bows, fell softly over the ruffled white corset that squeezed Sally oh-so-tight. White maribou-trimmed slippers complemented the ensemble. Sandra shimmied into a black fishnet catsuit, extravagant heels, and her trademark huge earrings. Could it have been only six weeks before that she quivered in the back of that taxi?

The Dressed to Thrill Ball was a celebration of fetish dressing. Several hundred guests arrived in leather clothes, rubber, corsets, super high heels . . . Many wore Antoinette's beloved p.v.c. fabric. Crossdressers were well represented. During dinner Antoinette invited all of the crossdressers who had come out for the first time in their lives to stand and be applauded. At tables around the room thirty men in women's clothes rose and took their bows while the crowd roared, "Brava!"

There were fashion competitions and awards determined by audience applause. The first place "Eroticism Award" went to two very sexy leather-clad men, lovers who had just been married. They got down on their knees and simulated some below-the-belt honeymoon moves. Second and third prizes went to "perma girls" (as in permanent, meaning born and bred) in outfits that were barely there. One wore a peekaboo dress of black leather cutouts and the other, named Helen Bed, displayed her breasts through a dress made of wire hoops and voile that encased her like a birdcage.

At last, the moment came for the cross-dressing competition. I held my breath as Sally, Jennifer, and Sandra made their appearances among a dozen contestants. Sally was first in the lineup. She was definitely the girl who most wanted to win, but even just walking down the runway, Sally was stepping beyond her dreams. She was the center of attention. She was beautiful. During the course of the ball, Sally had blossomed by following Jennifer's lead and making many new friends, among them a dancer named Jill. "You've got to walk like you believe you are *Miss It*," Jill advised her. I felt like the proud mother hen as radiant Sally spread her lace and maribou wings. Neophyte Sandra wobbled in her high heels, but made a brave presentation. A few other contestants looked like competition, but the real challenge came from Jennifer, who was a whiz at making friends at parties like this and so had lots of votes in the audience. (The little wiggle she added to her stroll did not hurt.) But in the end, it was Sally, the girl who needed it the most, who took the large trophy bearing the plaque "Best Cross-dresser" home with her. I suggested he put it in his office. The next time the FBI came to call, he was ready. Emboldened by his success at the ball, Jack informed the investigators that he was no longer in the closet. Coming out meant he was not vulnerable to intimidation from any quarter, friends or enemies. He also told them that having won the competition he thought he might hang up his stilettos and let Sally retire a champion. He had them stonewalled. When Jack rose to usher the investigators out the door, he stood extra tall. He was not wearing pumps but he said that he felt like it. Jack knew he was Miss It.

Pride and Prejudice

Not all excursions into the outside world are met with acceptance. Sometimes the challenge comes from the most unexpected places. Since the Stonewall riot in 1969, each spring in New York and in major cities in this country and now around the world, gays and lesbians celebrate a day of Pride. The Stonewall is a gay bar in Sheridan Square, the heart of the West Village, that was the subject of frequent raids by the police. In that summer of 1969, led by the bars drag queens, the patrons and then all of Sheridan Square fought back. In 1994, the twenty-fifth anniversary of Stonewall, the title of this annual festival and parade was expanded to include the transgendered population: transvestites and transsexuals, and in reality the festival includes other alternative lifestyles as well. As a sex rights activist, I had always felt a strong allegiance to this celebration and its principles and I had marched in many of the parades, often with Annie Sprinkle. We loved to come up with our own crazy contingent. A few years ago we celebrated our friendship and marched down Fifth Avenue as bride and bride. She wore the veil, I wore the top hat. We both wore wedding gowns. In 1986 we marched with my friend Robert Maxwell, who would die the next year, and actor "Little Mike" Anderson, a dwarf. We carried placards that read on one side, "Bisexual exhibitionists into midgets and proud" and on the flip side, "We love and respect our friends with AIDS." In 1994, with our finishing school in full swing, student Sandra Peters, who had now changed her name to Zondra, presented us with a banner in the hope that she would inspire me to organize an academy contingent. Our small but enthusiastic group consisted of Jennifer James, Patti Harrington, Zondra, and me. Jennifer James wore flesh-colored tights, pink short shorts, a white ruffled blouse, pink sequined vest, and white go-go boots—a sort of Las Vegas cheerleader look. Patti Harrington, whose ensemble recalled the sixties and seventies, wore a long, daisy-covered granny dress that skimmed over the tops of her sensible clogs. Zondra managed, once again, to make me cringe in her Tina Turner wig and black bikini bathing suit. I warned her high-heeled sandals were not a wise choice for any three-mile hike, but, as usual, Zondra stuck to her fashion statement. The parade took many hours—the route had been extended that year in honor of the anniversary celebration and would end in Central Park with lots of fanfare and speeches. We had begun marching with the transgender contingent but broke ranks to position ourselves in front of a band. This worked to our advantage because at regular intervals along the route, the parade was halted to let traffic pass through. The traffic patrolmen in charge always stopped the band so that they could listen to music while they directed the traffic and we stood in front, like the band's majorettes, dancing in step and passing out academy business cards to New York's Finest, truly the world's greatest policemen.

All of this marching took its toll on Sandra. Her feet were on fire. She had actually removed her shoes for the last few blocks and was now standing barefoot with me and her sorority sisters at the parade's conclusion in Central Park as we watched the crowds circle Bethesda Fountain. "Go soak your feet," I suggested, pointing her in the direction of the cool, inviting waters of the fountain. When she hesitated, Jennifer piped up, "Zondra, I think this is one time you need to definitely heed Miss Vera's advice." Steam practically rose from the water as Zondra submerged her tootsies.

Later that day, after saying good-bye to a limping Zondra, Jennifer, Patti, and I took a walk from the center of the Village along Christopher Street, the heart of the festival. As we neared the West Side Highway and the end of the road, we spotted a crowd of young men right in our path. Most of those assembled were dressed in the style of grunge/home boys: big baggy shorts, gold chains, big sneakers, and hats turned around backward. A few of them began to eye us viciously, then one of them began to hoot and laugh and point. Each of these homeboys, too, was trying to establish an identity by dressing in a peculiar style. Would they succumb now to a pack mentality and try to intimidate those who were different? Who were these boys to laugh at my girls? In a split second, I made my decision. I stepped up to the lead hyena, pointed my finger at him, and doubled over hooting and laughing, louder and harder, overcoming his laughter with my own, until people started laughing at him. Then we all laughed together, until the laughter turned to music. Patti was the first to speak. "Miss Vera, I don't believe you did that," she said as we held our heads high and strolled safely out of harm's way. "Sometimes you just have to fight fire with fire," I said, feeling the adrenaline pulse through my veins. "I've wanted to do that for a long time."

I was always the big sister, the eldest of three: Mary, Georgia, and Connie. Connie was four years my junior and a smart and sassy kid sister. Georgia, who was born with Down's syndrome, was a year younger then me. We three were always very close. Connie, now a wife and mother to her own daughters, Meredith and Maureen, has always been my rock of support. Georgia was a gift through whom I have learned many lessons—the number-one lesson being to never, ever make fun of another human being. I can say that now but at age ten, Georgia presented quite a challenge. In church her joyful voice would ring out with hymns that she seemed to be singing in a different language. Heads would turn, necks craned to see who was making all that racket. I'd gently nudge Georgia to lower her voice, which just caused her to laugh and sing all the louder, so I'd put my arm around her and we'd both sing away.

One day, the three of us were playing in the park when some boys took notice of Georgia and began to make fun of her. We tried to ignore them, but when they came after us with sticks dipped in doggie do, I grabbed my sisters and we high-tailed it out of there. That day on Christopher Street was my second chance. I was no longer a child. The years fell away, as I felt a courage well up from deep inside of me.

A bully is motivated by fear and ignorance and is very insecure. Laugh in his face and he often melts away like the Wicked Witch of the East in the *Wizard of Oz,* not even a cackle left behind. But these particular bullies were still within sight, so rather than gloat in triumph, I encouraged the girls to step lively.

Taking It on the Road

Toward the end of 1994, I received a special invitation from Dr. Vern Bullough to make a presentation at the gender conference sponsored by the University of California at Northridge in February 1995. Our academy had received much favorable publicity and there was curiosity among the organized gender community to discover more about the hoopla. I was honored and very, very excited. Until the death of Dr. Bonnie Bullough in 1996, the Bulloughs, a famed husband and wife sexologist team, had co-authored many books on different aspects of human sexuality, including *Crossdressing, Sex and Gender,* a book that ranks high on our academy list of recommended reading. The Bulloughs' style was a combination of academic brilliance, thorough knowledge of their subjects, and accessible prose. The conference would reflect that style, for it was one of the first of its kind to bring together academic scholars, accredited professionals, leaders of various gender organizations like the International Foundation for Gender Education (IFGE), the Society for the Second Self (Tri-Ess), and Renaissance as well as individuals representing a broad spectrum of gender options, along with some wives and partners. Female to male transsexuals made a strong showing. One participant would later comment that there might be as many gender categories as there are people.

I invited students Jennifer James and Patricia Harrington to accompany me, reasoning that the conference would broaden their horizons and their presence would be a tremendous support for me. Jennifer loves to socialize and is the academy's best press agent. Patricia, an avid reader, had become more and more eager for knowledge on the entire subject of cross-dressing. I encouraged the girls to think of this as our academy road show and promised if they were good and if they chose, they could fly home *en femme*. For Patricia, that trip home was reason enough to go. Off we went with slides, video clips, a plan to transform a volunteer, and lots of spunk. Northridge is right in the heart of earthquake territory and we hoped to shake things up.

Jennifer and Patricia looked gorgeous, thanks to the expertise of Valerie Driscoll, proprietor of the Hair to Wear salon in Torrance, California, and our academy's West Coast makeup connection. Patricia is actually very good at her own makeup but could not do it with the speed of Valerie. Jennifer still needs more makeup classes since our Student Council President has spent more of her time on field trips rather than on practicing lipstick application. Miss Valerie provided a much needed and lovely set of helping hands when faced with our busy schedule. But then, Valerie is used to speed and drag, for on her off-duty hours she races her own cars on that other kind of drag strip, sometimes posing in a mini and thigh-high boots.

I challenged the bounds of political correctness by having Jennifer appear on-stage in her new pink and ultra frilly French maid's uniform. There is a line of thinking in what has become the organized cross-dressing movement of eschewing any image that might give transvestism a sexual or fetishistic connotation. Some cross-dressers, especially those who identify as transsexual, are tired of the "kinky" image and want to be taken more seriously. My experience with students has shown me that there is always an erotic element to cross-dressing, though how much that registers with the individual student depends on how connected that person is to her sexuality. One of my favorite comments on this subject occurs in photographer Mariette Pathy Allen's beautiful book of portraits and interviews *Transformations: Cross-dressers and Those Who Love Them.* Bob aka Malinda says, "The gender scene is a love-hate relationship for me . . . They're just interested in a respectable image, but a woman has the right to be a tramp or a whore. They think that to legitimize transvestism, they all have to emulate the D.A.R. [Daughters of the American Revolution]!"

Since the sissy maid is the first image with which many of our students identify, I thought it important that sissydom be represented. By way of explanation, I informed the large audience that at the academy we promote sissy power and told them the story of how the academy came out in the media and the role our sissy maids played in that turning point.

I had initially placed academy ads in magazines that marketed themselves directly to cross-dressers and in adults-only sex publications. Then I decided to try the mainstream press. I had noticed that in the back of *New York,* the widely circulated weekly, there was a section called "Role-Play" in which houses of domination, whose names I recognized, and other erotic entrepreneurs could be found. Since cross-dressers comprise a large part of the clientele of such places, I knew the ladies-in-waiting I wanted to reach must be thumbing through these pages. Our academy name is self-explanatory, but a bit long, so to save money I decided the ad would read, "Miss Vera's Cross-dressing Academy," with our phone number. (These ads are sold at premium rates.) This rattled the ad taker, who said we could not be so specific. They did not allow the word cross-dresser in the ads. I thought this was ridiculous but tried to conform by placing an ad that was as vague as the others I read in their pages: "Pursue your dreams in an uplifting environment. Call 212-242-6449."

I was astonished when the ad taker and then her supervisor told me, "I'm sorry, now that we know what you do, we cannot accept your ad." This really angered me. So I sat down and wrote the publisher a letter in which I informed him that I was very proud of our work and since his magazine was already catering to my clientele, it made no sense to me why I could not place my ad.

New York decided to run the vague "Pursue your dreams" ad. We were flooded with calls from people who wanted to be whipped, humiliated, or have intercourse. Obviously, there is a big disparity among dreamers. Since those were not among our course offerings, I considered the ad to be a waste of time, both mine and the callers, and I decided to forget *New York* magazine. Six months later, we threw our first academy party with

Jennifer James, June G. Edwards, and Raquel serving as sissy maids. My friend Amy Rosemarin, an early supporter of our endeavors, mentioned the party and our serving girls to her friend, writer George Rush, who has since, with his wife, Chris Molloy, created one of this city's preeminent gossip pages. At the time, one of George's freelance clients was *New York.* George pitched the party to his editor at *New York.* She asked if they might also send a photographer. Our sissy maids consented. The result was that a full-page story entitled "Crossdress with Success" appeared in *New York* magazine, complete with photos. Mr. Rush treated the subject with dignity, compassion, and humor. In the week of February 8, 1993, the week that issue went on the stands, I again telephoned the classified-ad department of *New York* magazine. In an example of the left hand not knowing what the right hand is doing, the ad taker recalled my earlier attempt and reiterated that we could not use the word cross-dress. I suggested she turn to page thirty-two of that week's issue and check the headline for herself. From that time on the word "cross-dress" was no longer censored from the classified pages. I was proud of our breakthrough and I knew much of our success was due to the tantalizing power of our brave sissy maids, who had not only served us but had served themselves, and in the long run, this gender community, proud.

At the gender conference, while Jennifer James represented the playful, kinky look during our onstage presentation, Patricia, our graceful long-legged lovely, represented the more sophisticated fashion model/career girl look. She taught Roger, the transformation candidate I chose from the audience, how to pose in pumps, thus displaying what she had learned from her diligent pursuit of her studies. Patricia is a real academy success story who shows what is possible when a student really applies himself. An interesting thing happened with Roger's transformation from he to she. In the end, Roger, who was not a cross-dresser but was curious and who was at the conference to present a workshop on a related subject, discovered that he was not so comfortable wearing a long-haired wig, but he loved the way he looked mid-process wearing eye makeup and lipstick, before we put on his party hat. I think men in lipstick and mascara is definitely a wave of the future.

Our schedule gave the students plenty of opportunity to be independent while dressed, such as on excursions into the city of Los Angeles. On Friday night, after our presentation, some attendees drove to a club called Peanuts, but since this was an hour away, Jennifer and I opted for the hotel bar where we danced with the locals. Often I take students to bars like Peanuts or New York City's Edelweiss, and the fab Jackie's 60, which are real transgender hubs, but what I really love to do is to take our girls out into the so-called straight world to create some excitement and challenge. Soon a few of the other conference attendees, including cross-dressers Christine, a real party girl from Southern California, and Terry Williams, an Atlanta beauty, joined Jennifer and me in the bar. While Jennifer chatted with the locals, Terry quizzed me on what life is like as Dean of Students. "Do you help students get dressed?" Terry asked. "Do you help them get into their gaffs?" I answered yes. "And does that turn you on?" she wanted

to know. I said honestly that this part of the class was not a big turn-on to me, but made me feel more like the maid. What really turns me on was not to see that manhood disappear but to see a hard penis straining to break through the confines of transparent panty hose or a flimsy pair of panties. I'm still more of a heterosexual girl than a lesbian. On some occasions it is more difficult than others to maintain the student-teacher relationship, but I make it a rule to do so even though our girls look sexy and vulnerable when in their femme personas. Because they are vulnerable in many ways, and I do not want to take advantage of that vulnerability.

"You are different from the way I imagined," said Terry. "How did you imagine me to be?" I asked. "I did not know there were women out there like you," he replied.

I think one of the major contributions our academy made to the conference was to discuss the sexual aspects of cross-dressing in a candid and mature manner, as well as keeping the subject fun and provocative, just as we do here during Sex Education class.

During that same evening in the disco, I chatted with a young woman who had come with her date and a group of friends. After some light conversation, she looked me in the eye and said, "You are a beautiful woman; you could have your pick of men, what are you doing here with these guys in dresses?" "Having fun," was my answer and that was certainly true, but her question raised some personal issues for me.

The success of the academy had come about because I had put a lot of hard work into it and it had paid off in so many ways. But I had also taken time from my personal social life. I was encouraging my students to strive toward a balance in their lives. I could not overlook my own. From that moment on, I decided, I would make a concerted effort to set some time aside for myself, to reinvigorate my own social life and my sex life—and I have, but that is another tale. This field trip had brought personal insights I had not expected.

For all of us, the gender conference also gave us the opportunity to meet some of the most well-known and dedicated members of the community. There was Dr. Peggy Rudd, who is the wife of a cross-dresser and the author of a number of books from the wife's point of view. Virginia Prince, who pioneered the organized transvestism movement, and whose efforts laid the groundwork for Tri-Ess, the Society for the Second Self, which now has dozens of chapters across the United States, was in attendance, as was Carol Beecroft, the current executive director of Tri-Ess, and others. Dr. Sandra Cole, of the Gender Institute at the University of Michigan, spoke, in particular, of the work she was doing with cross-dressers' wives and partners. Dallas Denny, who created the relatively new group AEGIS (American Educational Gender Information Service), was present, as was cross-dresser JoAnn Roberts, who runs the highly successful Renaissance education/social group and publishing network. Dr. Stanley Biber, famed sex-reassignment surgeon, received a commendation at the conference luncheon, as did Virginia Prince. Also there were Drs. Vern and Bonnie Bullough and their colleagues at Cal State, organizers of the conference; James Green, who runs the female to male group; along with a host of other academicians, psychologists, and cross-dressers of all persuasions.

At conference end, Jennifer flew home as James because of his work schedule but Patti Harrington took her flight home *en femme*. She was amazed because, for the very first time, she was not nervous in an airplane—her white knuckles subdued by red fingernails.

Chapter 13

Etiquette
for
Macho
Girls

*E*tiquette is nothing more or less than the standards of behavior that govern life in polite society. The word etiquette, which is French in origin, means "ticket" and refers to the set of rules a monarch would set forth for the court. An academy student is encouraged to think of his etiquette lessons as an admission ticket to a new world, a world that, by his altered presence, he has helped to create. Some might argue, and have, that the act of cross-dressing violates the rules of propriety. It was not long ago that sumptuary laws against transvestism were imposed to keep the huddled masses in place. Cross-dressing, a threat to the status quo, was considered not merely impolite, but immoral and illegal. But as my friend Annie Sprinkle likes to say, "It's not easy being avant garde."

Etiquette is one of the most basic areas of study here at Miss Vera's Finishing School. When I began to instruct the students of the academy, I noticed how many of the corrections I made to their behavior had to do with refinement and decorum. The first lesson in Voice Class was not how to raise the voice but simply how to say a clear and definite "yes" rather than an affirmative grunt. The more I interacted with students, the more I felt that the worst of their behavior involved a crudeness that had become all too acceptable in the fast-paced and rapidly declining modern male world. I still believe this to be so. I also believe that refining this crudeness offers new options to all of us.

No student of the academy can hope to be a lady without being a gentleman. Like the knights of old, even dressed in male garb, the student carries the symbols of his lady, her manners with him at all times. And when *en femme,* those silk scarves and undies, like the colors Guinevere gave to Lancelot, help give her strength and keep her gallant under fire. The philosopher Kierkegaard describes a "knight of faith" who walks within the social order and yet apart from its social norms, mores, customs, and status. The students of the academy are knights of faith, harbingers of a new social order that values politeness as much as politics.

There is some aspect of etiquette involved in every lesson. We teach a student to occupy a smaller space at the table, not just to camouflage her big hands or long arms, but to make sure that she does not send those long arms flying into her tablemate's teacup. We teach her to do her own makeup not just for camouflage purposes but to help her be neat and well groomed and to bring more beauty into the world. Etiquette is not a long list of impossible rules that confine us and keep us from being free and having fun, but the rules of a game that make each play more intense. In her tell-all book What Falls Away, Mia Farrow relates that when she was in the presence of the Queen of England, she took the opportunity to ask what the Queen thought was the most important thing to teach children. "Manners," responded Her Majesty. Cornelia Guest—who is called "the last debutante," though I think not—states that when growing up she learned etiquette as her most important lesson. In the case of cross-dressing, some established rules must be amended, others must be created.

Etiquette can become somewhat confusing when our student goes from man to miss. Say he has finally convinced his wife to take his femmeself out on the town? Who opens the door to the restaurant? Who hails the taxi? Who helps whom with her coat? When the deans and I take a student out, we treat her like the lady we want him to be, a process that by observance can also hone his skills as a gentleman. We hail the cab, open the doors. We appreciate that these are treats that she may have never before experienced. To keep our student in the femme role, we want to give him all of the perks that go with the territory. If we are doing this over a prolonged period, say a two-day Femme Intensive, the deans and I might tire of being gentlemen. Being a man can be a drag. So we reverse roles for a while and encourage the student to be of more service. It also does our girl good to get out there in the street, stick up his arm, let his dress rise up a little, show off those gams of which we know he is so proud, and bring that taxi to halt at his high heel.

The basis of etiquette is to treat others the way in which we ourselves would like to be treated. It is the golden rule: "Do unto others as you would have others do unto you." If a student just remembers that, she will know all she needs to know about etiquette. It is also important to do what feels most comfortable to the people involved. When a student shares his femmeself with his female partner, he will want to be particularly sensitive to his partner's needs. Our student's wife or girlfriend may be prepared to help her cross-dressed husband on with his coat—women and men exchange this simple courtesy all the time; it can also be a lovely sign of affection—but pulling out a chair could be too much to expect, unless the wife, too, is cross-dressed and playing the male role to the hilt. Keep the lines of communication open. It is a

good idea to talk about these things before going out. Strategize.

While our girl must be mindful of how she treats and is treated by those she knows, she must also be careful with strangers and no place is caution more required than in the ladies' room.

Ladies' Room Techniques

Congratulations, Miss Debutante. You have finally defied nature and made it out in a dress, but Mother Nature has thrown another challenge your way. When you've got to go, you've got to go, and, in most cases, you've got to do it in the ladies' room. Even Dear Abby agrees.

Dear Abby,
I have often wanted to write about the following, but hoped that someone else would write and provide the answer first.

I am a pre-op transsexual and usually dress in women's clothing complete with wig and makeup.

My question is, which rest room should I use when I go out in public?

Abby, please inform your readers that most of us transsexuals and transvestites are in the ladies' room to use the facilities or to repair our makeup—nothing more.

—Miss "X"

Dear Miss "X": When you are dressed like a woman, you should use the women's room.

Lip-lining, a task for the ladies' room.

never will, especially with more and more cross-dressers joining the flow of everyday life. To maximize the safety of our student and to minimize any misinterpretation of his aims, we try, at all times, to accompany our girls to the ladies' room. It is best to have a buddy in this situation. But make sure that buddy is a genetic female. To have some genetic girlfriends as your chaperones can help defuse what might otherwise be a volatile situation, sort of like having an interpreter in a foreign land. Slowly but surely, we are all learning to speak the same language. Two cross-dressers entering the ladies' room is dicey since this could be seen as more intimidating to the other ladies. If it is not possible to have a genetic female chaperone, or if our girl really wants to try going it alone, we suggest that she not linger a moment longer than necessary. Proceed into the stall (whatever you do, don't forget to leave that seat down), wash your hands, apply hand lotion if available. Check yourself out in the mirror, fix whatever needs to

Anytime a student visits the ladies' room, it is both exciting and scary. We have never encountered a problem in the ladies' room, but that is not to say that we

be fixed—lip liner, lipstick, lip brush. Primp your wig, give yourself a tiny spritz of perfume, make sure your skirt is not tucked into your panty hose and no paper is attached to your pump, then out the door. If at any time during this procedure you feel uncomfortable due to the scrutiny of another patron of the amenities, you might choose to cut your visit short. This is treacherous territory, even for genetic girls, and some locations are more dangerous than others. In almost every theater in the land, toilet facilities for women are woefully inadequate. Are you woman enough to join that line of irate genetic girls that snakes out of the bathroom, each woman awaiting her turn while tapping her toe, glancing at her watch, and casting a malevolent gaze at the men's room patrons who enter and exit with ease? A student who because of absolute necessity puts his femmeself in this situation must exude confidence, even if she is faking it, because if her maleness is detected, women who would otherwise be serene and tolerant can get ugly. Expanded ladies' room facilities would help this situation. Increased public awareness could make it possible for men in dresses, as well as men in pants, to visit the men's room. New construction plans that require "potty parity" will help. Three types of toilet facilities would be ideal: ladies, gentlemen, and uncommitted. Until that happens, in a pinch, do like a drag queen and (quietly) brazen it out, or look for the handicapped facilities, girlfriend.

Tea Party Manners

An academy tea party gives the perfect opportunity to learn the rules of etiquette. We are in the tea salon called Tea & Sympathy. It is a cozy little neighborhood café run by Nicki, an enterprising British lady with a cockney twang she plays to the hilt. Miss Viqui, our Assistant Headmistress, is in charge of the class. Having grown up in a home where she learned from her mother, her aunt, and her grandmother that the way to solve a problem was over "a cuppa," Miss Viqui became expert in the tea ritual from an early age. The contrast between Miss Viqui, our most diminutive dean, and student June G. Edwards, a six-foot-two, squared-jawed, double black belt karate champ in her chic red suit, is quite striking. June is struggling to plop a dollop of cream into the center of a scone. Compared to the he-man size portions our girl is used to devouring, the scone is a thimble full of food. Seated next to June is Student Council President Jennifer James, who after being told to remove his dainty white gloves while he eats, has revealed, much to his chagrin, grease-covered fingernails. (No wonder this girl identifies as a Tomboy.) Miss Viqui and I, and especially June—who, like most of the students enjoys watching one of her sorority sisters squirm—utter a resounding "ycck." The combination of hairy knuckles and unkempt nails almost leads to the return of the gloves, but not quite. We make a note to give Jennifer further training with the nail brush, orange stick, and a discussion of hair-removal options. After sending her to the loo for another go with the soap, the lesson continues. Jennifer gets in trouble again when he opens his mouth to speak before she has swallowed her cucumber sandwich. June keeps her mouth closed when she chews but that is about the only time, otherwise he speaks end-lessly about his favorite subject, June G. Edwards. Clearly, we have our work cut out for us.

Miss Viqui has demonstrated to our girls the proper way to pour. 1) Place the individual tea strainer over the guest's teacup. 2) With the teacup on the table, pour tea up to one inch from the rim to al-low room for milk or cream and sugar. (Be careful not to drip tea on the table and do not let a drop hang from the spout.)

Our girls have been to tea at the Plaza (a favorite stop after shopping in Saks), the Helmsley Palace, and the Soho Tea Salon. Journalist Rebecca Meade, on assignment for British *Elle,* treated us to tea at the Stanhope, where we celebrated Patti Harrington's first anniversary with the academy, her one-year birthday. Follow-ing Miss Viqui's instructions, Patti learned to pour with aplomb.

Gifts

A woman can spend her life receiving gifts from men. (I know that I have.) Flowers, clothing, jewelry, cars . . . academy girls love to receive gifts; even the littlest, most casual, thing means a lot to girls who've been starved for such signs of affection. During class, we've given a student that special lipstick that looks so good on him or the earrings that so perfectly match a dress he ordered by mail and brought with him. When a student arrives for a two-day Femme Intensive, we prepare a bedroom for the femmeself, using the herstory assignment he has already com-pleted. We leave beautifully wrapped presents: a slinky nightie, a favorite per-fume. By standing order, our friends at

McManus Florist create the Sissy Bouquet, an assortment of pink flowers trimmed with pink ribbons and bows. The bouquet was named in honor of Sally Sissyribbons, its very first recipient, and the name stuck. The response of our students to the Sissy Bouquet has prompted me to send flowers to other men friends of mine who have no interest whatsoever in cross-dressing. When my friend Phil Berger, America's foremost boxing writer, celebrated the publication of *Blood Season,* his bio of Mike Tyson (to whom I issue an open invitation to visit this academy), I sent Mr. Berger a bouquet of red roses and a card that read, "Real men deserve flowers." He was tickled pink.

Thank-You Notes

One area in which academy girls shine is in bread-and-butter notes. Their gratitude comes winging in via mail in pink en-velopes on pink stationery. These unso-licited testimonials mean a lot to the deans and me.

Gala Performance

Since our inception, each year a group from Miss Vera's Finishing School has at-tended the dazzling Night of 1000 Gowns, the annual charity drag gala that is also a coronation. Students, escorts, the deans, and friends of the academy cele-brate at this lavishly elegant formal dinner dance sponsored by the Imperial Court of New York, an organization of commu-nity-minded gay men from all walks of life who love to dress in drag. Their motto is "Do good and look fabulous." (Chapter 15.)

In preparation for this event, besides

lessons in table manners and how to dance backward, students must also learn how to curtsy and when to wear which gloves.

Curtsies have always been a part of society life. Throughout the South, where grand debutante balls are most popular, the lower the curtsy the higher the praise. Texas girls pride themselves on taking the lowest bows. After months of practice some are able to touch their foreheads to the floor. Though many of our girls would love to emulate that graceful sweeping move, and given considerably more hours spent in tutus a few would stand a good chance, most do not have the luxury of that time. In the basic no-frills classic curtsy, according to Grand Duchess Swana, the Imperial Court's Mistress of Protocol, the debutante disengages herself from her escort; she steps back with her right foot, then across and down, so that her right knee approaches her left ankle. She goes as low as she can while keeping her back straight and her arms extended to both sides. The head is then bowed, starting from the neck. G.D. Swana advises that students practice, practice, practice until the entire curtsy is performed in one fluid motion. Older girls or a Cinderella still unsure in her slippers may use the arm of an escort for support. He will bow as she curtsies. The depth of her dip depends on the suppleness of our debutante and, in the case of our girls, on the length of her dress. Curtsies are always part of formal affairs and a formal gown is floor-length, but academy students so enjoy showing off their legs that I am lenient with them and allow their dresses to be cocktail-length, which calls for a more modest dip.

Countess Swana grants this concession, but prefers the floor-length side-slit-sheath option.

I Glove You

Gloves are essential items in any cross-dresser's wardrobe and satin spandex has proved a boone to our girls. This fabric makes any style "one size fits all." I have always been a proponent of gloves because they are so evocative. Long, fingerless, opera-length (to the shoulder) gloves are ideal for our girls and I favor them myself on occasion. These make it possible to show off a manicure while camouflaging arm hair. Unlike finger gloves, these do not have to be removed while eating. Otherwise gloves must always be removed when eating, but may remain on when dancing or during cocktail hour. Rules on glove length have relaxed somewhat over the years, but I am still a traditionalist. The longer the dress, the longer the gloves and vice versa. But, of course, we must make an exception to the rule for academy girls in sleeveless cocktail-length dresses. Tradition would have them wear wrist- or elbow-length gloves but if our girl has arm hair to hide, she'll wear opera-length gloves that reach to her shoulders with that thigh-cut rock-and-roll mini.

Charity benefits like the Night of 1000 Gowns encourage the student to allow his femmeself to be of service as a society dame. We are proud when our girls can not only make their dreams come true but help others in the process.

Our girls tend to make their dress and their makeup a first priority, but etiquette is just as important in their education, for they must always remember, *beauty is as beauty does.*

Homework Assignment. Successful completion of this assignment qualifies the student to receive the Amy Vanderbilt Etiquette Letter of Commendation.

1. Learn to curtsy. (Send me a picture of you in action.)

2. Compose a handwritten thank-you note to someone who has been of service to you and send it, on perfumed pink stationery.

3. Make a donation to a charity of your choice. Give money or time or a note of encouragement.

4. Engage in a conversation in which you turn the attention on the other person.

Chapter 14

Sex Education

Facts About Fantasies

*M*ost students acknowledge that they feel sexier as their femmeselves. If I ask our girl, "When can you most rely on your penis to get hard, when you are dressed in female clothes or when you are not dressed in them?" The answer is always, "When I am dressed."

Only recently have men been allowed to take on the role of desired sex objects. Gay porno stars led the way, with shirtless male hunks on the soaps and Calvin Klein underwear models close behind. But it is really the female image that is the one we have been encouraged to

think of as the object of desire, so it is not hard to understand why, when a man feels sexy, he might identify that feeling as feminine. Put some lingerie on those feelings and his juices will really flow.

The femmeself is relatively less sexually inhibited, particularly when it comes to fantasies. When a student's fantasies disturb him, I assure him that he is not alone. One of my dear friends is Candida Royalle, creator of Femme, Inc., maker of erotic videos from a woman's point of view. Candida gives many lectures both here and internationally. Afterward, the women and men in her audience have the opportunity to ask her questions. I asked Candida what is the number-one question that she hears. She did not hesitate a moment before she said, "People always ask me if their particular fantasy is okay."

Fantasies are meant to be disturbing, to shake us up, and they are often not politically correct. I consider myself a very liberated, take-charge woman, but nothing brings me to orgasm faster than the idea that I am taken, preferably suspended in imaginative positions, while being brought to orgasm after orgasm usually by more than one person.

If our girl enjoys the fantasy of being taken, she is not alone. According to a report that appeared several years ago in the *New York Times,* enough men and women enjoy the dream of being ravaged to make it the number-one fantasy of all time. At Miss Vera's Finishing School if Rhett Butler feels more like Scarlett O'Hara, we'll release the Southern belle in him and squeeze her into a corset, too.

As I have stated earlier, the majority of students at present identifies as heterosexual, about 60 percent are married.

Many will tell me, "I am heterosexual in my daily life"—"but when I am dressed, anything goes." Some speak only of fantasy, others are ready to be more adventuresome. Part of our philosophy is that the line between who is heterosexual, gay, or bisexual is a very blurry one, particularly when it comes to fantasy. That little sex kitten, the femmeself, may want to inspire both men and women to drool over her rump and long legs in a mini-skirt. Remember, sex is not always about being horny; it is also a desire for attention and affection from men and from women. We all have the physical capacity to experience bisexual pleasure and many of us have and do, a fact that will become more and more evident as time goes on. Bisexuality is common in the rest of the animal kingdom. Whether we exercise that option depends on our own personal sexual evolution, a product of heredity and environment; development and experience; nature and nurture. You can bet that Daddy and Mommy are usually somewhere lurking about, the unseen and/or unwitting puppeteers in the dance of our wet dreams.

Welcome to the Evolution

When people ask what led me to a career in sex research, I credit the inspiration to a good Catholic education. Becoming a star in the erotic galaxy helped me to shed light on my personal sexual issues. It was a way to break from the domination of my parents; it was a way to stay tightly linked to them by my rebellion. I went from being a girl who was afraid to say "yes" to sex to one who was almost afraid to say, "no." What I finally learned was that I have a

choice. I have taken the opportunity to find my own answers, to explore myself as a sexual human being, and I want to pass that opportunity on to my students.

In visual terms, our sexuality is a path or, as sexologist Dr. John Money has said in his book of the same name, a *Lovemap*. For example, a child is abused, the road turns here; he gets spanked and ejaculates, another bend in the road; he sees Mommy and Daddy making love, turn here; he never sees Mommy and Daddy being tender, turn there; he is seduced by an older woman, turn again; he puts on a pair of panties and feels like the girl in *Playboy,* another turning point . . . and so his sexuality evolves. Sex is simple, sexuality is complex. At the academy, one of our aims is to work from the complex to the simple.

A man may think of his femmeself as a bizarre aberration, but in terms of his development and experience, she makes absolute sense. So we explore her, experience her to the fullest. We discover what she has to tell him so that he can have more information, more options, and more directions for growth. Each of us deserves choices and self-acceptance is empowering. The femmeself may have dreams and desires that the students find disturbing, but these dreams and desires reflect unfulfilled needs and avenues of self-expression. Her very existence depends on this. She is his lover, his mother, his teacher, his friend. She is Joan of Arc, Marilyn Monroe, Mother Teresa, his very own centerfold. But the student must never forget: She is him.

Penetrating Observation

The academy's sex education course, which is taught by me, has gone through a number of evolutions, just as people do. Originally, I thought that the desire to cross-dress was simply motivated by an acknowledged or unacknowledged desire for penetration, that Venus Envy is at its core. When a new student arrived, even before the makeup session, I instructed him to strip off his male clothes and slip into a bra and panties. I had him lie down and began to massage his shoulders and entire back, from head to toe. Many of the students had never been touched by another person when they were in lingerie. I used fragrant oils and played Puccini's *Madame Butterfly.* After about twenty minutes, the student was ready to melt. As I approached his buttocks, if he tightened his cheeks, I kept my hands moving down his legs. But if he started to wriggle his buttocks, invitingly, under my touch, I knew he might be ready to go further and deeper. An opportunity to take our girls further appeared when a handy invention came my way. One of the last parties Annie Sprinkle held at her Sprinkle Salon was an all-female gathering. Annie's parties have never been simply chat groups, there are always activities. This night Annie brought out a large machine called the Simian Vibrator. The machine was a large, firm, curved cushion with a replaceable simulated penis, or "dildo," in the center of the seat. A person employing the Simian Vibrator would ease herself down and let the dildo enter her. The dildo was a vibrator that danced at various speeds. The controls were in a panel that was held by the rider.

Annie explained that she was safekeeping the machine for Dell Williams, owner of Eve's Garden, the first erotic boutique for women, which Dell had created in the seventies. The machine had been sent to Dell by the manufacturer for a trial run. "Are there any volunteers?" asked Annie. A woman named Gloria was the first to raise her hand. The machine was fitted with a condom. Gloria mounted and rode, at first cautiously and then with the wild abandon of a Texan on Gilley's mechanical bull. There it was, the perfect device for our girls. I could not believe my luck when Annie later mentioned that the machine took up lots of space and she was thinking of giving it back to Dell. "I'll take it off your hands," I said, knowing we might have one or two cowgirls back at the ranch.

If our student enjoyed penetration or the fantasy of it—and many do—I wanted to encourage him to sashay down that avenue of pleasure. Penetration is one of my favorite subjects and one of deep consequence. Speaking as a genetic girl, I will say penetration feels lovely. It feels so good to be opened, to be filled, to be at the receiving end of a long, slow, thrust of passion, or short quick ones, for that matter. When a person is penetrated, the body is like a furnace that has been stoked, and the heat, which is the sexual energy, starts to rise, carried on the breath to other parts of the body. This rising of energy is always part of the sexual process, but penetration starts that process in the most swift and sure way. The student also needed to be reminded that this is the rubber age. He must always use condoms. He could experiment with toys—but be careful about sharing them and always play safe. If the direction of the feminist movement is women on top, what follows is men on bottom.

Tao Now

There was so much to learn, I decided that sex education would be a separate class through which I could impart more of the knowledge I had acquired in my years of research through the elysian fields. During an eighty-day trip around the world, I had visited the erotic temples of Khajuraho, India, which were built by the Tantric yogis, a sect that reached its high point during the thirteenth and fourteenth centuries. The Tantrics believed that sexual energy or kundalini was the source of life and they decorated their temples with relief sculptures depicting humans and animals in sexual positions. The term tantra was described by the modern guru Rajneesh as sex with intelligence—enlightened sex. The Tantrics, like the Taoists, believe that all energy is carried through the body on the breath. They identify the kundalini as a female form of energy. I decided to incorporate breathing exercises and an exploration of tantric yoga into our sex education curriculum.

Sex Ed. at the academy is now a course entitled "Exploring your Female Sexual Energy." Makeup Application, maid training, Ballet One and Tutu, and the other courses that involve cosmetics and costumes receive a lot of attention from students, from the media, and from those who are just curious. Sex education is a touchy and controversial subject, but too important to be overlooked. The whole concept of cross-dressing can be seen as a way to avoid sex. But to not explore and communicate about the sexual aspects of cross-dressing would be a mistake.

Our goals in sex education are AAA to increase our students *awareness,* influence their *attitudes,* and inspire positive *action.* We honor the student's trust by appreciating her limits but not selling her short. Whether the class is Makeup Application or Female Sexual Energy, we support the student—introduce the student to expert teachers, give her a wide range of tools, and show her how to use them. We present our neophyte with increased options and encourage her to make the most of them.

Veronica Vera

MY BODY IS A TEMPLE

In the Tantric temple, Khajuraho, India.

Are We Having Sex, Yet?

The student needs to understand that he is not alone. Millions of men all over the world get turned on by dressing up. And it's okay, as long as the student does not ignore other needs. Cross-dressing is a relaxing, satisfying, nourishing, and immensely pleasurable sensual experience. How overtly sexual it gets, depends on our girl.

Class Is in Session

What is a typical Female Sexual Energy class at the academy? First we pick out a vulva for the student. In our academy library is a book called *Femalia,* which was published by Joani Blank and the all-female-owned, San Francisco-based, Down There Press. *Femalia* is a book of photographs that illustrate the genitals or *femalia* of thirty-one different women. There are several reasons why our ladies-in-waiting study this book. First, I do not assume that all are well acquainted with female anatomy. A few students have never before seen a vulva. Steve, a student at NYU, a neighboring academic institution, asked our help in fulfilling his student film requirement by allowing him to document a Miracle Miss class in which we would transform him to Peach Steele. Peach, nee Steve, took one look at those juicy, full-color vulvae and turned as red as a cherry. Fortunately, his blush, as well as his gulp, were filmed for posterity. Some of our girls are familiar with one vulva—their wife's. Some have seen many but could still learn more about what to do with one. If the student fantasizes about having a vulva, it will be a good idea to learn about her care and feeding. So we go through a chart that shows the clitoris and the labia and the clitoral hood . . . As proved by the thirty-one vulvae pictured in our textbook, each vulva looks unique. Some have large clitoral hoods that may need to be pushed aside to increase sensitivity; some are not so protected and so may need less stimulation. We go through the pictures one by one: this one is very symmetrical and looks like a pansy; this one is the color of barbecued spareribs and looks just as mouthwatering; turn this one sideways and she looks like a mouth (recalling that Rolling Stones album cover); this one is very dark on the outside and shocking pink on the inside; this one looks like a statue of the Virgin Mary . . . here is her head and here are her arms extended in her cloak. This part of Female Sexual Energy class puts a new twist on the concept "think pink." By encouraging our girl to "think pink," we are also not pussyfooting around the genitals. Often, dressing is a fetish, a way to avoid actual human sexual contact. So we begin by demystifying the genitals and moving right to the source. Since many of our students identify as lesbians—when *en femme,* they choose female sexual partners—this study of femalia will assure that when our student meets a vulva-carrying female she will know how to bring her pleasure. It is interesting to note that of the thirty-one photographs that comprise the varied bouquet in *Femalia,* the one that the majority of students have picked for themselves is the most delicate, the least hairy, the most symmetrical—perhaps the least threatening of the bunch, or the least likely to have teeth.

After choosing a vulva, the student is probably ready for the more hands-on portion of sex education class. The guided meditation that follows is one that I created to encourage the student to release his inhibitions and follow his femmeself to increased pleasure and fulfillment. I invite you to follow along—I have tried to include something for everyone. So lean back, get comfy, and imagine yourself in this situation. Now study hard:

The lights in the academy are turned low. You are dressed in bra, panties, and a slip as you lie on a divan. You may wear prosthetic breast forms inside your bra, but other than the breast forms, no additional padding, no gaff, no corset . . . nothing that would get in the way of your being able to touch yourself or feel the smooth fabric against your skin. Incense burns and the haunting Irish voice of the singer Enya floats on the air; she is an accompaniment to my instructions. You listen to my every word:

"Breathe. Feel your juices stir. Feel the kundalini, your female sexual energy, coiled like a snake, start to rise from your genitals, your femalia, that beautiful vulva that you have picked out for yourself. She begins to uncoil, and travel up your spine, spreading each vertebra as you breathe, breathe, breathe. Feel your breasts rise and fall. Lick your lips, your lovely red-stained mouth. Touch your full breasts, move your

Barbara Nitke

A student feels his female sexual energy.

to dry them with big fluffy towels, help the women into silk kimonas, and give massages upon request. In return, the women teach you to be a totally uninhibited sexpot, an instrument of their and your pleasure. They teach you to delight them with your tongue, learning their individual preferences. The more you drink of their juices, the more feminine your body becomes. Your breasts and hips enlarge; your waist gets tiny. Inside your panties, your penis gets larger and larger until it bursts forth in the form of a beautiful dewy flower. When one of the women feels really horny she straps on a dildo and as you kneel between the legs of one woman, another one takes you from behind, easing that dildo in and out of you, in and out. The women play with your body, squeezing and sucking your nipples, taking turns to enter you from behind. Those who cannot get close enough to touch you begin to make love to each other, inspired by the scene in front of them. Proud of their charge, they decide to continue your education and invite a beautiful, muscular man to join the party. (Lesbians might stop here.) Before you go out as a girl about town, you must demonstrate that you know how to put on a condom. You open the packet, pinch the tip of the condom to squeeze out any air, place the condom on this guest's stiff, waiting penis, and roll the rubber down his shaft. While the women continue to skewer you at one end, the man slides his sheathed penis into your mouth. Breathe, breathe. Feel those good feelings all over your body. As you approach orgasm, remember to dedicate your orgasm to something that you really want. This can be something tangible, like a new car, or something intangible, like better understanding of yourself. You can wish for a lover with whom you can share your

hands along your body, over that silken slip, and continue to breathe, breathe, breathe as those delicious sensations travel from the tips of your toes to the top of your head, into your long, flowing hair. Feel your femmeself wrap her arms around you, holding you close to her until you melt into her, become one with her and she with you . . .

"Imagine yourself the harem girl at a bathhouse. As the beautiful women lounge in the warm pools of the marbled bath, your job is

femmeself. But put this energy to use because it is very, very powerful.

The energy released during this class has been known to make the walls of the academy vibrate with excitement as it did during the class of Tony aka Ginger. My first impression of Tony was that he looked as if he had not spent much time in the sun. His complexion was clear, but very, very white. He was slim, about five ten, and forty-five years old. I was attracted to his hands, which were immaculately clean and alabaster. His nails were cut extremely short. They reminded me of nun's hands. But there was a part of Tony that felt more like Ginger from "Gilligan's Island"—his role model. The more time we spent with Tony, the more Ginger began to emerge. We photographed Ginger in sexy poses and she really began to come alive. At the start of Female Sexual Energy class, Tony informed me that he had not had sex with another person since 1968. I talked him through the sex meditation. Ginger became more and more excited. As the orgasm started to build the student reached his hands out to hold on to the walls. The air was so thick, like Jell-O. The room never looked more pink. All of the statues, the flowers, the furniture stood out as if they were outlined in black. Tony rocked back and forth as he shouted, "Move over, Captain, Ginger's in charge." It was the first time he had an orgasm in the presence of another person in twenty-five years.

Practice Makes Perfect

Because Patti Harrington is a student who comes to the academy once a month, she has been able to make great progress in her education, particularly sex education. She knows the words of the dedication ritual by heart and has shown by her actions that she means every one, particularly the section about trust. In his herstory, Pat described himself as a computer nerd, and implied that he was a loner, with few friends and fewer opportunities for fun. But from the beginning, Pat showed qualities that he did not appreciate. To say he suffered from low self-esteem is an understatement. He was the original Mr. Gloom and Doom, always ready to look on the dark side of things, never able to accept a compliment. He was anal retentive, but when that nervous persistence was directed away from himself and channeled into his lessons, he became a star student: a whiz at makeup, a graceful walker, and an incredible seamstress. His ingenuousness allowed him to be honest, open, and appreciative, in short, a joy to teach. Was it any wonder that his sexuality, too, would blossom?

Pat arrived at the academy a virgin. Other than joining his buddies on what for Pat was an unsuccessful visit to a brothel, he had no sexual experience. "Whenever I felt sexy, I immediately connected it with feelings of being a girl," said Pat, "and I felt guilty about thinking of myself as a girl, so I pushed those feelings away." It was not until Pat began to let Patti out that he was able to get in touch with his sexuality.

When asked if he considered himself straight or gay, Pat said that having had no sexual experience made him not sure. So I orchestrated Pat's experiences. I decided to augment classes at the academy with visits to some associate professors. Massage seemed the perfect way for the students to experience touch. I was especially curious to see how some of the students would respond to the touch of a man. Patti and I went to see a male counselor named Samuel Kirschner, creator of In Touch/Mind Body Therapy. He incorporated light touching into a program that consisted mostly of conversation. I thought meeting Samuel would also be a good experience for Patti because Samuel's state of being is a lesson in itself. After years of practice this generous teacher has his male and female energies almost perfectly in balance.

At one point Samuel touched Patti's palm with his fingers, sending shivers of electricity through the student. Later, back at the academy after Patti changed back to Pat and just before leaving, he confided with a big smile, "Patricia wants a boyfriend."

After work one day, Pat dropped into Uncle Charlie's, one of Greenwich Village's most popular gay bars, but he was so shy he did not speak to anyone. "At least you made it inside," I said. I realized that one reason why Pat might be shy was because he had no experience

Marty Fishman

Patti and date Den Follington.

with which to inspire confidence. And if he was going to be cruising gay bars, I'd better make sure he was prepared—and quick. It was time for another class.

We visited Hank, a sensitive masseur I had known for several years, who was a sex therapist in his own right. I explained Patti's experience, or rather, lack of it. Patti had gotten a lot out of just holding hands with Samuel; Hank picked up the pace.

"Would you like me to be nude or clothed while I massage you?" he asked Patti. She was noncommittal. Off came Hank's shirt, down came his shorts, up went his penis. The masseur enjoyed being naked. I kissed Patti, handed her a sack of condoms and her dildo, which we called Mr. Right because of its size, and told her to have fun. This is the way it can always be, I thought, sex as an initiation in a positive atmosphere, with a caring, enthusiastic, and talented practitioner, and some preparation. While Patti and the masseur enjoyed class, I relaxed in the next room and listened to the pregnant silence. Well??? I demanded. "Tell me all." The class had consisted mostly of fondling. Patti was thrilled that Hank could have an erection in her presence. She felt accepted in a way she had never experienced before. When she recounted that she had caused him to ejaculate, her grin was even wider, "I'm a slut," Patti said proudly. "Good for you, I knew you had it in you," I said.

The Other Woman

Many of our students would love to share their femmeselves with their wives or female partners, but are not sure how to go about communicating their desires. Often a student will tell me, "My wife would never understand." I cannot count how many times I have heard that sad sentence. Each time I hear it, I think that what the student really means is that he himself does not understand, so how could anyone else? Our goal is to help the student to accept and understand his femmeself so that he can share his knowledge with his partner. Dealing with cross-dressing, like dealing with any other aspect of a relationship, takes communication and compromise.

It was some months before student Bob's wife Eileen felt comfortable enough to have sex with Bob's femmeself Renee Roberts. At first, Eileen told Bob that while she could go out dancing with Renee she was not interested in her as a sex partner. Bob accepted her limit. After Eileen had gotten to know Renee and felt secure in Renee's love rather than threatened by this *other woman,* she invited her into their bed. "She just does not like the mess involved with Renee's makeup," says Bob.

Following John White's debut as Joan Hazelnut at the Learning Annex seminar, he and Viqui went home to make love. They, too, encountered cosmetic complications. He wrote:

I kissed her neck, her chin, her cheeks, leaving rouge splotches from painted lips. We laughed joyfully; her face looked like the special effects of a poorly made horror movie. Without seeing myself, I know I was melting. She unzipped my dress and I awkwardly wobbled in my painful heels to help her strip me from the bondage of womanhood. The corset loosened: I gasped in relief. Viqui touched my breasts as we admired them in the mirror, but the silicone had no sensation for me. What a pity. She went under them, reaching and caressing the real thing.

I responded, finally. Visually, we remained active, as layer after layer unfolded.

Still, foreplay can have its drawbacks when you're candy-coated. The garter belt down, the hose off, the hip pads dropped, hairy masculine leg uncovered; the gaff that had been riding and digging into my ass was free at last and, finally, my manhood stuck up, some kind of foreplay! She couldn't carry me into the bedroom, but I went willingly. We did the beast-with-two backs with great passion. I kept saying the kinds of things that men always hope their women will say, like "Stick it to me, baby! Fuck me! Ahh!" I was a real moaner.

To make love with a husband who is cross-dressed presents more challenges than the makeup. Dr. Sandra Cole, in her talk at the Cal-State Gender Conference the students and I attended, said that many of the women she counseled in the Gender Institute in Ann Arbor, who were wives of cross-dressers, found that as their husbands evolved in their sexuality, the women, evolved too. They confronted things like power exchanges, lesbianism, introduction of toys, and primarily, the need to speak openly and candidly about their emotions, their own sexual needs and preferences.

Student Louise told me he had recently started dating a woman to whom he was very attracted but he said that he thought he might not be communicating his admiration because he feared her reaction to his cross-dressing. I asked him for more information and learned that he had only recently met the woman, did not know her very well, and the attraction, at this point, was still superficial. "Are you looking for a person with whom to have an emotionally committed relationship or is your priority anyone who will

share your cross-dressing with you?" He answered that he was looking for a relationship. I suggested he get to know this woman better and vice versa. Goddess knows, there are lots of reasons two people might not be compatible; by taking some time to get to know one another the student and his partner can eliminate some of the frequent hazards. If he makes sharing his cross-dressing the first priority, and things don't work out, his poor femmeself is likely to take all the blame, when, for some other reason, the romance may have been doomed from the start. He needs to learn to have some respect for himself and be mindful of all of his needs. My advice was that he take it slow. Get to know this potential partner first, rather than rush into a dinner at home where he answers the door in his prettiest dress. This move, resorted to by more than one eager beaver, is likely to sabotage a romance at the threshhold rather than result in our girl's being carried across one.

Still, the student did not want to feel that he had to hide who she was, so the question remained how could he be open and upfront about an aspect of his sexuality that is important to him. There need not be only one answer to this question, but many options he might consider.

The Pantie Preview

I advised Louise to be more casual about his cross-dressing. "Do you enjoy wearing female panties?" I asked, knowing his probable response. When he answered with an enthusiastic "yes," I suggested he give himself permission to wear panties under his male clothes. When he had the opportunity to get naked with this woman and she asked about the panties, he should tell her, as casually as possible, that he enjoys wearing them and that they turn him on and so does she. It is important that he keeps the emphasis on her, shows his interest in her and her pleasure. Then she will be more inclined to want to spend more time with him.

The student is advised not to start off a new relationship with a confession. Guilt is boring. If he hangs his head and gives her the old, "There is something that I have to tell you" routine, he will scare her away pretty quick. If he thinks that she may be special, he wants her to know it and not feel that he is just looking for someone, anyone, who will accept him as a crossdresser and who she is does not matter.

"Believe me, you are not the only man in the world who loves to wear female clothes," I told him. "We receive hundreds of requests for information each year and there seems to be no let up in sight. It is just not that unusual." The student Louise did wear his panties on the second date. Afterward, he told me, "I must have had an extra twinkle in my eye because she kissed me soon after I walked in the door." The romance has continued at a slow, but steady pace for over a year.

I advise any student who would like to wear ladies underwear, such as bras, panties, or panty hose, under their male clothes, to do so. Because these clothes are connected to feelings of security and safety, they can help him to be more effective. Most likely, he is not going to be walking around with a constant erection—well, maybe in the beginning, but eventually, he will just be too busy. He will discover that when he gives himself permission to wear panties—when he owns his underwear—the student

feels less like a child and more like an adult, potent in every sense of the word.

Many of our girls dream of living full time as a female, but for most this is a fantasy, a very strong fantasy, but still a fantasy. If the student keeps his desire secret, it often becomes more and more powerful until it seems to take over his life. At the academy, by giving our lady-in-waiting the chance to make fantasy a reality, we help him to differentiate between the two. Preoperative transsexuals, meaning those who identify as the opposite sex and may be taking hormones but have had no surgery, seem to represent the best of both worlds and so have a powerful allure. I have met and interviewed many pre-op transsexuals, especially those who frequented night clubs and supported themselves through performance or prostitution or both. These are not our students, though you may find our students or a potential student visiting gender-bender night spots like Edelweiss or Sally's.

JoAnn Finds a Man

JoAnn, the fetish doll I introduced in Chapter 9, wanted her entire look to inspire lust, her own as well as any observer's. Her leather mini, bare shoulders, and corseted waist, and those impossibly high six-inch platform stilettos were chosen to mark her as a sexual object. Eric, who was in his mid thirties, had been dressing off and on since the age of ten and with increased frequency for the last five years, since his marriage.

On his first visit to the academy he asked that we transform him in preparation for his own night on the town. This would not be JoAnn's first time out. She was a

Dear Miss Vera,

I would like to thank you and the deans for the wonderful class . . . This feeling that you gave me is one that is hard to describe; but I'll do my best . . . It fills the heart and the whole being with a tingling sensation that makes me smile all day long. I took a month to tell you this because I needed to see if this feeling would last, and it has.

I would like to tell you about that night. As we were applying my makeup, you asked to hear JoAnn's voice. I felt a little apprehensive, but I spoke. As time passed and the makeup neared completion, JoAnn began to come out. You sat there looking at me and I noticed something in your eyes . . . JoAnn's reflection. Wow, what a sexy thing I've become. You then started talking about a man's penis. The size and the shape . . . I began to want it. I mean really want it as a woman would. This was great! I then started to dress and now JoAnn was ready to go out. I didn't have much time, Sally's was dead, so I decided to stay dressed and head home, a drive that would take me several hours.

Well, on the road a truck driver noticed me and began to slow down and we rode side by side. He took out his flashlight and directed it at my crotch. Of course, he could see the top of my stockings and garters. He followed me for fifteen miles. I pulled off the highway, he pulled off the highway. I got back on, he got back on. Finally, I lost this guy. Even though I was a little scared, I felt like he wanted me . . . That's what I wanted to feel . . .

very self-sufficient girl and had already visited Sally's and Edelweiss, but never with the professional makeup job she learned she could get at the academy. We fulfilled her request and she responded with a letter.

JoAnn continued her letter cit-

. . . By this time, I needed something or someone. I sat down and pulled out the pictures you took of me . . . Wow! Now I had a hard-on. I looked and looked. JoAnn began to masturbate . . .

ing encounters with a waitress who called her "ma'am," a young gas station attendant who filled her tank and seemed inclined to pump more, and the man in the neighboring hotel room who dropped his briefcase at the sight of her.

Reading JoAnn's letter, I wondered how much was true and how much was fantasy. On her next visit to the academy, I did not have to wonder about her sexual adventures because I was part of them.

Some months later, when JoAnn returned she asked that we go to Edelweiss together, so that I might observe her in action. I had begun the evening feeling tired, but JoAnn's excitement was infectious and I found myself dressing up and looking a lot sexier than I had planned. JoAnn wore her beloved leather mini ensemble: big hair, big lips, long nails, and four-inch pumps. I wore form-fitting trousers and a tuxedo-type jacket with a provocative low-cut neckline. She was determined that this night she would actually pick up a man. We entered the bar and JoAnn and I perched provocatively on two stools. JoAnn crossed her legs and dangled her red four-inch stiletto-clad feet like shark bait. Within five minutes a young man approached and began chatting us up. He was very good-looking and resembled Robert Redford with brown hair. As smoothly as if she were pitching a sales account, JoAnn offered to buy him a drink. I thought this a bit forward—but then JoAnn had intended it to be. The man, Dennis, scored lots of points when he turned the offer around and treated us instead. JoAnn was a tall girl, over six feet in heels, and very, very pretty. In other circumstances, she would have had a good chance to pass as a biological female, but in her fetish gear and

in this bar, which is famous for its gender-bender clientele, we knew it likely that Dennis understood she was a girl with something extra. Just to be sure, JoAnn, who is very, very honest, told him she was an academy student and asked if Dennis had ever had the urge to dress. Dennis said he had not, but that he was game for anything. I thought he looked just fine the way he was, but I did recognize an opportunity when I heard one, so I invited him back with us for a nightcap and gown. Dennis dropped us at the entrance to the academy. While he parked his car, JoAnn and I entered the lobby alone. I turned to her, and taking advantage of this private moment, I quickly conveyed what I thought would be an excellent plan: "I'll kiss him and you pleasure his member."

She sensed its merits immediately and gasped, "Yes, Miss Vera."

With all of the academy's frocks and props at our disposal, it took no time at all to get Dennis out of his clothes. "Would you like to feel the sensation of wearing a corset?" I asked. "If you remove your belt, we could put one on over your clothes, but for maximum effect you can remove your sweater, shirt, and trousers."

Dennis stripped down to his white jockey shorts.

"Would you like to see how I look in my corset?" asked JoAnn.

While I laced the gentleman in, JoAnn slipped out of her ensemble to show off her wasp-waist figure in a scarlet corset. Her legs were encased in sheer black nylon hose, attached to the corset by a dozen garters.

Dennis sat in a chair as JoAnn twirled around for his inspection. The corset inspired our guest to sit up nice and straight, but more than the gentleman's posture was erect. I sat a chair next to him, and according to plan, brought my mouth very close to his lips. JoAnn knelt at his feet and stroked his shaft with her long red talons. His mouth reached out to mine and while we kissed JoAnn ripped open the condom and put it in place. She looked up into his face and they made eye contact then she took what she hungered for. He leaned back, sighed into my mouth, and petted the top of her bobbing hairdo.

Before Dennis left, JoAnn went to her wallet and pulled out a picture. "This is me," she said, showing it to Dennis, who looked at the picture with mild curiosity. The person JoAnn really showed the picture to was himself.

For me, this escapade with JoAnn was totally unplanned and unexpected. I would not make it a practice to get so physically involved or even to let it happen again, but I was glad it had happened because I was reminded of how sexy our students can be, how much lust they can inspire in themselves and in others—and the experience was fun.

For JoAnn, it was a turning point in understanding who he was. Eric worked very hard and was good at his job, which like that of many of our students required him to travel. He had a young son, of whom he was very proud. Eric loved his wife but he had difficulty discussing his sexual feelings with her. He said that she enjoyed her friendships with gay men but that any hint that her husband might be something other than super straight was met with such fury he cut the conversation short, terrified of the consequences. He felt trapped and he hated being dishonest. Eric needed support. I suggested he talk to a therapist on a regular basis.

The back pages of the magazine that was then called *Tapestry* and is now *Transgender* contain a great resource directory. We lucked out in Eric's case because there was a listing for a therapist located just two towns over from where he lived. He began to see the therapist on a regular basis.

June's Story

Only one of the academy's students has had a sex change operation, or as it is now called, a "genital congruency procedure." June G. Edwards at six two, with a square jaw, deep voice, and a second-degree black belt in karate had a tougher road to hoe and a tougher beard, too.

June was in her late thirties before she decided to make the change. She had entered the academy, taken her classes, and then gone

Miss Vera

June G. Edwards.

off on her own. She was taking hormones and had begun to lose some of her male power. She had even been mugged on the street, something that would not have happened so easily to karate expert Ed. As a result of the mugging, she met a sexy female detective who wanted to know all about June. About two years after our initial meeting, which was also two years after she came out as a cross-dresser, June announced her decision for surgery. She was tired of living in limbo. The turning point for Ed had been when a transsexual woman happened to visit his place of business. He recognized her as such, and they had a heart-to-heart. The woman sympathized with Ed when he told her that he was unhappy in his present situation and that his life did not seem to be in focus. She told him that she had felt the same way before her surgery. She advised, if you are really serious, go ahead and do it, and then get on with your life.

I was not thrilled when June told me her plan. I was afraid it was all too soon. Had she really spent enough time in therapy? But June was determined. She told me that her parents would be traveling with her to Montreal where her surgeon was located. "Traveling for ten hours with her mom and dad who are not exactly gung-ho about all this, should be a test of her mettle," I thought. She arrived at the hospital, as determined as ever. So I sent her a bouquet of irises, her favorite flower, to her apartment as a welcome-home present and waited.

June came to see me and showed me the new her. The surgery was amazing. Had I not known her story, I would have seen nothing amiss. There was a big change I did notice in June. She was calmer, and there was more of a maturity about her. The June I knew before talked endlessly about her exploits and was very self-absorbed. The person I met now had a lot more understanding. I realized that the surgery itself can be a great therapy. June is part of a new breed, a transgendered female, and she enjoys that transgendered status. She told me that she had experienced her first orgasms as a female under the direction of Betty Dodson. What better initiation! Now she was really one of the girls.

Thank You, Ma'am

No course at the academy is entirely separate from every other. An important part of sex education is sex etiquette. Sex is a gift that humans can give to each other. It is good to say thank you. After one student had his first sexual experience with another cross-dresser, he proceeded to make light of the event, acting as if this was a tryst like any other. The student had removed his femme clothes, he told me. In other words, he was the man, while the other cross-dresser remained dressed and was thus, the femme. "That's nice in theory," I told him, "but in reality you were a man having sex with another man." I congratulated him on giving himself that liberty. "You seem to think it should make more of an impression on me," he said. "Yes, I think that often we are too quick to pass on our feelings, to not let things register." I urged him to celebrate this new experience by sending a thank-you note to his partner of the night. "There's no need to profess undying love. You both live in other cities. It was a one-night stand. But it was memorable and enjoyable and it was a first in your life. In celebrating the experience, you celebrate yourself."

Chapter 15

Coming Out

A debutante "comes out" when she is presented to society at a gala soiree or coming-out party. A girl might have her very own event or be presented along with a number of other young ladies at a cotillion. Coming out means that she is ready to assume the duties and responsibilities of being an adult woman. She is ready to have suitors. She is mating material.

Coming out in our academy lexicon has this social but also a sexio-political definition. It means the student is honoring who he is and being honest about what has been hidden. Most of us have something to "come out" with in little ways, others of us have more big-ticket items. I knew that in having "come out" to my dad a dozen years earlier about my quite unin-

Viqui Maggio

**Lady Stefania Luisa Augusta and Mr.
Gerard Flynn.**

asking the same questions and getting the same answers and together we reshape the world.

An academy girl might come out several times. He comes out to himself that first time he puts on some feminine gear and looks in the mirror, but it is not until he shares his femmeself with another person that the student really comes out. For many students, that first moment of sharing occurs here at the academy. For others it might occur at a shopping mall. Don, an accountant who described himself as shy and quiet, told of his first time out as Donna. "I went to a mall. I wore a short skirt, a wig, and heels. I did my own makeup. I guess I looked kind of rough, kind of slutty, but I didn't care. This was who I was and I just wanted to say, 'Here I am.' " It takes courage to come out and even more courage to stay out. Some debutantes never get beyond the thrill of a one-time excursion, like Donna's trip to the mall, because keeping it up has been known to result in more than her development being arrested. It is important to carefully pick and choose the people, and, as much as possible, the time of this revelation. Not all of our girls are "out," most are not. But the ones who have consciously revealed themselves to one or more people in their lives have benefited greatly. I wanted to help our girls celebrate coming out in a big way, just like any other debutantes. I wanted curtsies and crinolines and class, and a night to remember.

hibited sexual writing and research, I had freed myself to be the best I could be. Such self-revelations are important empowering steps. As each of our girls learns to walk in his high heels, I hope her academy education will lead him to such personal freedom and inspire others to do the same.

The personal truly is political. When we give ourselves permission to be who we are, we give ourselves permission to feel and to speak, to ask questions and to have opinions. We meet others who are

Night of 1000 Gowns

In 1991, while paying for some personal frillies at Lee's Mardi Gras (a department store with great lingerie for perma girls, too), I could not help but notice the stack of campy postcards strategically placed at my fingertips. On the front of the cards a very large, Divine-style drag queen, wearing a skintight gold lamé gown and matching flying-saucer chapeau, slouched against a baby grand piano which she seemed to dwarf. Below her a banner read, "We're still here and we're still fabulous!"

The card announced the fifth annual Night of 1000 Gowns, the charity ball presented by the Imperial Court of New York, which promised a candlelit procession and coronation ball. With the word procession, they were definitely speaking my language. I recalled the May processions of my childhood and imagined beyond to a rhinestone-studded extravaganza with all of the pomp and circumstance accorded true royalty—a scene to rival the wedding of Diana and Charles or the coronation scene from the filmed version of *The Prisoner of Zenda*. As it happened, I was not to be disappointed.

I attended my first "Night" that year as a journalist, after having convinced Jared Rutter, the editor of my monthly column in the adult magazine *Adam,* that our straight male readership (and by now, you know that covers a lot of territory) would enjoy reading about drag queens. The ball appealed to Jared's eclectic tastes, as well as to his knowledge that my previous columns on transgender subjects had elicited a great amount of fan mail, second only to that of stories about female wrestlers who pin male opponents to the floor in scissor locks.

From their press clippings, I learned that the New York court was one of fifty royal courts in the Imperial Court System, a humanitarian foundation, that spans the United States, Mexico, and Canada. The first of these royal courts had been founded in 1965 in San Francisco by José Sarria, this country's first openly gay political candidate (for San Francisco supervisor). Battling discrimination and disease, the courts became a source of pride and pizazz created within the gay community but reaching out to everyone. I was eager to participate in an event that might give me some insight into an important sector of sexual politics, while providing me with some great fashion tips.

When I asked Miss Viqui to be my photographer and showed her the previous year's lavishly illustrated souvenir booklet, she got really excited, for she recognized the outgoing Empress Camille Beauchamps (the name the character played by Bette Davis adopts as part of her ugly-duckling-to-swan transformation in *Now, Voyager*) as Ben Freeman, once her art institute classmate at Parsons. She was quite impressed with Ben's ascension to the throne; from queen about town, he'd become empress of New York.

Except for the fact that down to their garter belts most members of the Imperial Court identify as homosexual, they are a lot like academy girls—many have very mainstream jobs and drag is a leisure activity. The court provides an innovative way to support needy causes, hence the group's motto, "Do good and look fabulous!" José, the Absolute Empress I José aka the Widow Norton, still travels the country making appearances at major court functions. (Just try and stop her!)

On that big night, in the grand ballroom of the Hotel Roosevelt, we saw the boldly beautiful, as well as the just plain bold. I had decided to downplay my image, just basic black, a flouncy skirt, corseted waist, and lace blouse that accentuated my breast attributes. These man-made girls were dressed to kill, and I did not want to be massacred. Viqui went in drag, she wore a tuxedo. We looked like the perfect couple.

It was a night of extravagance. With so many frocks trailing on the floor, there was serious danger from high-speed trains. Everyone glittered in diamantés, sequins, silks, satins, and beads. But no one glittered like the Empress Camille Beauchamps. She made her very last official entrance in a foot-high tiara and jeweled black leather gown.

Amid the throng of photographers and lights, she spotted Miss Viqui with her camera and whispered, "Psst, Viqui, it's me . . . Ben." Then she popped her hand to her hairdo and turned a swift pirouette in the direction of Miss Viqui's ready flash. There was no way we would have missed her. She sparkled like the crystal floor at Tiffany's. She glittered like the chandeliers at Tavern on the Green. She lit the room like the Chrysler Building illuminates the sky. What Camille reflected was more than baubles. It was the community spirit that went into her creation, including her proud parents, who attended the ball and took an ad in the souvenir program, which they dedicated with pride to "Our Son the Empress."

I recognized other members of what is now widely known as the gender community. Dr. Sheila Kirk of IFGE and *Transgender* magazine was excited about her upcoming treatise on hormones. Photo-portrait artist Mariette Pathy Allen socialized and looked for more subjects like those who had collaborated on her landmark book. Carla, lady of the night who had purchased the title Baroness of Hoboken and Weehawken, chatted up her Sunday night socials at the kinky night club the Vault, which were the successors to her Silk Stocking Club. Selling titles for dollars was another way the court raised contributions. I took the opportunity to purchase the title of lady as a gift for Sally Sissyribbons. The next year, Sally became the first of our ladies-in-waiting

Miss Vera

Miss Viqui and Sir Anthony McAulay.

Viqui Maggio

Empress Saleen and consort Prince Chuckie.

to attend the Imperial Court ball. As the academy grew, I recognized the ball as our coming-out party. Where else could a man pay $25 and become a lady (a bargain at any price) or a duchess ($35), or a maharani ($75), or tsarina ($200)?

Academy debutantes in 1993 included Jennifer James, June G. Edwards, and Susan Sargent. June had already experienced one "coming out" following the academy's initial publicity in a *New York* magazine article. Though the biographical facts mentioned in that article were few, along with the picture of June in her French maid's uniform, they were enough for friends and acquaintances to identify this hometown girl. Now, a few months later, after having survived the loss of one job as a result of the article, having withstood the varied questions and responses of family and friends, and made quantum leaps in her own self-respect, June was ready to cel-

ebrate in a glamorous new party dress that showed off her corseted waist, broad back muscles, and the fleur-de-lis Spider Webb had tattooed near her heart as part of her academy Femme Intensive. On the way to becoming a lady, he had become quite a man and she wasn't finished yet.

Jennifer James loved a party and she practically skipped down the runway. The formal grandeur of the coronation ceremony appealed to Jennifer's love of chivalry. The Night of 1000 Gowns took Jennifer to another level. Little girl Jennifer, our most exhuberant sissy maid, had blossomed into an ingenue. She was not just a lady, she was a fairy tale princess. Though the intimate circle who knew both James and Jennifer was still small, it would, slowly but surely, expand.

Vietnam vet Susan Sargent's response to the magnificent ball quelled any fears I had that our girls might feel uncomfortable at such a gay event. No matter how many talk shows he watches, no matter how many articles he reads, in his heart a cross-dresser can still believe that he is the only girl in town. When Susan walked into that ballroom in her red-sequined cocktail dress and was confronted by hundreds of others celebrating the freedom to cross-dress, she no longer felt lonely, she felt lucky.

It was appropriate that 1993 saw our first academy contingent, for it was also the year of Coco Le Chine's ascension to the throne. HIH Coco, the Celestial Dragon Empress, became the gracious ambassadress who brought the court to the attention of everyone from Joan Rivers to President Clinton. It was a big year for drag.

I initiated the tradition of our girls having escorts the next year. We had a gaggle of Japanese paparazzi on our tails and our group included student Yvette, a librarian, who was so awestruck she uttered almost no words the entire night. In 1995 Patti Harrington invited her mom. Until then Mrs. Harrington had no knowledge of this daughter. She chatted especially amiably with Melanie, an Irish colleen and banker working in Europe. This was Melanie's first visit to the academy and we had scheduled it to coincide with the memorable event. For Melanie and Mrs. Harrington to meet was an unexpected bonus for both. Melanie was able to imagine what it might be like to have her own mother sitting in Mrs. Harrington's place and Mrs. Harrington met a likable fellow similar to her son in many ways: quiet, respectful, smart, successful, shy, responsible, and happiest in a dress. A year later, Pat's participation in an HBO "Real Sex" segment on our school made him the target of a not-so-well-meaning busybody who went running to Pat's mother for her reaction. Having been to the ball, Mrs. Harrington calmly replied that she not only knew about Patti but that she applauded his taste in friends and in fashion, thus defusing the effects of the gossip.

Another student had actually saved a sister's marriage by coming out to his family. The sister, a newlywed, came down hard and often on her husband for what she saw as flaws in his family tree. "Well, your brother's a transvestite," the husband retorted. That student's coming out granted a sort of liberation to the

Miss Vera

Faculty members: Miss Viqui (en famille), Miss Maria, and Miss Tiger.

Lemmon's memorable "Daphne," "Nobody's perfect."

In 1997, I was finishing our academy book. Miss Viqui, our Assistant Headmistress, was now Mrs. John White and they were very pregnant. Jennifer James was busy completing his last semester in preparation for a new career as a veterinarian. With all of these other demands on our time, it seemed as if it might be best to skip the festivities, but how could we resist? Patti Harrington organized everything and was our hostess. Though the ball itself had grown to 600 revelers at the New York Hilton, it was a beautiful and more low-key night for the academy, considerably different, I am sure, from the nights that lie ahead and from the amazing previous year.

A Night to Remember

With springtime and prom season in New York came the tenth annual Night of 1000 Gowns. The core of 1996's academy contingent began with five lucky students, which was quite a handful considering we were in charge of their dresses, their dates, and their dreams. The expression "drag time" refers to the fact that drag queens are notoriously late. There is a lot of preparation for a girl with something extra. We had the first girl in the makeup chair at one in the afternoon and by cocktail hour they all looked like real princesses. Each had sparkling jewelry, a lush fragrant orchid corsage, and her own male or female escort. For weeks prior to the ball the girls had been preparing. Shopping, shopping, shopping . . . for dresses, jewels, gloves. Patti Harrington learned enough in sewing classes with Miss

Viqui to create her own gown, complete with long train from a *très difficile* Vogue pattern. She proved a student can begin a task knowing nothing and build something. It was the same lesson that I learned at Kate Millett's farm—when I learned to lay a floor. Kate had instilled me with butch training. At the academy we instill men with femme training. Patti was a great example to her sorority sisters.

Student Carole Kent's dream was to wear a mink stole. Prior to the ball, we found one at a rental house. Carole requested that she be the first transformation of the day, so that she could go off to a nail salon just like the society deb she longed to be. Melanie had had such a great time the previous year, she returned from Germany. Both Melanie and Carole chose to have female escorts. Sexy women in tuxedoes held their chairs out from the table and held them close as they led the students in waltzes around the floor.

It was right after the ball that year that student Roberta Jennings attended the academy for the very first time. When we told her about the ball she made me promise to let her know when it was coming up again so that she might attend. Roberta engaged a male escort and said that she hoped she would get lucky. Patti chose to have a male escort and Miss Viqui suggested her friend David.

Jennifer James had two beautiful women as escorts. James has developed a new tack with the women in his life, both old friends and new—he tells them about Jennifer. Not in a scared way but with understanding and enthusiasm. Most were intrigued, as was Louise, a woman he had befriended and begun dating when he left his job and returned to college. When

James invited Louise to be Jennifer's date for the ball, she put on a slinky black gown and she came. James had also come out to his best friends Tom and his wife Janice. The couple had asked plenty of questions: Was James gay? No. Why was he doing it, was it for the money? No, he actually paid to come to class. He did it because it was fun and because Jennifer had been a part of him for almost as long as he could remember. The three remained friends; twenty years of friendship and the mutual respect that the three shared would not be torn apart like too tight panty hose. There was plenty of room for growth, expansion, and support. Janice was so intrigued she decided to come to the ball. Tom said he would be more comfortable at home with the kids, but as the day grew near and James' and Janice's excitement grew, Tom seemed a bit envious. Jennifer was a busy girl with a lady on each arm.

The academy contingent filled two tables including the deans, the students, our male and female escorts, my editor Bruce Tracy and his partner Mickey Rolfe, my best friend Annie Sprinkle and Kim Silver, who was then her dear wife. So many different couples in combination and permutation.

Midnight drew near and, as was the custom, the royal procession began. The flamboyant crown jewels were carried in on velvet pillows. Picture a skyscraper interpreted as a tiara and you will have an inkling of the size of these jewels. Then the royal courtiers and courtesans, followed by past imperial majesties—among them dowager Empress Billie Ann Miller VIII, the Empress of Peace and Love, with Dowager Emperor V Ron, the Lionhearted, the Em-

Viqui Maggio

Janice, Louise, Jennifer, and John.

Viqui Maggio

The fan club.

peror of Social Change—at his and Billie Ann's coronation Ron had invited me to be part of his entourage, with the title Favored Lady of the Evening in recognition of my brilliant erotic career—Empress VII Coco LeChine; and that year's outgoing Empress IX Philomena, the Empress of Faith, Hope and Cartier, whose delicate bone structure was beauty that ran more than skin deep.

Robert Sorrell aka Grand Duchess Swana Swaroski, Imperial Jeweler and Mistress of Protocol, was the academy's best friend at court. The countess stopped at our tables to invite us to assemble and be ready for our presentation to the new imperial majesties, who entered to the tune of the march from *Aida*. We would lead the presentations of those who had

purchased titles in the name of charity and would have a chance to strut proudly for all to see. As we rose from our seats we were joined by academy students who were seated at other tables, those whose lives we had been privileged to touch. Lady June G. Edwards (now a full-fledged girl with the equipment to prove it) walked with her good friend Lady Barbara Nitke, who had photographed so many of our students and was documenting June's incredible journey; Renee Roberts walked alone, but his wife Eileen cheered him from the sidelines. Student Zondra, who had not only stepped out of the closet but kicked the door off its hinges, had become an official member of the court, which gave her lots more opportunities to display her unique style.

Carole Kent, the accountant so careful with dollars, glittered in bijoux and was caressed by her mink stole. In his business, Ken had many clients, but Carole now had her first, the academy, and we had a brilliant accountant to keep us sitting pretty into old age. Roberta Jennings scurried in from the corridor, having just completed still another phone call to his wife in which they professed their love for each other. Patricia Harrington smiled shyly at David. They had been chatting all night. Several months later Pat and David began dating for real.

I noticed a change in the lineup. Jennifer James' escorts Louise and Janice were there but where was Jennifer? Then I saw. Among the crowd of people who had forgone the dinner and arrived just for the coronation ceremony was a person I had not expected to see. Jennifer James stared into the face of his best friend Tom. Tom chuckled while shaking his head, then he held out

his arm to Jennifer James, who curtsied low and took it. Their free hands came together in a high-five salute.

The deans and I, with our escorts, beamed at our beautiful students. The girls needed a little practice on their curtsies. Their high heels sometimes landed a bit heavily. But those things matter little compared to their courage, the lessons they continue to learn and by their examples continue to teach. There's more to being a man than just being a man; it takes balls to be a lady; and the path of humanity runs in-between. Sissyhood is powerful.

Cherchez la femme!

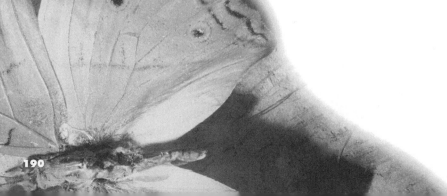

How to Become an Academy Debutante

*Y*ou are invited to call us at 212-242-6449 to receive our brochure and enrollment application, which will be discreetly sent in a pink envelope.

Students may also study via prerecorded classes at 1-900-884-VERA (8372). Cost of these classes is $2.99/minute. Adults only. Private tutorials with Miss Vera and the deans are available at 1-900-288-VERA. Cost of these private tutorials is $4.99/minute. Adults only.

Our Web address is http://www.missvera.com.

Recommended Reading and Sources

Many of the books in our academy library are mentioned in the text, but I would like to single out some of those I consider most helpful.

Books

Crossdressing, Sex and Gender by Drs. Vern and Bonnie Bullough (University of Pennsylvania Press, 1993). Presents a great overall picture that's easy to read. At bookstores and through IFGE.

Transformations, Crossdressers and Those Who Love Them by Mariette Pathy Allen. (Dutton, 1989). Portraits and interviews.

Crossdressing with Dignity by Dr. Peggy Rudd, the wife of a cross-dresser. (PM Publishers, Katy, TX, 1990). Through IFGE (see address under "Sources").

The Man in the Red Velvet Dress by J. J. Allen, a cross-dresser and past president of the California Powder Puffs (River Head Press, 1996.)

Femalia is just one of the many books published by Joani Blank, the Human Sexuality Library, and Down There Press. For catalog contact Good Vibrations Mail Order 1-800-289-8423.

Gender Outlaw: On Men, Women, and the Rest of Us by Kate Bornstein (Vintage Books, 1995).

Gender Shock by Phyllis Burke (Doubleday, 1997). Revealing look at changing attitudes. Includes a visit to the academy.

Sex Changes by Pat Califia (Cleis Press, 1997). Provacative and political analysis of transgenderism.

Magazines

Transformation. Largest circulation. Some photos contain nudity. (Subscriptions, $29.95 plus $12 shipping outside U.S.) By credit card at 714-775-0238 or mail to Transformation, Vista Station, P.O. Box 51480, Sparks, Nevada 89434. All forms accepted.

Sissy Maid Quarterly. Written and edited by Deborah Rose, a real afficionado. Recommended for its excellent domestic tips. Contact: Sandy Thomas Publications, P.O. Box 2309, Capistrano Beach, CA 92624.

Dragazine. One issue per year, $5.95 ea. Check or money order to Dragazine, P.O. Box 461795, West Hollywood, CA 90046.

Transgender. Quarterly magazine. $40/year included with membership in IFGE. (See below.)

Femme Mirror. (See Tri-Ess, below.)

Skin Two. Beautifully printed fashion and fetish resource published in London. Tim Woodward Publishing, 14 Grand Union Centre West Row, London W10 5AS. Tel 011 44 181 968 0234 www.skintwo.co.uk.

Sources

Networks

IFGE, the International Foundation for Gender Education. Spreads an umbrella over the gender spectrum. Great information resource, publishes *Transgender* magazine, and offers books. IFGE, P.O. Box 229, Waltham, MA 02254-0229; (1-617)-899-2212; e-mail: http://wwwifge@world.com.

SPICE for wives and partners. Sponsors yearly conference. Contact Dr. Peggy Rudd, P.O. Box 5304, Katy, TX 77491.

Renaissance Education Association: 214-630-1347; http://www.cds.pub.com.

AEGIS(American Education Gender Information Service): 404-939-0244.

Imperial Court of New York. Sponsors Night of 1000 Gowns. The best coming-out party; 212-475-0838; Box 149, 61 East Eighth Street, New York, NY 10003.

Tri-Ess, the Society for the Second Self, has chapters all over the country. Holds conventions that can keep a lady-in-waiting busy throughout the year. Publishes *Femme Mirror.* For a chapter near you, contact Tri-Ess, P.O. Box 194, Tulare, CA 93275; 209-688-9246.

Advisers

Dr. Patti Britton, gender counseling on-line, http://www.sexclinic.com.

Samuel Kirschner, In Touch/Mind Body

Therapy, 148 East 28th Street, New York, NY 10016; 212-683-0219.

Loughlin and Latimer, Legal Counsels, 9 Kansas Street, Hackensack, NJ 07601; 201-487-9797; for questions of gender law.

Shops

Versatile Productions. Ms. Antoinette's treasure trove of fashions, corsets, and accoutrements; 714-538-0257 for brochures; http://www.versatile fashions.com.

Lee's Mardi Gras, the TV department store, 400 West Fourteenth Street, New York, NY 10014. Books, clothing, and accessories; http://www.lmgnyc.com.

Classic Curves. Padded derrieres. Ms. Espy Lopez, owner. P.O. Box 115, Wilmington, CA 90748; 310-549-8787; http://classiccurv.aol.com.

Come Again Erotic Emporium. Lingerie, books, and shoes, 212-308-9394, 353 East 53rd Street, New York, NY 10023.

Cosmetics Plus, the fabulous makeup emporiums located throughout Manhattan and in California, welcomes academy girls. Just tell them Ingrid sent you.

Photographers

The great photographers whose work appears in this book may be contacted at:

Annie Sprinkle: http://www.heck.com.

Eric Kroll: http://www.fetish-usa.com.

Jeff Griffith Advertising, New York, NY: 212-633-8161.

Abe Frajndlich: (fax) 212-995-1688.

Barbara Nitke: through the academy.

Marty Fishman: 718-797-0927.

James Stiles: 212-627-1766.

Viqui Maggio: through the academy.

List of Courses

*H*ere is an abbreviated version of the academy's curriculum. For your very own enrollment application and brochure, *see* "How to Become an Academy Debutante"

Sudden Beauty

2½ hours on campus: 2–4:30 P.M. or 8–10:30 P.M. We concentrate on finding a look for you. Great for busy girls or budget-conscious beauties.

Miracle Miss

4 hours on campus: 2–6 P.M. or 7–11 P.M. Makeup and walking classes, plus an elective. The ideal introduc-

tion to your femmeself and great preparation for those of you who dream of going out one day, and that day may be
sooner than you think!

Dining Debutante

6 hours on and off campus: 5–11 P.M. A
restaurant is the perfect place to make your
first public appearance. We prepare you with
makeup and high-heel classes. Relax and be
gorgeous while seeing the world with new
eyes and new eyelashes.

Campus Co-ed

8 hours on campus: 10 A.M.–6 P.M. or 12
noon–8 P.M. (for late risers). Live in your
own private dormitory for a full day of
classes taught by glamorous, caring teachers. You'll never want to graduate.

Girl on the Go

10 hours on campus w/field trip: 10
A.M.–8 P.M. or noon to 10 P.M. Transformation with makeup class. Body sculpting
with corsets. Polaroid pinups and outdoor
shots. High-heel walking, posing, and taxi
class. Voice Class. Sensuality seminar. On
campus lunch. Restaurant dinner w/ladies'
room lesson and Broadway show. Stay up
late and be a Playgirl After Hours.

Modeling Assignment

10 hours w/studio photo shoot: Learn to
be a centerfold model or enjoy a full day
of photo therapy and go from baby to
bride and beyond!

Maid to Order

8 hours on campus. Washing lingerie,
giving pedicures, working your way up to
manicures. Wearing the proper uniform.
Would you like to be the serving girl at
the dean's tea party? We don't just fall for

any man in uniform, we teach you how to
look cute *and* be of service.

Fem Intensives, "The Cinderfella Experience."

*At least 2 full days and evenings on and
off campus.* Can include photo shoot.
Great for out-of-town students who
want to experience a lot in a little time.
Schedule is similar to "Girl on the Go"
and other full-day and evening experiences.

All classes include Polaroid souvenirs
and most include personal video for home
study.

Acknowledgments

*I*n making this book a reality, I have been guided and encouraged by my editor, Bruce Tracy, who constantly amazes me with the scope of his knowledge and understanding. It is a privilege and a pleasure to work with him.

Thank you also to Ms. Nancy Tuckerman, who brought Bruce and me together. Mario Pulice designed a great and politically strong cover. Ruedi Hofmann's photograph was perfect. Amanda R. Kavanagh's interior design turned the book into a little jewel.

Doubleday attorneys Katherine Trager and M. K. Moore provided welcome support. Eliza Truitt, assistant to Bruce Tracy, made sure all ran smoothly. Thank you to all those essential to making this book a thing of beauty in every way and for getting it into your hands.

My agent, Mitch Douglas at ICM, had faith even before I had the idea. His responsiveness and integrity give me confidence. Helen Shabason, Esq., at ICM gave service above and beyond the call of duty.

Marilyn G. Haft, Esq., my personal Joan of Arc, has helped me to protect what is so valuable, my intellectual property. The counsel of Mary Dorman, Esq., was goddess-sent.

Advanced Telecom Services in Wayne, Pa., the best 900 service bureau, helped me to not run out of lipstick, nylons, or peace of mind in the slow months. Suzanne Joseph gave financial guidance. Susie Bright held my hand via e-mail early on and gave me the benefit of her publishing experiences. Phil Berger, who has absolutely no desire to cross-dress, gave me his love, and as a generous perk, shared his expertise. His dedication to his craft helped me see what writing is all about.

Lou Kessel, doctor of chiropractic, made it possible for me to sit at my desk. My pussy cats, Ashley and Archie, our academy mascots, let me squeeze them when I felt the need, which was often.

Amy Rosemarin, who helped bring the academy out in the media; and Jeff Griffith and Joe Lovering, who created our award-winning ad campaign—all understood the amazing possibilities of art and business. Our neighbors and the staff, especially Betty and Ruben at the Thomas Eddy Building, have been essential in their support of this incredible adventure. Thanks to Jennifer Fillipelli for her courtesy and Dina Mendros for the videography.

Merci to the editors who kept me writing intelligently about human sexuality: Jared Rutter, Jack Heidenry, V.K. Mc-Carty, and Stan Bernstein. And to Tuppy Owens, a beacon of erotic light. Publishers Al Goldstein and Kat Sunlove helped us reach the public on a continuing basis. When it was time to expand my horizons, Joe Conason and Eric Etheridge put me in *The New York Observer* (my favorite paper along with the *National Enquirer),* and helped me to grow. I am grateful for the business acumen and intuition of Dominique D'Anthony, the loyalty and wisdom of Ms. Antoinette, and for Annie Sprinkle, who was and will always be there.

Our faculty of deans, all named in this book, along with Patrick Roger-Binet of Paris, honorary dean of decor, are my team, my colleagues, and my friends. Thank you all so much. Of all the deans, I must single out Viqui Maggio, my friend and confidante and a woman of many talents. She eases the pressure and quadruples the pleasure.

This book would not have been possible without the students of the academy, the campus coeds and telephone extension students, especially James Byrnes, Pat Harrington, Sally, and June, who faced the fear and did it anyway. I owe a debt of gratitude to John White, who became Joan, for fun and friendship. The photographers, artists, and models whose work graces these pages are an elegant complement to us all. They are named and rethanked in the Sources.

Right from the get-go, I believed this project would be a success. (My mantra is: "The book, the show, the movie, the home-shopping club.") I always felt the tremendous love and support of the cross-dressers, from the very public ones to those who are very private, and that has made all the difference.

My family wished that I used my real name rather than my professional name on the cover, so for them I gratefully sign below.

M. V. Antonakos aka Veronica Vera
New York City, August 1997

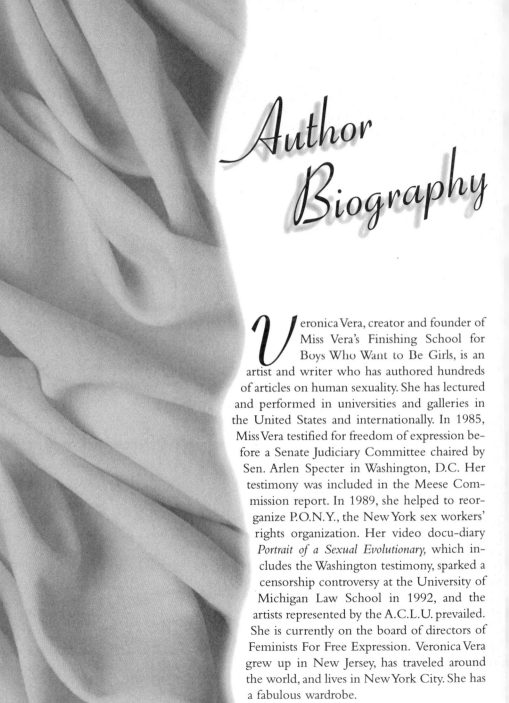

Author Biography

*V*eronica Vera, creator and founder of Miss Vera's Finishing School for Boys Who Want to Be Girls, is an artist and writer who has authored hundreds of articles on human sexuality. She has lectured and performed in universities and galleries in the United States and internationally. In 1985, Miss Vera testified for freedom of expression before a Senate Judiciary Committee chaired by Sen. Arlen Specter in Washington, D.C. Her testimony was included in the Meese Commission report. In 1989, she helped to reorganize P.O.N.Y., the New York sex workers' rights organization. Her video docu-diary *Portrait of a Sexual Evolutionary,* which includes the Washington testimony, sparked a censorship controversy at the University of Michigan Law School in 1992, and the artists represented by the A.C.L.U. prevailed. She is currently on the board of directors of Feminists For Free Expression. Veronica Vera grew up in New Jersey, has traveled around the world, and lives in New York City. She has a fabulous wardrobe.